REGIONAL POWERS AND BRITISH EXPANSION

Encyclopaedic History of India Series

REGIONAL POWERS AND BRITISH EXPANSION

Dr. Mahesh Vikram Singh
Professor, Deptt. of History
Mahatma Gandhi Kashi Vidyapeeth
Varanasi (UP)

Dr. Brij Bhushan Shrivastava
Head of Deptt., Ancient History, Archeology & Culture
SMMTPG College, Ballia (UP)

CENTRUM PRESS
NEW DELHI-110002 (INDIA)

CENTRUM PRESS
H.O.: 4360/4, Ansari Road, Daryaganj,
New Delhi-110002 (India)
Tel: 23278000, 23261597, 23255577, 23286875
B.O.: No. 1015, Ist Main Road, BSK IIIrd Stage,
IIIrd Phase, IIIrd Block, Bangalore-560085 (INDIA)
Tel: 080-41723429
Email: centrumpress@gmail.com
Visit us at: www.centrumpress.com

Regional Powers and British Expansion

First Edition, 2011

ISBN 978-93-80836-81-2

PRINTED IN INDIA

Printed at Mehra Offset Press, Delhi

प्रो. विपिन चंद्रा
अध्यक्ष
Prof. Bipan Chandra
Chairman

नेशनल बुक ट्रस्ट, इंडिया
नेहरू भवन
5 इंस्टीट्यूशनल एरिया, फेज़-II, वसंत कुंज, नई दिल्ली-110 070
फोन/ Phone: 011-26121880 फैक्स/ Fax: 011-26121883

NATIONAL BOOK TRUST, INDIA
Nehru Bhawan
5 Institutional Area, Phase II, Vasant Kunj, New Delhi-110 070
ई-मेल / E-mail: chairman@nbtindia.org.in
वेबसाइट / Website: www.nbtindia.org.in

FOREWORD

The term 'history' is derived from the Greek word 'historia' that means knowledge acquired through investigation. Obviously, this knowledge can be correct if the method of investigation is objective and not vitiated by any kind of bias. In other words, if the study of human past is comprehensive and obtained through scientific inquiry, it can provide perspective on the present day problems and help one plan for the future.

A true historian has to identify the sources that can be most useful in a given context. Documents, coins, archaeology, anthropology, geography, travel accounts, oral traditions, mythology and so on can be useful but they can be used only after their veracity is tested and they are critically examined. They should be checked and counter-checked.

Over the centuries, one finds the study and writing of history vitiated by biases. There are numerous instances in which historical data have been distorted to support or oppose certain preconceived ideas and purposes. Strictly speaking such history is just like fiction to accord with preconceived notions and serve some ulterior purposes.

The study of the past has never been static. Conclusions go on changing because of the discovery of new materials and tools of investigation. To give a concrete example, the carbon 14 or radiocarbon dating test has revolutionized the study of civilizations and settlements, especially of prehistoric times, for which written documents, coins, etc. are seldom available. This method has enabled historians to determine more accurately than before the time period of a particular civilization or settlement. This method was discovered only 70 years ago by American scientists.

In our country, excavations brought to light the Indus Valley Civilization and its various features, hitherto unknown. Similarly, no complete text of Kautilya's Arthashastra was available before it was discovered by Shamasastry, the chief of the Mysore Government Oriental Library in the first decade of the last century. Likewise, people's knowledge of the history of the Buddhist period got extended after excavations at Sarnath and the ruins of the Asokan period at Patna. In the future, if the Harappan inscriptions are deciphered, our knowledge of the Indus Valley Civilization will increase enormously. All these instances underline the fact that our knowledge of history is never static and its frontiers go on extending.

In the light of what has been said above the encyclopedic history is going to be of great help to students interested in Indian history. It is comprehensive and as far as possible free from biases. It includes the latest materials, and objective conclusions.

Prof . Bipan Chandra

Professor Emeritus, JNU

Chairman, National Book Trust, India

Contents

Preface

The people of India have had a continuous civilization since 2500 B.C., when the inhabitants of the Indus River valley developed an urban culture based on commerce and sustained by agricultural trade. This civilization declined around 1500 B.C., probably due to ecological changes. During the second millennium B.C., pastoral, Aryan-speaking tribes migrated from the northwest into the subcontinent. As they settled in the middle Ganges River valley, they adapted to antecedent cultures.

The political map of ancient and medieval India was made up of myriad kingdoms with fluctuating boundaries. In the 4th and 5th centuries A.D., northern India was unified under the Gupta Dynasty. During this period, known as India's Golden Age, Hindu culture and political administration reached new heights. Islam spread across the Indian subcontinent over a period of 500 years. In the 10th and 11th centuries, Turks and Afghans invaded India and established sultanates in Delhi. In the early 16th century, descendants of Genghis Khan swept across the Khyber Pass and established the Mughal (Mogul) Dynasty, which lasted for 200 years. From the 11th to the 15th centuries, southern India was dominated by Hindu Chola and Vijayanagar Dynasties. During this time, the two systems—the prevailing Hindu and Muslim—mingled, leaving lasting cultural influences on each other.

The first British outpost in South Asia was established in 1619 at Surat on the northwestern coast. Later in the century, the East India Company opened permanent trading stations at Madras, Bombay, and Calcutta, each under the protection of native rulers. The British expanded their influence from these footholds until, by the 1850s, they controlled most of present-day India, Pakistan, and Bangladesh. In 1857, a rebellion in north India led by mutinous Indian soldiers caused the British Parliament to transfer all political power from the East India Company to the Crown. Great Britain began administering most of India directly while controlling the rest through treaties with local rulers.

In the late 1800s, the first steps were taken toward self-government in British India with the appointment of Indian councillors to advise the British viceroy and the establishment of provincial councils with Indian members; the British subsequently widened participation in legislative councils. Beginning in 1920, Indian leader Mohandas K. Gandhi transformed the Indian National Congress political party into a mass movement to campaign against British colonial rule.

—Authors

1

Nawabs of Bengal

The Nawabs of Bengal were the hereditary *nazims* or *subadars* (provincial governors) of the *subah* (province) of Bengal during the Mughal rule and the de-facto rulers of the province.

History

From 1717 until 1880, three successive Islamic dynasties-the Nasiri, Afshar and Najafi-ruled Bengal:

The first dynasty, the Nasiri, ruled from 1717 until 1740. The founder of the Nasiri, Murshid Quli Jafar Khan, was born a poor Deccani Brahmin before being sold into slavery and bought by one Haji Shafi Isfahani, a Persian merchant from Isfahan who converted him to Islam. He entered the service of the Emperor Aurangzeb and rose through the ranks before becoming Nazim of Bengal in 1717, a post he held until his death in 1727. He in turn was succeeded by his grandson and son-in law until his grandson was killed in battle and succeeded by Alivardi Khan of the Afshar Dynasty in 1740.

The second dynasty, the Afshar, ruled from 1740 to 1757. They were succeeded by the third and final dynasty to rule Bengal, the Najafi, after Siraj Ud Daula, the last of the Afshar rulers was killed at the Battle of Plassey in 1757.

The Najafi Dynasty of Bengal were *sayyid* and were descended from the Prophet Muhammad through Imam Hassan ibn Ali, ruling from 1757 until 1880.

Under the Mughal Rule

Bengal *subah* was one of the wealthiest parts of the Mughal empire. As the Mughal empire began to decline, the Nawabs grew in power, although nominally sub-ordinate to the Mughal emperor. They wielded great power in their own right and ruled the *subah* as independent rulers for all practical purposes.

Under the British Rule

After the Nawab Siraj Ud Daulah (the last independent ruler of Bengal) was defeated by the British forces of Sir Robert Clive at Palashi in 1757, the Nawabs became puppet rulers dependent on the British. The Nawab who replaced Siraj-ud-daula was Mir Jafar. He was personally led to the throne by Robert Clive after triumph of the British in battle. He briefly tried to re-assert his power by allying with the Dutch, but this plan was ended by the [illegible] le of Chinsurah. After the grant of the *Diwani* of Bengal, Bihar and Orissa by the Mughal emperor Shah Alam II to the British East India Company in 1765 and the appointment of Hastings by the East India Company as their first Governor General of Bengal in 1771, the Nawabs were deprived of any real power, and finally in 1793, when the *nizamat* (governorship) was also taken away from them, they remained as the mere pensioners of the British East India Company. In 1880, Mansur Ali Khan, the last Nawab of Bengal was forced to relinquish his title. His son, Nawab Sayyid Hassan Ali Mirza Khan Bahadur, who succeeded him, was given the lesser title of Nawab of Murshidabad by the British. Hassan's descendants continued the title until 1969 when the last Nawab of the dynasty died; since then the title has been in dispute.

Nasiri (1717-1740)

Murshid Quli Khan

Murshid Quli Khan was the first Nawab of Bengal. In fact circumstances resulted in his being the first independent ruler of Bengal post the death of Emperor Aurangzeb. Though he continued to recognize the nominal overlordship of the Mughal Emperor, for all practical purposes he was the de facto ruler of Bengal.

Evolution of the Position of the Nawab of Bengal

The decay and downfall of the Mughal Empire began in right earnest after the reign of Aurangzeb. The Peacock Throne in Delhi became a "musical chair" for the successors of Aurangzeb and fuelled by court intrigues of numerous nobles the tenure between 1707 and 1719 saw no less than eight Mughal Emperors (more than the sum of the last 180 years) namely Bahadur Shah I, Jahandar Shah, Farrukh Siyar, Rafi ud-Darajat, Rafi ud-Daulah, Neku Siyar, Muhammad Ibrahim and finally some stability came in the form of Muhammad Shah in 1719.

Such instability saw the rise of three notable nobles; Saadat Ali Khan the Subahdar of Oudh, Murshid Quli Khan the Subahdar of Orissa and Nazim of Bengal and Qamar ud-din Khan (also known as Asaf Jah I) the Subahdar of Deccan.

The distinguishing factor in these three nobles were that all were decorated generals of Aurangazeb and were old timers and unlike the "newer" nobles in the Red Fort; never got actively involved in court intrigues and were always on the "right" side of the Mughal Emperor, however weak the emperor might be. In stead these three nobles concentrated in entrenching themselves in their respective territories. Gradually while Delhi became weaker Oudh, Hyderabad/Deccan and Bengal became strong and prosperous. This was the direct outcome of the resources in Delhi getting strained due to the frequent changes of Emperors in Delhi. Every Mughal Emperor henceforth became more and more dependent on the three nobles and the nobles cleverly and tactfully extracted more and more for their "loyalty" till the time they became de-facto and then the de-jure rulers or Nawabs of the territories. The final blow came in 1724, when Nizam ul-Mulk, Asaf Jah I declared himself the Nizam of Hyderabad.

Meanwhile Murshid Quli Khan was gradually consolidating his position. In 1717, he renamed his capital city from Makhsusabad to Murshidabad (after himself). The then Mughal Emperor Farrukh Siyar granted formal approval to this (symbolic) change of name, paving the way for Murshid Quli Khan to become the de-facto Nawab of Bengal. He however continued to "act and function" as the viceroy of the ever weakening Mughal Emperor.

Early Life

There are quite a few versions of his early life. About his family and parenthood nothing is known for certain. One version is that he was grandson of the Maratha general Mohammed Quli Khan (formerly Netaji Palkar) by his Iranian wife Nusrat Banu, daughter of Mughal Vazir Asad Khan. The other is that Haji Shafi of Ispahan, formerly a high-ranking Mughal officer, brought him up in Iran with paternal affection and gave him useful education.

After Haji Shafi's death, he came back to India, and under the name *Mirza Hadi* entered the service of the Mughal Emperor as the Diwan and Faujdar of Golconda and received a Mansab or rank.

The third and most reliable version is that he was born a poor Brahmin in the Deccan, bought by Haji Shafi Isfahani, a merchant from Isfahan, converted and renamed Muhammad Hadi/Mirza Hadi. He entered the service of Haji Abdullah, Diwan of Berar, later transferring to Royal service under Emperor Aurangzeb.

Rise to Power

When Aurangzeb was looking for an honest and efficient Diwan for Bengal, his choice fell on this young man. He was transferred in 1701 to Bengal as diwan and was honoured with the title of *Kartalab Khan* meaning "the seeker of challenges" in Persian.

The Mirza was a sagacious (strictly Muslim) man, and an officer of honesty and integrity. He had already held the office of Diwan of the Subah of Orissa. In several Mahals pertaining to Orissa he had effected retrenchments in expenditure, and had thus become prominent amongst the Imperial officials. He was held matchless in probity and rectitude of purpose. Rendering eminent services, in periods of siege and war, he had got into the good graces of Emperor Aurangzeb. At that period, the reins of the administration of Financial and Revenue affairs, the power over the assessment and collection of revenue, and payments into and disbursements from the Imperial Treasury lay in the hands of the Diwan of the Subah. Imperial Treasury lay in the hands of the Diwan of the Subah. The Nazim had jurisdiction over the Procedure and Administration of Political affairs, such as the repression and chastisement of the refractory and the disobedient, and the extirpation of rebels and tyrants.

Imperial Treasury lay in the hands of the Diwan of the Subah. The Nazim had jurisdiction over the Procedure and Administration of Political affairs, such as the repression and chastisement of the refractory and the disobedient, and the extirpation of rebels and tyrants. Except with regard to the Jagirs attached to the Nizamat and personal Mansabs and presents, the Nazim had no power to meddle with the Imperial revenue. Both the Nazim and the Diwan Kar Talab Khan, being appointed by Emperor to be Diwan of the

Subah of Bengal, arrived at Jahangir Nagar (Dhaka). After waiting on the Prince Azim-us-Shan, (the grandson of the Mughal Emperor, Aurangzeb; he devoted himself to the administration of the fiscal affairs. And the remittances into, and disbursements from, the Treasury being in charge of the abovementioned Khan, the Prince's control over the income and expenditure ceased.

This led him to the path of direct conflict with Prince Azim-us-Shan wherein the Prince attempted to assassinate Kar Talab Khan, who in all humility reported the matter to the Mughal Emperor, Aurangzeb. The emperor acted quickly shifting Azim-us-Shan to Patna (which was renamed to Azimabad) and Kar Talab Khan to Makhsusabad (later known as Murshidabad). This happened in 1703. This is sometimes erroneously referred to as the transfer of the capital of the Subah Bengal from Dhaka to Murshidabad. The whole process actually took fifteen years (1703-1717). Murshidabad was the capital from 1717 to 1780.

His efficient Revenue administration and in proving his good and faithful services, the Khan became the recipient of further Imperial favours. He was appointed Deputy to the Prince in the Nizam at of the Subah of Bengal and Orissa, in addition to the office of Diwan, by the Emperor Aurangzeb. He was also given the title of Murshid Quli Khan, and further received a valuable Khilat, with a standard and a kettle-drum. His mansab was also raised.

During the reign of Aurangzeb and after it, Murshid Quli's rise was meteoric. From the Dewan of Hyderabad, Bengal (1700-1708 and 1710-1713), of Bihar, and of the Deccan (1708-1710), Naib Nazim of Bengal (1713-1717), Subahdar of Orissa (1714), and Nazim of Bengal (1717). Removed his headqaurters from Dacca (Jahangir Nagar/Dhaka) to Makhsusabad in 1703, and renamed it Murshidabad in 1717. The then Mughal Emperor, Farrukh Siyar granted formal approval to this (symbollic) change of name and from then on Murshid Quli Khan became the de-facto Nawab of Bengal. He celebrated this by opening a mint in Murshidabad and introduced the *Zurbe Murshedabad* coin.

Reign

Murshid Quli never formally severed his links to the Mughals and continued to send annual tribute to Delhi. Although he laid the foundation of a well-run and economically viable state, it was his successor who made the rupture with Delhi. Post 1717, Mushid Quli set about resolving matters of state, with an "iron fist", very aggressively most of the times and with an undue heavy hand on others. As an administrative decision, Midnapore was separated from Orissa and annexed to the Subah of Bengal.

Revenue Collection

On matters of Revenue Collection Murshid Quli was absolutely non-compromising to the extent of being ruthless. Hindu Zamindars especially suffered under his rule and were terrorized by the Nawab and his 'Amils' (Collectors of Revenue). In aggressively collecting revenue, both current and arrears he put a complete stop to the authority of Zamindars over the collection and disbursement of the Imperial Revenue, he limited their source of income to profits of *Nankar* (tax-free lands give in consideration for services rendered) tenures. Accordingly a new Revenue Roll (some say a "Perfect Roll" before the Permanent Settlement of Bengal) was drawn up.

Land and Agrarian Reforms

On matters of Land Reforms, the *Amils* (Collectors of Revenue) under his orders, sent *Shiqdars* and *Amins* to every village of the *Parganas,* measured the cultivated and waste-lands, and leased them back to tenants, plot by plot, and advanced agricultural loans (Taqavi) to the poorer tenantry, and put forth exertions for increase in the produce of the lands. Thus Murshid Quli affected not only increase in revenue, but also increase in their 'areas'.

He ensured that a part of the revenues were remitted to the Imperial Treasury in Delhi. Till the time of Aurangzeb the entirety was remitted to Delhi but post 1717 this remittance was limited to the annual tribute or *nazrana.*

His administration was so vigorous and successful that there was neither foreign incursion nor internal disturbance, and consequently the military expenditure was nearly abolished.

Cruelty Aspect in Administration

In this matter it is important to note that various records have suggested his extreme harsh treatment towards affluent Hindus in general and Zamindars in particular. There are records (in Riyaz us-Salatin) of his torture of the Zamindar of Bishnupur for collection of revenue arrears. His Diwan for sometime, Syed Razi Khan was especially known to be a bigot and short-tempered man *(read: Riyaz us-Salatin)*, and in collection of dues was extremely strict, and by adopting harsh measures collected the revenue. It is said he prepared a reservoir full of filth (human excreta??), and he sneeringly named this reservoir 'Baikunth' (on Vaikunta the Hindu name for Paradise/the Muslim equivalent of Jannat). He used to thrust into this reservoir the defaulting Zamindars and defaulting *Amils* (Collectors of Revenue). After torturing them in various ways, and making them undergo various privations, he used to collect in entirety the arrears.

Legend (local word of mouth without documented support) also has it that Murshid Quli tore down eighteen Hindu temples to construct *Katra Masjid*, the mosque which was later to be his mausoleum. (More details follow in the Trivia section). Murshid Quli was in the service of the Mughal Emperor, Aurangzeb for quite some time and a big reason for his treatment of his Hindu subjects could be attributed to the influence of the policies of the former. It is also said that he adopted a moderate path on the last year of his rule. There are however no records suggesting repression towards the poor, be it Hindu or Muslim. It is also notable that there were quite a few important Hindu officers in the Revenue Administration of Murshid Quli Khan.

It is important to note that most of these (so-called) bigot and harsh practices were immediately discontinued by Shuja-ud-Din Muhammad Khan, on his ascent to the position of Nawab. Shuja was a practical man who had the experience and vision to adopt an inclusive policy towards the antagonized *affluent* Hindus.

His Personality

Murshid Quli Khan was very powerful as a personality and his commands were so overawing, that his peons sufficed to keep peace in the country, and to overawe the refractory. And fear of his personality was so deeply impressed on the hearts of all, both the high and the low, that the courage of lion-hearted persons quailed in his presence. The Khan did not allow petty Zamindars access to his presence. The "Mutsadis" and "Amils" and leading Zamindars had not the heart to sit down in his presence; on the contrary, they remained standing breathless like statues. Hindu Zamindars were forbidden to ride on *Palkis*. The Mutasadis, in his presence, did not ride on horseback ; whilst the Mansabdars attended at state functions in their military uniforms. In his presence one could not salute another; and if anything opposed to etiquette occurred on the part of anyone, he was immediately censured. Every week he held court on two days to listen to complaints, and used to mete out justice to the complainants.

Amongst his deeds of justice, it may be mentioned, that to avenge the wrong done to another, obeying the sacred Islamic law, he executed his own son.

In administration of justice, in administration of the political affairs of the country, and in maintenance of the respect due to the Mughal Emperor, he spared no one. Murshid Quli Khan's uprightness in administration of justice (regardless of all family ties of attachment) is remarkable.

In brief Murshid Quli was no better or no worse than quite a few Muslim Rulers who set up kingdoms in India but most certainly he enhanced the material prosperity of Bengal in terms of Revenue.

Death and Succession

Murshid Quli Khan passed died in 1139 A.H. (30 June, 1727), (according to Riyaz-us-Salatin by Ghulam Hussein Salim). However some sources like the *Encyclopaedia Britannica* suggest that the year was 1726.

In absence of a direct heir he nominated his maternal grandson Sarfaraz Khan to succeed him. It is highly likely that Sarfaraz Khan ascended to the Masnad as Nawab Nazim before abdicating in favour of his father Shuja-ud-Din Muhammad Khan. On hearing of Sarfaraz's accession to the Masnad, his fatherShuja-ud-Din Muhammad Khan, the Dewan Nazim of Orissa, marched at the head of a large army towards Murshidabad. To avoid a conflict in the family, the dowager Begum of Murshid Quli Khan intervened; and her son-in-law Shuja-ud-Din Muhammad Khan ascended to the masnad of Bengal.

By the end of 1727, Shuja-ud-Din Muhammad Khan was firmly established as the Nawab of Bengal.

Murshid Quli Khan lies buried below the steps of Katra Masjid (mosque) in Murshidabad. He laid the foundation of the Nasiri Dynasty which would last for another thirteen years.

Trivia

It would be interesting to know a few things (trivia) on Murshid Quli Khan and his times.

1. The British East India Company, like the French, Dutch and Danes had the simple status of Zamindar or Bania (trader) during his rule. Things changed rapidly in the next two decades.
2. Murshid Quli Khan was a pious Muslim and it is believed that while on his death-bed, he deeply regretted the excesses committed by him. Accordingly his death wish was that he be buried under the stairs of the mausoleum 'Katra Masjid' he had constructed for himself in 1723. The hope was that the dust from the feet of worshippers would cleanse his sin and give him eternal peace.
3. It is believed that Murshid Quli tore down eighteen Hindu temples to construct the 'Katra Masjid', in 1723. The mosque which was later to be his mausoleum in 1727. Ironically it's domes and a large part of the mausoleum were struck down by lightning within years of his passing away. The remaining part was destroyed by an earthquake in 1897. The other ironic part is that the remaining part used for 'Namaaz' remained 'strongly' intact (unlike other contemporary buildings/structures) and is in use today. It is now one of the two sets of mausoleums in Murshidabad "protected" by the Government of India. The other being Khoshbag, the final resting place of Alivardi Khan and his grandson, Siraj-ud-Daulah.
4. It is believed that during the rule of Murshid Quli, rice sold at five "maunds" to the "rupiyah" or rupee and a man making a rupee a month could have had two full meals for his family with "pulao" and "kalia"; the former a Bengali rice delicacy and the latter a river fish delicacy.
5. Murshid Quli Khan is also known as "Jaffer Khan, Zinda Peer" or the "Living Saint". It is believed that cholera (common in Bengal till recently) never breaks out in the vicinity of this sacred building through its blessings and benedictions.

Shuja-ud-Din Muhammad Khan

Shuja-ud-Din Muhammad Khan was the second Nawab of Bengal. He married Zainab un-nisa Begum, the daughter of Murshid Quli Khan and after the death of his father-in-law in June 30, 1727, he became the Nawab Nazim (Governor) of Bengal Subah (which became hereditary with his ascent to the throne).

Early Life

Born at Burhanpur, Deccan, as Mirza Shuja ud-din Muhammad Khan (Mirza Deccani), son of Nawab Jan Muhammad Khan (Mirza Nur ud-din Muhammad), he was appointed Subahdar of Orissa 1719. Appointed as Nazim of Bengal and Orissa, July 1727. Subahdar of Bihar 1731. The title of Subahdar was bestowed by the Mughal Emperor of Delhi.

Rise to Power

In absence of a direct heir, Murshid Quli Khan nominated his maternal grandson Sarfaraz Khan to the Masnad of Bengal. Murshid Quli Khan died in 1727 and Sarfaraz Khan was to (had he??) ascended to the Masnad as Nawab Nazim.

Shuja ud-din Muhammad Khan was the 'Subahdar' of Orissa with 'Alivardi Khan' as his Naib (Deputy). Murshid Quli was not generally pleased of the inclusive and people friendly policies of Shuja. Accordingly when Sarfaraz Khan was announced heir, Shuja was disturbed at the idea of being in the employment of his son. Alivardi Khan and his brother Haji Ahmed convinced Shuja that merit should be the deciding guideline for the position of Nawab and that Shuja was more than suitable for this position. With support from Alivardi and Haji he made preparations for a take over. He sent deputations to the Mughal Emperor, Muhammad Shah and his Vazir, Khan Dauran in Delhi to accord formal permission and request for support. All his trustees save Alivardi were asked to resign from their duties and take up 'positions' in Murshidabad if the need may arise. Alivardi was to be in stand-by with him.

Shuja was stationed at Katak (Cuttack) and in preparation for action crossed the river Mahanadi. On hearing that Murshid Quli had but a few days to leave he secretly started his march. Three days into the march he heard of Murshid Quli's death. He doubled speed and reached Murshidabad in another three days and enthroned himself as the Nawab. In the interim a formal approval from Vazir Khan Dauran in Delhi had arrived and the Mughal Emperor had supported his cause.

The speed of Shuja took Sarfaraz Khan by surprise. In the interim Alivardi had arrived with an army in support of Shuja. Sarfaraz might have decided to contest however to avoid a conflict in the family, the Dowager Begum of Murshid Quli Khan intervened, Sarfaraz Khan in favour of his father, Shuja-ud-Din Muhammad Khan, and her son-in-law Shuja-ud-Din Muhammad Khan ascended to the Masnad of Bengal.

It is certain that by August, 1727 Shuja-ud-Din Muhammad Khan was firmly established as the Nawab of Bengal.

As a sign of gratitude for supporting him, he sent a huge amount of money from his revenue collection to the Mughal Emperor Muhammad Shah and in return received the title of "Mutaman-ul-Mulk Shuja-ud-Daula Asad Jang". He also received the personal Mansab of a Haft Hazari, with seven thousand troopers, besides a fringed *Palki*, together with the insignia of the *Mahi Order*, and a Khilat consistiug of six pieces of robes, precious stones, a jewel-mounted sword, and a *Royal* elephant with a horse. He was further confirmed in the office of *Nazim of Bengal*.

Reign

Shuja ud-Din was known to be brave, liberal and generous. The only factor that went against him in terms of having a long rule, was his age.

Administration

The Siyar-ul-Mutakherin mentions that with regard to private disputes between man and man, he trusted no one ; but sending for the parties, he would listen patiently and leisurely to the story of each, and with much judgment drew his conclusion, and pronouncing the decree, caused it to be executed with punctuality. Constantly animated by a scrupulous regard for justice, and always inspired by fear of God, he uprooted from his realm the foundations of oppressions and tyrannies.

It is important to note here that Shuja detested the high handed policies of Murshid Quli Khan and had them reversed (in totality) immediately. His detest was so extreme that he went to the extent of auctioning the household goods of Murshid Quli Khan to his arch enemies, the Hindu Zamindars. By this act he raised four million rupees. He had Nazir Ahmad and Murad Farrash, the employes of Murshid Quli Khan, who were notorious for their highhandedness, executed and confiscated their effects. He tore down most of the buildings cunstructed by Murshid Quli and had newer and bigger constructions done in their place. He allowed the growth and prosperity of his subordinates who respected and gave him fullest loyal services in return. Unlike Murshid Quli, he was not feared and never extracted loyalty but rather commanded the same.

Re-alignment of Administrative Districts

In 1733, he merged Bihar Subah with Bengal and divided the merged territory into four administrative divisions: (a) Central division consisting of west Bengal, north Bengal and central Bengal; (b) Dhaka division consisting of east and south Bengal, a small portion of north Bengal and the districts of Sylhet and Chittagong (c) Bihar and (d) Orissa.

The Central division was administered directly by the Nawab who was assisted by a council of advisers. Other divisions were placed in charge of a Naib Nazim or Naib Subahdar.

He made the following changes in the administrative positions:

1. Elder son, Sarfaraz Khan: Nazim (Dewan) of the Subah of Bengal
2. Younger son, Muhammad Taqi : Naib (Deputy) Subahdar of Orissa
3. Younger son-in-law, Mirza Lutfullah: Naib (Deputy) Nazim of Dacca
4. Haji Ahmed (brother of Alivardi Khan): Chief Counsellor
5. Nawazish Muhammad Khan: Mir Bakshi (Paymaster General)
6. Syed Ahmed Khan: Faujdar of Rangpur
7. Zain ud-Deen Ahmed Khan: Faujdar of Rajmahal (Akbar Nagar)
8. Pir Khan: Faujdar of Hooghly.

By the end of his reign major re-alignments in positions had to be effected. They were very important in context of the times to come.

1. Alivardi Khan: Naib Subahdar of Azimabad (Patna/Bihar)
2. Elder son, Sarfaraz Khan: Naib (Deputy) Subahdar of Dacca
3. Younger son-in-law, Mirza Lutfullah: Naib (Deputy) Subahdar of Orissa.

Revenue Relief and Settlement

Re-settlement of Deprived Hindu Zamindars

The Siyar-ul-Mutakherin also mentions that his equity was no less conspicuous towards the Zamindars and other landholders of Bengal. These persons, under Murshid Quli's administration, had been mostly kept in confinement, and tormented in such a variety of ways, that it would be a pity to spend paper and ink in describing them. Shuja after having firmly established his government, released such of the Zamindars and other landholders as he found on enquiry free from crime or fraud ; as to the others, he ordered them to be all brought into his presence, and to form a circle round his person. This being done, he asked them, how they would behave in future, should he release them. These poor people, who had been for years languishing in dungeons, surprised at this address, burst forth into encomiums on his goodness, and after supplicating heaven to grant him a long and prosperous government, promised that henceforward they would pay the revenue with punctuality, and would prove obedient and dutiful servants. Engagements in their own handwriting, authenticated by the proper formalities, being taken from them, they confirmed them by the most solemn oaths. Shujah now sent for a number of rich dresses for each, according to his respective rank and station, so that there was not one in that assembly who did not receive a suitable present. This ceremony being over they were all released, with injunctions to transmit henceforward the revenue through the house of Jagat Seth, Fateh Chand.

Revenue Settlement

By this stroke of policy, over and above the profits of 'Jagirs' and fees on ware-houses and factories, he easily raised one crore and fifty lakhs (fifteen million) of rupees, which he remitted to the Imperial Treasury through the Banking Agency of Jagat Seth Fatih Chand. By selling off at fancy prices to Zamindars the jaded horses, cattle, and other livestock, as well as damaged carpets and curtains belonging to the private estate of Nawab Murshid Quli

Khan, he sent another forty lakhs (four million) of rupees, besides elephants, to Emperor Muhammad Shah. And after the Abstract Balance Sheet of the Annual Accounts was prepared, he remitted to the Imperial Capital the stipulated annual tribute of the Nizamat, besides the Imperial Revenue, according to the established

Prosperity and Public Welfare

Shuja-ud-Din Muhammad Khan, inherited (from Murshid Quli Khan) a treasury which was full. He enhanced it further and spent liberally on public welfare.

He surpassed his predecessors in office in paraphernalia of royalty and armaments, and though his prime of life had passed, he did not scorn life's pleasures. Dismantling the public buildings erected by Murshid Quli Khan, as they seemed too small according to his lofty ideals, he built instead a grand and spacious Palace, an Arsenal, a lofty Gateway, a Revenue Court, a Public Audience-Hall, a Private Office, a Boudoir for Ladies, a Reception-Hall, a Court of Exchequer and a Court of Justice. He lived in magnificent splendour, and used to ride out in right regal state. He attended constantly to the well-being of his Army, and to the happiness of his subjects. On his officers, he lavished largesses amounting to no less than one thousand or five hundred rupees in each case.

Nazir Ahmad (an official of Murshid Quli) had laid the foundation of a Mosque with a garden on the banks of the river Bhagirathi. Shuja, after executing him, finished the mosque and garden, and named them after himself. He tastefully embellished the garden by building therein grand palaces with reservoirs, canals and numerous fountains. It was a splendid garden, compared with which the spring-houses of Kashmir paled like withering autumn-gardens ; nay, the garden of *Iram* itself seemed to draw its inspiration of freshness and sweetness from it. Shuja ud-Din used frequently to resort for promenades and picnics to that paradise-like garden, and held there pleasure-parties and other entertainments. Every year in that beautiful garden, he used to give a State Banquet to the educated section of his State Officers.

Rise of Powerful Advisors

This period saw the rise of important state officials like:

- Alivardi Khan who was the Naib Nazim of Azimabad (once annexed to Bengal)

- Haji Ahmed (brother of Alivardi Khan) who was the Chief Counsellor to the Nizamat
- Rai Alam Chand who became Diwan of Bengal (was given the tille of Ray-Rayan)
- Jagat Seth, Fateh Chand became the Banker to the Nawab

Their power came from the fact that the Nawab trusted them and mostly left them unsupervised, concentrating on matters of his please. These aides turned out to be very able, efficient and loyal and executed their responsibilities to the satisfaction of the Nawab. The experience would come in good stead as they would play a very active role in the future of Bengal for the next two to three decades. Shuja trusted and rewarded their loyalty but was wise enough to keep their ambitions under a check through proper balances. He was largely unsuccessful and this his successor Sarfaraz Khan would experience in 1740.

First Altercation with the British East India Company

The new Faujdar of Hugli, Pir Khan (Shuja Quli Khan), commenced exactions and oppressions. The Port of Hugli from his acts of omission and commission was ruined; and he commenced quarreling with the European merchants. On the pretext of collecting the customs-duties of the Imperial Customs House, he requisitioned troops from the Emperor, commenced hostility with the English, Dutch, and French, and levied *Nazars* and taxes.

It is said that once while unloading from English vessels bales of silk and cotton, and placing these below the fort he unfairly confiscated them. The English troops advancing from Calcutta, arrived near the fort. Pir Khan finding himself an unequal match for them climbed down, when the English troops carried off their goods.

The aforesaid Khan; writing to Nawab Shuja ud-Daulah requisitioned troops to attack the English and by cutting off supplies of Qasimbazar (Cossimbazar/Cassimbazar) and Calcutta, he reduced them to straits. The Chief of the English Factory at Qasimbazar was compelled in consequence to arrange terms of peace, by agreeing to pay three lakhs (three hundred thousand) of rupees as *nazar* to the Nawab. The Chief of the English Factory in Calcutta, borrowing the *nazarana* money from the Calcutta bankers, remitted it to Murshidabad.

Personality

Shuja-ud-Din is remembered as the most successful Nawab of Bengal who ushered in a reign of "rare" prosperity in Bengal, in the 18th century. He had the experience and the tact to handle a vast array of circumstances and learnt well from Murshid Quli Khan. He was known to be shrewd, firm, a well educated and well mannered person. He started an era of secularism in Bengal (in the 18th century) wherein, realizing their potential, very important positions were given to Hindus. While Murshid Quli hailed from the "Aurangzeb school of thought", Shuja was more of a realist, practical and a mild mannered person.

Siyar-ul-Mutakherin by Mir Gholam Hussein-Khan Tabtabai *(translated into English by Lieutenant Colonel John Briggs, M.R.A.S., The British East India Company (Madras Army) in May, 1831.)* notes that the reign of Nawab Shuja-ud-din Muhammad was one of the best (twelve) years of the 18th century for the Subah of Bengal. Well known to be a mild, just, secular and God fearing person Shuja was always interested in learning, jurisprudence and meeting new people who visited Murshidabad from other parts of the world. He was an able administrator and was tactful in dealing with the Mughal Emperor, Nawab of Oudh, Marathas, East India Company, his ambitious Nazims, his own son Sarfaraz Khan and ensured proper checks, balances and controls. He was vastly popular among his subjects as well as with the Mughal Emperor Muhammad Shah.

It is important to note that Shuja never engaged in conflict but managed his resources and manpower well enough to posture, never to attack. He had at his disposal the richest province in the country but had "problems" like Oudh, marauding Marathas and a weak Mughal Emperor. He preferred sending "supplies" to Delhi rather than "armies" to fight for the declining Mughals. He had advised caution while dealing with Nadir Shah and adopted a "hands off" approach on learning that Nadir had left Persia for Delhi. He however kept on sending a part of his revenue collection to Delhi and unlike the Nawab of Oudh kept away from the court intrigues in the Red Fort.

Death and Succession

After his death (of natural causes) in 1739, leaving behind two sons and two daughters. He was succeeded by his son Sarfaraz

Khan. He lies buried in Roshnibag in Murshidabad. His death coincided with the invasion of Delhi by Nadir Shah.

Shuja-ud-Din left behind a very rich and prosperous Bengal to a very average successor, Sarfaraz Khan who had contenders (certainly) better than him. The Nasiri Dynasty lasted for another thirteen months and ended with Sarfaraz Khan.

Trivia

It is believed that during the rule of Shuja-ud-Din Muhammad Khan, rice sold at eight "maunds" to the "rupiyah" or rupee. During Murshid Quli's time, rice sold at five "maunds" to the "rupiyah" or rupee.

Sarfaraz Khan

Early Life

Born Mirza Asadullah, sometime after 1700, he ascended as the Nawab of Bengal under the title Mutaman ul-Mulk, Ala ud-Daula, Nawab Sarfaraz Khan Bahadur, Haidar Jang [Mirza Asadullah], Nawab Nazim of Bengal, Bihar and Orissa. He was earlier raised to the title of Sarfaraz Khan by the Mughal Emperor Farrukh Siyar in 1720 and was the Diwan of Bengal from 1720-1726.

He was the elder son of Mutamad ul-Mulk, Shuja ud-Daula, Nawab Muhammad Shuja Khan Bahadur (Shuja-ud-Din Muhammad Khan), Asad Jang, Nawab Nazim of Bengal, Bihar and Orissa, by his first wife, Zainab un-nisa Begum Sahiba, daughter of Mutamad ul-Mulk, Ala ud-Daula, Nawab Murshid Quli Khan Bahadur Nasiri, Nasir Jang, Nawab Nazim of Bengal and Orissa.

Succession

Sarfaraz Khan succeeded on the death of his maternal grandfather, 30 June 1727 but was deposed in favour of his own father, July 1727. He succeeded his father on his death, 13 March 1739 and remained the Nawab of Bengal between 1739 and 1740 until being defeated by Alivardi Khan in 1740.

Reign

Known to be an extremely pious, religious and moderate ruler he left the administration into the hands of his Nazims and Naib Nazims. Religious matters was his priority. This neglect in administrative matters resulted the gradual rise of Alivardi Khan the Nazim of Azimabad (Patna).

Sarfaraz Khan became the Diwan of Bengal for sometime early into the reign of his father Shuja-ud-Din Muhammad Khan and later became the Nazim of Jahangir Nagar (Dhaka). Sarfaraz, however, did never live in Dhaka and administered it by his adviser Syed Galib Ali Khan. This was because of his disinterest in administrative and economic matters. Such negligence would cost him dearly towards the end of his life.

Sarfaraz Khan was a pious man, full of the outward forms of devotion, and extremely regular in his stated prayers and ablutions. He moreover fasted three full months besides the blessed month of Ramzan, and was scrupulous in the discharge of the several forms of worship to be attended to at different periods throughout the year. He was, however, totally deficient in those great qualities of mind, so indispensably necessary in sovereigns. Wholly engrossed in the little forms of religion, he neglected the affairs of state, and paid no attention to the observance of those duties requisite in a man of his high station and rank. It is true, he offered no injury to the persons of Ray-Rayan, Alam Chand, the Dewan of his father, nor to Jagat Seth or Haji Ahmed, his two other ministers, the latter, men of great abilities and influence, who, together with the Ray-Rayan, had the absolute direction of affairs in the late reign ; but he resigned the reins of government into the hands of a few interested men, who had personal wrongs to revenge.

Among these were Haji Lutfullah, Mardan Ali Khan, Mir Murtaza, and others, who, long incensed against Haji Ahmed, depreciated his character everywhere, and insulted him with taunting expressions. These incensed noblemen, intent on giving vent to their enmity and hatred against Haji Ahmed, caused caricatures to be drawn of him, and eventually effected in Sarfaraz Khan's mind a total alienation of regard towards him. Haji Ahmed was accordingly removed from the office of Dewan, which he had held ever since Shuja-ud-Din Muhammad Khan's accession ; and the office was now bestowed on Mir Murtaza. The viceroy wanted also to deprive Ataullah Khan, son-in-law of the Haji, of the military command of Rajmahal, in order to give it to his own son-in-law Hassan Muhammad Khan.

Intrigues in his Durbar

Haji Ahmed dreading the influence of his numerous enemies, endeavoured to gain strength to oppose them; he therefore wrote every thing to his brother Alivardi Khan, magnifying trifles exceedingly in the representation. Haji Ahmed had the art, too, to persuade the new viceroy to disband great part of his forces, and otherwise to retrench his expenses. Advice so consonant to his feelings was adopted without hesitation ; but while he listened to the counsel of Haji Ahmed to effect reduction, he allowed the arrest of Haji Ahmed's two sons Zain-ud-Din Ahmed Khan, who was on the road from Patna (Azimabad), and Syed Ahmed Khan, who had just arrived from his command of Rangpur.

Sarfaraz Khan now set on foot an inquiry into the management of the public revenue of Azimabad (Patna), and recalled the troops that had been placed by his father under Alivardi Khan, and for whom during many years they had conceived an attachment. On their seeming to hesitate about being removed, he resumed the grant of land which his father Shuja bestowed on them. All these acts were minutely reported by Haji Ahmed, and assiduously trans mitted to his brother Alivardi Khan with the usual exaggeration ; and to give more weight to his own assertions, he used to superadd the testimony of his son Syed Ahmed Khan, who on such occasions submitted to the influence of paternal authority.

Conspiracy of Alivardi Khan

Alivardi Khan daily informed of these events, resolved to avail himself of his acquaintance and connection with his friend Ishaq Khan, at the court of Delhi, a nobleman who was now in *complete possession of the Mughal Emperor's ear*. He wrote him a secret letter, in which he requested to have the patents of the three provinces transferred to himself, under promise of sending to court a present of a crore (ten million) of rupees, besides the whole of Sarfaraz Khan's wealth. To effect this, he required an imperial commission directed to himself, empowering him to wrest the three provinces out of the hands of the present viceroy, Sarfaraz Khan. After having dispatched these letters, he gave out that he intended marching against the zamindars of Bhojpur, and under that pretence he mustered his troops, which he always kept in constant readiness. At the same time, he had the art to give Sarfaraz Khan public notice of his project, though he in reality waited ready to avail himself of the first opportunity to effect his true purpose. At length, ten months after Nadir-shah's departure for Persia, and just thirteen months after Shuja-ud-Din Muhammad Khan's decease, he received the imperialcommission, drawn up in the style he had requested. Being now resolved on marching against Sarfaraz Khan, he wrote secretly to Jagat Seth Fateh Chand, that on a certain day he would commence his march. In March, 1740; Alivardi Khan, set out for Murshidabad, on the context of expedition to Bhojpur, and encamped at some distance from the city of Patna.

Alivardi Khan in a message to Sarfaraz Khan suggested that he was not marching on him but was arriving to pay homage to the Nawab. Initially satisfied, Sarfaraz Khan eventually decided to march on the head of his army and arrived at the town of Comrah on the 9th of April, 1740. Alivardi in the interim, secured the Teliagarhi pass and camped at Rajmahal. The Nawab's army was being led by a seasoned general, Ghaus Khan and Ray-Rayan, Alam Chand also accompanied. The rebel army was being led by Alivardi Khan with Nandalal and Nawazish Muhammad Khan as his deputys. They opposing armies marched on to Giria (Battle of Giria), a village on the banks of the river Bhagirathi for a showdown on the 26th of April, 1740.

Defeat and Death

Sarfaraz was stark unlucky to have an opponent like Alivardi who besides being an excellent leader even at the age of 70, knew Sarfaraz's weaknesses. Sarfaraz Khan was defeated and killed in the Battle of Giria on the banks of the river Bhagirathi. The incumbent Alivardi Khan, the Nazim of Azimabad (Patna) defeated him in a direct conflict. The battle was short but bloody and intense given the "loyalty standards" of the time. The outcome was decided early by Sarfaraz Khan falling to a bullet. The remnants of his army continued to put up a brave resistance but Alivardi Khan was too good a general for them. The conspiracy angle of the battle is covered in detail on the page, Battle of Giria.

Summary

The primary cause for this debacle was that Sarfaraz never saw what was coming in the form of Alivardi Khan and did not take precautionary measures in time. Besides, Alivardi did not give him much time to settle down. Sarfaraz was more concerned of the "bigger threat" Nadir Shah who was vandalizing Delhi and Punjab. Nadir had in fact written to Sarfaraz which aggravated matters further. He can be best described as mild mannered person who neither had the opportunity nor the exceptional merit required to leave a "mark" on history on such troubled times and was consigned to the footnotes of history.

Sarfaraz Khan's reign was for a little over 13 months. The Nasiri Dynasty of Murshid Quli Khan ended with the death of Sarfaraz Khan. Sarfaraz Khan had five sons and five daughters who never made it to the doors of power. He lies buried at Naginabag in Murshidabad.

Afshar (1740-1757)

Alivardi Khan

Ali Vardi Khan was the Nawab of Bengal between 1740 and 1756.

Birth

Ali Vardi was born on May 10, 1671 to Shah Quli Khan Mirza Muhammad Madani and the daughter of Nawab Aqil Khan Afshar. He was named Mirza Muhammad Ali.

Official Name

His official title was *Shuja ul-Mulk, Husam ud-Daula, Nawab Muhammad Alahvirdi Khan Bahadur, Mahabat Jang, Nawab Nazim of Bengal, Bihar and Orissa.*

Life

He was a Shiite Muslim and his father Mirza Muhammad Madani was an employee of Azam Shah, the son of Mughal emperor Aurangzeb. Azam Shah also employed the sons of Mirza Muhammad, but after the death of Azam Shah the family fell into poverty.

His two sons Muhammad Ali and Mirza Ahmed managed to find employment under Orissa's Subdedar Suza-ud-Din. After Suza-ud-din was promoted to nawab the two brothers' future prospects widened. In 1728, Suza-ud-din promoted Muhammad Ali to 'Fauzdar' (General) and entitled him as *Ali Vardi*. In 1733, he was assigned as Bihar's assistant Subedar (governor).

Rise to Power

Ali Vardi Khan however wanted to become the ruler of Bengal himself, on 29 April 1740 he deposed Shuja-ud-din's succesor, Sarfaraz Khan from power, becoming Nawab of Bengal and also got recognition from Mughal emperor Muhammad Shah.

Reign

During his reign Bengal was attacked twice by the Nagpur Kingdom under Raghoji I Bhonsle in 1746 and 1750. This caused the loss of Cuttack to Nagpur in 1750.

Death

He died in 16 April 1756. His grandson Siraj-ud-Daula succeeded Ali Vardi Khan as the Nawab of Bengal in April 1756 at the age of 23.

Siraj ud-Daulah

Mirza Muhammad Siraj-ud-Daulah, more commonly known as *Siraj ud-Daulah* (1733 – July 2, 1757), was the last independent Nawab of Bengal, Bihar and Orissa. The end of his reign marks the start of British East India Company rule over Bengal and later almost all of South Asia. He was also called "Sir Roger Dowlett" by many of the British who were unable to pronounce his name correctly in Hindustani.

Early Years

Siraj's father Zain Uddin was the ruler of Bihar and his mother Amina Begum was the youngest daughter of Nawab Ali Vardi Khan. Since Ali Vardi had no son, Siraj, as his grandson, became very close to him and since his childhood was seen by many as successor to the throne of Murshidabad. Accordingly, he was raised at the nawab's palace with all necessary education and training suitable for a future nawab. Young Siraj also accompanied Ali Vardi in his military ventures against the Marathas in 1746.

Ali Vardi Khan in 1752 officially declared his grandson Crown Prince and successor to the throne, creating no small amount of division in the family and the royal court.

Reign as Nawab

Mirza Mohammad Siraj succeeded Ali Vardi Khan as the Nawab of Bengal in April 1756 at the age of 23, and took the name

Siraj-Ud-Daulah. Siraj-Ud-Daulah's nomination to the nawabship aroused the jealousy and enmity of Ghaseti Begum (the eldest sister of Siraj's mother), Raja Rajballabh, Mir Jafar Ali Khan and Shawkat Jang (Siraj's cousin). Ghaseti Begam possessed huge wealth, which was the source of her influence and strength. Apprehending serious opposition from her, Sirajuddaula seized her wealth from Motijheel Palace and placed her in confinement. The Nawab also gave high government positions to his favourites. Mir Mardan was appointed Bakshi (Paymaster of the army) in place of Mir Jafar. Mohanlal was elevated to the post of peshkar of his Dewan Khana and he exercised great influence in the administration. Eventually Siraj suppressed Shaukat Jang, governor of Purnia, who was killed in a clash.

Black Hole of Calcutta

He, as the direct political disciple of his grandfather, was aware of the global British interest in colonization and hence, resented the British politico-military presence in Bengal represented by the British East India Company. He was annoyed at the company's alleged involvement with and instigation of some members of his own court in a conspiracy to oust him. His charges against the company were mainly threefold. Firstly, that they strengthened the fortification around the Fort William without any intimation and approval; secondly, that they grossly abused the trade privileges granted to them by the Mughal rulers, which caused heavy loss of customs duties for the government; and thirdly, that they gave shelter to some of his officers, for example Krishnadas, son of Rajballav, who fled Dhaka after misappropriating government funds. Hence, when the East India Company started further enhancement of military preparedness at Fort William in Calcutta, Siraj asked them to stop. The Company did not heed his directives, so Siraj-Ud-Daulah retaliated and captured Kolkata (Shortly renamed as Alinagar) from the British in June 1756. During this time, he is alleged to have put 146 British subjects in a 20 by 20 foot chamber, known as the infamous Black Hole of Calcutta; only 23 were said to have survived the overnight ordeal. The real facts around the incident are disputed by later historians, but at that time the lurid account of this incident by one survivor – Holwell – obtained wide circulation in England and helped gain support for the East India Company's continued conquest of India.

The Battle of Plassey

The Battle of Plassey (or Palashi) is widely considered the turning point in the history of India, and opened the way to eventual British domination. After Siraj-Ud-Daulah's conquest of Calcutta, the British responded by sending fresh troops from Madras to recapture the fort and avenge the attack. A retreating Siraj-Ud-Daulah met the British at Plassey, but betrayed by a conspiracy hatched by Jagat Seth, Mir Jafar, Krishna Chandra, Umi Chand etc., he lost the battle and had to escape. He went first to Murshidabad and then to Patna by boat, but was eventually arrested by Mir Jafar's soldiers. Siraj-Ud-Daulah was executed on July 2, 1757 by Mohammad Ali Beg under orders from Mir Jafar.

The Character of Siraj-Ud-Daulah

Siraj-Ud-Daulah is usually proclaimed as a freedom fighter in modern India, Bangladesh, and Pakistan for his opposition to the British annexation. As a teenager, he led a reckless life, which came to the notice of his grandfather. But keeping a promise he made to his dear grandfather on his death bed, he gave up gambling and drinking alcohol totally after becoming the nawab. He was a fierce fighter against the Marathas and the pirates of Southern Bengal as a prince during 1740s, but his forces were later totally routed by the greatly outnumbered British.

"Siraj-ud-daula has been pictured", says the biographer of Robert Clive, *"as a monster of vice, cruelty and depravity."*. In 1778, Robert Orme wrote of the relationship with his maternal grandfather Ali Vardi Khan:

> *"Mirza Mahmud Siraj, a youth of seventeen years, had discovered the most vicious propensities, at an age when only follies are expected from princes. But the great affection which Allaverdy [Ali Vardi] had borne to the father was transferred to this son, whom he had for some years bred in his own palace; where instead of correcting the evil dispositions of his nature, he suffered them to increase by overweening indulgence: taught by his minions to regard himself as of a superior order of being, his natural cruelty, hardened by habit, in conception he was not slow, but absurd; obstinate, sullen, and impatient of contradiction; but notwithstanding this insolent contempt of mankind,the confusion of his ideas rendered him suspicious of all those who approached him, excepting his favourites, who*

were buffoons and profligate men, raised from menial servants to be his companions: with these he lived in every kind of intemperance and debauchery, and more especially in drinking spiritous liquors to an excess, which inflamed his passions and impaired the little understanding with which he was born. He had, however, cunning enough to carry himself with much demureness in the presence of Allaverdy, whom no one ventured to inform of his real character; for in despotic states the sovereign is always the last to hear what it concerns him most to know."

Two Muslim historians of the period wrote of him, and both made specific mention of his exceptional cruelty and arrogance.

Ghulam Husain Salim wrote :

"Owing to Siraj ud Dowla's harshness of temper and indulgence, fear and terror had settled on the hearts of everyone to such an extent that no one among his generals of the army or the noblemen of the city was free from anxiety. Amongst his officers, whoever went to wait on Siraj ud Dowla despaired of life and honour, and whoever returned without being disgraced and ill-treated offered thanks to God. Siraj ud Dowla treated all the noblemen and generals of Mahabat Jang [Ali Vardi Khan] with ridicule and drollery, and bestowed on each some contemptuous nickname that ill-suited any of them. And whatever harsh expressions and abusive epithet came to his lips, Siraj ud Dowla uttered them unhesitatingly in the face of everyone, and no one had the boldness to breath freely in his presence."[1]

Ghulam Husain Tabatabai had this to say about him:

"Making no distinction between vice and virtue, he carried defilement wherever he went, and, like a man alienated in his mind, he made the house of men and women of distinction the scenes of his depravity, without minding either rank or station. In a little time he became detested as Pharaoh, and people on meeting him by chance used to say, 'God save us from him!'"

Najafi (1757-1880)

Mir Jafar

Sayyid Mir Muhammed Jafar Ali Khan, formal title *Shuja ul-Mulk, Hashim ud-Daula, Nawab Ja'afar 'Ali Khan Bahadur, Mahabat*

Jang commonly known as *Mir Jafar*, second son of Sayyid Ahmad Najafi, (1691 –February 5, 1765) was Nawab of Bengal, Bihar and Orissa. He is also known by Indians as *Gaddar-e-Hind* (which translates in English as 'The Traitor of India'). He succeeded Siraj-Ud-Daulah as the eighth Nawab of Bengal, and the first of the Najafi dynasty after deceiving Nawab Siraj-Ud-Daulah and surrendering his army in battle field against Robert Clive. His rule is widely considered the start of British rule in India; it was, however, a key step in eventual British domination of the country.

Mir Jafar is generally regarded in the same manner as Vidkun Quisling in Norway, Benedict Arnold in the United States, and Philippe Petain in France. His memory is widely reviled by the people of Bengal, India and Pakistan; the word *"mirjafar"* in Bengali and the phrase *"meer Jafar"* in Urdu are now synonymous with traitor, used much as *quisling* is used in English, and Jaichand in Indian history.

Early Life

Mir Jafar came to Bengal as a penniless adventurer. He took up a job in Nawab's army and slowly promoted himself. Nawab Ali Vardi Khan later gave him the hand of his half-sister (Shah Khanam) and seven thousand horses to command.

Mir Jafar's initial military career was not without glory. He rescued Ali Vardi Khan's nephew, the hapless Sauqat Jung, from the clutches of Mirza Baqir at Katak. He played a prominent role in Ali Vardi Khan's many military campaigns, specially against the grandson of the earlier nawab Murshid Quli Khan, and the Marathas.

However, Mir Jafar had higher ambitions. Arrogant in his position he took advantage of an Ali Vardi Khan weakened by a decade of fighting with Marathas to enter into a conspiracy with Ataullah (the faujdar of Rajmahal) to overthrow and murder the Nawab. However, the conspiracy was unearthed and he was stripped of most of his powers. He returned to Murshidabad, where he regained the trust of the Nawab's grandson, Siraj-Ud-Daulah, and slowly returned to power and prominence.

The Overthrow of Siraj-Ud-Daulah

Soon after Ali Vardi Khan's natural death, Siraj Ud Daulah became the Nawab of Bengal at Murshidabad. On ascending the throne, he made the controversial decision of elevating a Kayastha named Mohanlal as his supreme Diwan. This elevation of a Hindu to such a prominent position caused the established nobility, and in particular Mir Jafar, great offence. He was then the *bakshi* or head of the armed forces, second only to the Nawab, and the elevation of Mohanlal to a post above him was taken almost as a personal insult. He became determined to overthrow Siraj-Ud-Daulah and gain the Nawabi for himself.

His opportunity came when Shiraj-Ud-Daulah was distracted in his campaign against the British. This was the time when the British contacted him (along with others in the Nawab's court) and offered him the throne if he betrayed Siraj-Ud-Daulah. The Nawab's behaviour had alienated many of his nobles, and many lent a sympathetic ear. However, Siraj-Ud-Daulah returned victorious from Kolkata and discovered the conspiracy; he demoted Mir Jafar and appointed Mir Madan, who was loyal to the Nawab, the new *bakshi*. Ghulam Husain says *"Siraju-d-daulah placing large batteries in front of Mir Jafar's palace was ready to blow him up, and ordered him to quit the City."* There is some question here as to why Mir Jafar was not more severely reprimanded, but its probable that Siraj-Ud-Daulah was wary of going too far given Mir Jafar's influence and widespread dissatisfaction in his court at the time. fact

Mir Jafar was left smarting under this new insult while Siraj-Ud-Daulah was busy with his campaign against the British. He now linked up with the rich bankers Jagat Seth, Umi Chand and the former Diwan, Rai Durlabh and sent out feelers to the British East India Company. Influenced nobles and other officials who joined hands were Mir Bakshi, Manickchand and Khadim Khan On 1 May 1757, the British Calcutta Council made a secret treaty with Mir Jafar, promising to place him on the throne of Bengal. William Watts, the chief of the British factory at Cossimbazar conducted the conspiracy with remarkable diplomatic skill and secrecy. On 5 June 1757 he personally visited Mir Jafar and obtained his oath of allegiance.

Meanwhile, the British had recovered from initial setbacks against Siraj-Ud-Daulah, received reinforcements from Madras, and regrouped under Robert Clive. Siraj-Ud-Daulah was forced to sign the Treaty of Alinagar and retreat to his capital at Murshidabad. He then attempted to win back the support of Mir

Jafar, and apparently thought he had successfully obtained the backing of the considerable military force still under Jafar's command (though no longer Bakshi, Mir Jafar retained a substantial number of foot soldiers and cavalry). Mir Jafar, it is recorded, was not particularly impressed by the promises of Siraj-Ud-Daulah but with some duplicity agreed to support him while continuing to encourage the British in their advances. Siraj-Ud-Daulah finally met the British forces at Plassey for the definitive stand. On the day of the Battle of Plassey, Siraj-Ud-Daulah had the advantage of overwhelming force, but at the critical time Mir Jafar's men stood watching passively rather than engage the enemy. This wiped out much of the numerical superiority that Siraj-Ud-Daulah enjoyed, and the soldiers of Siraj-Ud-Daula were decimated by the smaller but much better armed and trained British forces. Siraj-Ud-Daulah fled but was eventually captured and executed.

The Nawab Years

After Siraj Ud Daulah's defeat and subsequent execution, Mir Jafar achieved his long-pursued dream of gaining the throne, and was propped up by the British as puppet Nawab. Mir Jaar paid a sum of Rs.17,700,000 as compensation for the attack on Calcutta to the company and the traders of the city. In addition, he paid large sums as gifts or bribes to the officials of the company. Clive, for example received over two million rupees, Watts over one million Soon, however, he realised that British expectations were boundless and tried to wriggle out from under them; this time with the help of the Dutch. However, the British defeated the Dutch at the Battle of Chinsurah in November 1759 and retaliated by forcing him to abdicate in favour of his son-in-law Mir Qasim. However, Mir Qasim proved to be both able and independent, willing to live with but not bow to the British. The Company soon went to war with him, and he was eventually overthrown. Mir Jafar managed to regain the good graces of the British; he was again appointed Nawab in 1763 and held the position until his death in 1765.

Descendants

- Mir Jafar probably was the last truly independent ruler of Bengal. After him British ruled Bengal for next 200 years. Interestingly, after 200 years, when British left the region, it was again Mir Jafar's direct descendent Iskandar

Mirza, who became the first independent ruler of Bengal (as East Paakistan).

Mir Qasim

Mir Qasim (also spelt Mir Kasim full name:Mir Kasim Ali Khan) (died 1777) was Nawab of Bengal from 1760 to 1764. He was installed as Nawab by the British East India Company replacing Mir Jafar, his father-in-law,.who had himself been installed by the British after his role in the Battle of Palashi. However, Mir Jafar had started to assert independence by trying to tie up with the Dutch East India Company. The British eventually overran the Dutch forces at Chinsura and replaced Mir Jafar with Mir Qasim. Qasim later fell out with the British and fought them at the Battle of Buxar. His defeat has been suggested as the last real chance of preventing a British-ruled India following Britain's victory in the Seven Years War.

Conflict with British

Upon ascending the throne, Mir Qasim repaid the British with lavish gifts. To please the British, Mir Qasim robbed everybody, confiscated lands, reduced Mir Jafar's purse and depleted the treasury. He also transferred the districts of Burdwan, Midnapur and Chittagong to the British East India Company. However, he soon tired of British interference and endless avarice and like Mir Jafar before him, yearned to break free of the British. He eventually shifted his capital from Murshidabad to Munger in present day Bihar where he raised an independent army, financing them by streamlining reforms in tax collection.

He opposed the British East India Company position that their imperial Mughal licence (*dastak*) meant that they could trade without paying taxes (other local merchants with *dastaks* were required to pay up to 40% of their revenue as tax). Frustrated at the British refusal to pay these taxes, Mir Qasim abolished all taxes on the local traders as well. This upset the advantage that the British traders had been enjoying so far, and hostilities built up. After losing a number of skirmishes, Mir Qasim overran the Company offices in Patna in 1763, killing several Europeans including the Resident. Mir Qasim teamed up with Shuja-ud-Daula of Avadh and Shah Alam II, the itinerant Mughal emperor, who were also threatened by growing British might. However, their combined forces were defeated in the Battle of Buxar in 1764, thus ceding control of the rich Gangetic plain to the British.

The short campaign against British of Mir Qasim was significant. It was a direct fight against outsider British by native Bengali. Unlike Siraj-ud-Daulah before him, Mir Qasim was an effective and popular ruler. The battle with Mir Qasim and the success at Buxar established the British as conquerors of Bengal in a much more real sense than the Battle of Plassey ten years ago.

Death

Mir Qasim died in obscurity, possibly in Delhi in 1777. He passed his last days in abject poverty. His shawl had to be sold for paying off his coroners.

Observation

Mir Qasim was the one of the affected parties of the indecisiveness and foolhardiness of the Nawab of Oudh, Shuja-ud-Daula the first being the Marhattas in the Third Battle of Panipat. Never fully committed to a cause, Shuja lost the Battle of Buxar in spite of having vast numerical superiority due to poor planning and the fact that he was trying to score a point over the Mughal Emperor and the Nawab of Bengal.

Najimuddin Ali Khan

Sayyid Najimuddin Ali Khan formally known as *Sujah-ul-Mulk Najimuddaula Nawab Nazim Najimuddin Ali Khan Bahadur Mahabat Jang* (c1747-1766) was Nawab of Bengal, Bihar and Orissa from 1765 to 1766. The son of Mir Jafar with his third wife Munui Begum, he was the ninth Nawab of Bengal and the second from the Najafi dynasty.

Najimuddin was installed as Nawab of Bengal following the death of his father Mir Jafar when only 18 years of old. He ascended to the throne on 3 March, 1765. He was, like his father, a puppet Nawab propped up by and subordinate to the Company.

In 1765, following victory in the Battle of Buxar the British had formally gained Diwani of Bengal, Bihar and Orissa from Shah Alam II. The Nawab formally conferred this Diwani to the British on 30 September, 1765. The British then proceeded to strip the Nawabi of all effective administrative and military powers, leaving the Nawab even more a puppet than before.

Najimuddin died soon afterwards, on 8 May, 1766, apparently from a fever caught at a formal party given on the grounds of Murshidabad fort in honour of Robert Clive. He was buried at Jaffraganj cemetery and was succeeded to the Nawab's throne by his younger brother Najabut Ali Khan.

Najabut Ali Khan

Sayyid Najabut Ali Khan formal title *"Saif-ul-Mulk Saifuddaula Nawab Nazim Syed Najabut Ali Khan Bahadur Shahamut Jang"* (c1750-1770), son of Mir Jafar and his third wife Munni Begum succeeded his elder brother Najimuddin Ali Khan was the Nawab of Bengal, Bihar and Orissa on 22 May, 1766.

He was the tenth Nawab of Bengal and the third from the Najafi dynasty. Only sixteen when he became Nawab, he reigned under the Regency of his mother. He died of smallpox on 10 March, 1770.

Ashraf Ali Khan

Sayyid Ashraf Ali Khan (1770 CE) was the eleventh Nawab of Bengal, Bihar and Orissa and the fourth of the Najafi dynasty. The son of Mir Jafar and Rahat-un-Nisa, he was adopted and reared by his aunt Nafisat-un-Nisa (Majhli Begum).

He ascended the throne on 21 March, 1770 and died a mere three days later on 24 March, 1770 of smallpox. He was succeeded by his brother Mubaraq Ali Khan.

- Mubaraq Ali Khan (1770-1793)
- Baber Ali Khan (1793-1810)
- Zainul Abedin Ali Khan (1810-1821)
- Ahmad Ali Khan (1821-1824)
- Mubarak Ali Khan II (1824-1838).

Mansur Ali Khan (Nawab of Bengal)

Nawab Sayyid Mansur Ali Khan (29 October 1830-4 November 1884) was Nawab of Bengal until his abdication in 1880, whereupon he renounced his titles and position as Nawab of Bengal. Bengal had already been under occupation of the British since 1773, when Hastings was appointed by the East India Company as first Governor General of Bengal, so he was nothing more than a puppet of the British.

Biography

Marriage and Children

Had total five wives:

1. Shams i Jehan Begum, died 1905
2. Malika Zamani
3. Shah-un nisa
4. Sarah Vennell (English woman)
5. Julia Lewis (English woman).

Mansur Ali Khan left a total of 101 children, of whom 19 sons and 20 daughters survived him.

Death and Afterward

Mansur Ali Khan died in 1884 from cholera. He was succeeded by his eldest son, Nawab Sayyid Hassan Ali Mirza Khan Bahadur as Nawab of Murshidabad. His great-grandson Iskander Mirza (through his son Bahadur Syed Iskander Ali and his son Mohammad Fateh Ali) became first president of Pakistan in 1956.

Nawabs of Murshidabad (Najafi) 1880-1969

- Nawab Sayyid Hassan Ali Mirza Khan Bahadur (1880-1906)
- Nawab Sayyid Wasif Ali Mirza Khan (1906-1959)
- Nawab Sayyid Waris Ali Mirza Khan Bahadur (1959-1969).

2

Nawabs of Awadh

The Nawab of Awadh is the title of rulers who governed the state of Awadh in India in the 18th and 19th century.

Establishment

As the Mughal power declined and the emperors lost their paramountcy and they became first the puppets and then the prisoners of their feudatories, so Awadh grew stronger and more independent. Its capital city was Faizabad. Of all the Muslim states and dependencies of the Mughal empire, Awadh had the newest royal family. They were descended from a Persian adventurer called Sa'adat Khan, originally from Khurasan in Persia. There were many Khurasanis in the service of the Mughals, mostly soldiers, and if successful, they could hope for rich rewards. Burhan ul Mulk Sa'adat Khan proved to be amongst the most successful of this group. In 1732, he was made governor of the province of Awadh. His original title was Nazim, which means Governor, but soon he was made Nawab. In 1740, the Nawab was called Wazir or vizier, which means Chief Minister, and thereafter he was known as the Nawab Wazir. In practice, from Sa'adat Khan onwards, the titles had been hereditary, though in theory they were in the gift of the Mughal emperor, to whom allegiance was paid. A nazar, or token tribute, was sent each year to Delhi, and members of the imperial family were treated with great deference; two of them actually lived in Lucknow after 1819, and were treated with great courtesy.

Inclination Towards British

Achieving a certain degree of independence from the Moghuls in Delhi did not, unfortunately, mean that the Nawabs could rule entirely as they pleased. They had merely exchanged one master for another. The British, in the form of the East India Company based in Calcutta, had long looked with predatory eyes at the wealth of Awadh. Excuses for interference in the province were not hard to find. The most catastrophic from the Awadh point of view came when Shuja-ud-Daula invaded Bengal, and actually briefly held Calcutta. But British military victories at Plassey in 1757 and Buxar in 1764 utterly routed the Nawab. When peace was made, Awadh had lost much land. But the enemies became friends, on the surface anyway, and the Nawab Wazir was extolled in the British Parliament as the Chief native allay of the East India Company in all India.

The Nawabs surrendered their independence little by little over many years. To pay for the protection of British forces and assistance in war, Awadh gave up first the fort of Chunar, then the districts of Benares and Ghazipur, then the fort at Allahabad; all the time the cash subsidy which the Nawab paid to the Company grew and grew.

In 1773, the fatal step was taken by the Nawab of accepting a British Resident at Lucknow, and surrendering to the Company all control over foreign policy. Soon the Resident, however much he might defer ceremonially to the Nawab, became the real ruler.

Move of Capital

Asaf-ud-Daula, son of Shuja-ud-Daula, moved the capital from Faizabad to Lucknow in 1775 and made it one of the most prosperous and glittering cities in all India. It is said, he moved because he wanted to get away from the control of a dominant mother. On such a thread did the fate of the great city of Lucknow depend!

Nawab Asaf-ud-Daula was a generous and sympathetic ruler, an inveterate builder of monuments and a discriminate patron of the arts. He built the Bara Imambara with its intricate bhul-bhulayya and adjoining mosque, primarily to create employment for his subjects during a time of drought. The Rumi Darwaza also testifies to his architectural zeal.

The British Interference

His son, Wazir Ali, was the one who most regretted his grandfather's acceptance of a British resident at Lucknow. In 1798, the Governor-General removed him from the throne, on the excuse that there was doubt as to whether he was a true son of Asaf-ud-Daula, but more probably because he was displaying tendencies to independence. They put Asaf's brother, Sadat Ali Khan, on the throne. Sadat Ali Khan, though economical in fiscal management, was nevertheless an enthusiastic builder and commissioned many grand palaces, including Dilkusha, Hayat Baksh and Farhat Baksh, as well as the famous Lal Baradari. Hereafter the dynasty had to look to Calcutta rather than to Delhi to settle the succession.

The assassination of a British Resident in 1798 in Benares by the deposed Wazir Ali gave further excuse for interference, and Lord Wellesley (brother of the Duke of Wellington) was just the man to exploit it. By the treaty of 1801, the Nawab had to give up his own army, and pay heavily for a British-led one in its place. The southern doab (Rohilkhand) was ceded, and the remainder of the district of Allahabad and other areas became part of British India. In thirty years, Awadh had lost half its territory to the British.

The Nawab demanded in return for these concessions that he should have a free hand in governing his remaining territory, unchecked by the advice or interference of the British. But in this, he was badly handicapped by the fact that he had to rely on British troops to enforce his orders. Wellesley had another trick up his sleeve: a clause of the treaty by which the Nawab under-took to establish a system of administration "by the advice of and acting in conformity to the counsel of the officers of the Honourable Company" which should be conducive to the prosperity of his subjects. It seemed a harmless clause, but was to be the means by which the British eventually annexed Awadh.

The Golden Age

From 1819 onwards, things ran their course in Avadh. Sadat Ali being gathered to his fathers, Ghazi his son, sat on the musnud, the throne, and took the cognomen "ud-Din", implying Defender of the Faith. He was formally invested with the title of King by the British, though ironically the proclamation of kingship coincided with a period of almost complete dependence on the British. He lent two millions of rupees to the British feringhee for the Nepal War, and at its close got the Nepalese Terai, a marshy forest extending along the foot of the Himalayas in liquidation of half the debt. Some might have thought it a poor bargain, but in fact the Terai eventually produced some very valuable timber.

Ghazi-ud-Din was a good monarch, responsible for much building and public works of all kinds, and he paid due attention to the administration of justice. He built the Mubarak Manzil and Shah Manzil as well as Hazari Bagh, in which he introduced Lucknow society to the sport of animal contests for the first time

However, his son Nasir-ud-Din who succeeded to the throne, had an attachment to the English, not founded upon those things the English would like to be admired for justice, liberty, democracy but upon their dress, their eating habits and, more unfortunately, the drinking habits of the more disreputable element of English adventurer with whom he surrounded himself.

Nasir-ud-Din, despite such a temperament, was a popular monarch, who was responsible for the construction of an astrological centre, Tarunvali Kothi. Equipped with sophisticated instruments, it was entrusted to the care of a British astronomer. When he died there was another disputed succession and the British insisted on Muhammed Ali, another son of Sadat Ali, being enthroned. Muhammed Ali was a just and popular ruler and under him, Lucknow regained its splendour for a brief spell. He was however sorely troubled by rheumatism. He died in 1842 and his son Amjad Ali succeeded, a man more inclined towards matters religious and spiritual, leading to the neglect of governance.

Annexation by British

Amjad Ali was succeeded by Wajid Ali Shah, poet, singer, avid patron of the arts and lover of Lucknow. Of him it was written, "He is entirely taken up in the pursuit of his personal gratifications. He has no desire to be thought to take any interest whatever in public affairs and is altogether regardless of the duties and responsibilities of his high office. He lives exclusively in the society of fiddlers, eunuchs and women: he has done so since his childhood, and is likely to do so till his last."

This portrait of Wajid Ali Shah was used to justify British annexation of Awadh. If the charges of mismanagement levied against Wajid Ali Shah were true, the British were as much responsible for this as the Nawab. They were more in control of the administration and finances of Awadh since the 1780's than the Nawab. In addition, Awadh had been impoverished by the incessant cash demands of the British on the Nawab. The excuse at last came for the British to invoke that clause of the 1801 Treaty. And the Governor General in 1856, Lord Dalhousie, was just the man to do it. Awadh was annexed, Wajid Ali Shah shipped off to virtual imprisonment in Matiyaburj in Calcutta and, though this was not on the British programme, the stage set for the greatest rebellion to date against their power in India.

Revolt of 1857

One of Wajid Ali Shah's wives, the Begum Hazrat Mahal, remained in Lucknow, and when the Mutiny came in 1857, she put herself at the head of those fighting for freedom.

The Begum never did surrender, she died in Nepal in 1879.

Saadat Ali Khan I

Saadat Ali Khan (b.c.1680-d.19 March 1739) was the Subedar Nawab of Oudh from 26 January 1775 to 21 September 1797, and the son of Muhammad Nasir.

Life

Sa'adat Khan whose former name was Muhammad Amin was originally a merchant of Khurasan. He is the progenitor of the Nawabs of Oudh. His father Nasir Khan came to India during the reign of Bahadur Shah I and after his death Muhammad Amin came also.

Career

At the commencement of the emperor Muhammad Shah's reign he held the *faujdari* (garrison commander) of Bayana..

He was given the title of "Sadat Khan Bahadur".

He was made governor of Agra on Oct 15, 1720 AD.

He was given the title of "Captain of the Imperial Body Guards" on Jan 12, 1721 AD.

He was also made the governor of Oudh and the army-in-charge of Gorakhpur on Sep 9, 1722 AD, with the title of Sa'adat Khan in place of Raja Girdhar who was appointed governor of Malwa.

Oudh under him included five districts Khalilabad, Faizabad, Gorakhpur, Bahraich and Lucknow. Boundaries of Oudh stretched to Himalayan hills in north, Bihar in east, in south unto Kara

Manikpur of Allahabad province and in west unto Kannauj. From Gorakhpur to Kannauj 270 miles long and from northern hills to Kara Manikpur the province was 230 miles wide, totaling to 1,01,71,080 Bigha in area.

Local kings, zamindars and jagirdars have created mismanagement and destroyed the peace of the area since the reign of Aurangzeb, specially the Sheikh Zadas. Sadat Khan tamed them, made his own palace near Ayodhya, and founded a new city Faizabad, which became the capital of the new government. Due to his management policy state's income rose from Rupees 70 lakhs to 2 crores.

On his success Muhammad Shah was very pleased and given him the title of "Burhan-ul-Mulk".

Sadat Khan enlarged the state boundary on eastern front by taking Banaras, Jaunpur, Ghazipur and Chunar under his control from Jagirdar Murtaza Khan in 1728 AD.

He was present in the Battle of Karnal with Nadir Shah.

Death

Sadat Khan died on the night previous to the massacre of Delhi by Nadir Shah on the March 19, 1739. He was buried at Delhi in the mausoleum of his brother Sayadat Khan. At the time of his death, there were 22 lakhs army men, 50 tanks and crores of Rupees.

Issue & Successor

His only child was a daughter who was married to his nephew *Abul Mansur Khan* Safdarjung the son of Sayadat Khan who succeeded him in the government of Oudh.

Safdarjung

Safdarjung (b.c. 1708-d. 05 October 1754) was the Subadar Nawab of Oudh from 19 March 1739 to 05 October 1754.

Life

Safdarjung was born as Muhammad Muqim in Khurasan, Persia and migrated to India in 1722.

Career

He succeeded his father-in-law and maternal uncle Burhan ul

Mulk Sa'adat Khan to the throne of Oudh, apparently by paying Nadir Shah two crores of rupees. The Mughal Emperor Muhammad Shah gave him the title of "Safdarjung".

Safdarjung was an able administrator. He was not only effective in keeping control of Oudh, but also managed to render valuable assistance to the weakened Muhammad Shah. He was soon given governorship of Kashmir as well, and became a central figure at the Delhi court. During the later years of Muhammad Shah, he gained complete control of administration in the Mughal Empire. When Ahmad Shah Bahadur ascended the throne at Delhi, Safdarjung became his *Wazir ul-Mamalik-i-Hindustan* or Chief Minister of India. However, court politics eventually overtook him and he was dismissed in 1753.

After the accession of Ahmad Shah in 1748, he made sufdarjung his Chief Minister and gave him the charge of "Harem". He was also made the governor of Ajmer and became the "Faujdar " of Narnaul. This was fact that all the power of Mughal Empire was bestowed upon Safdarjung by the end of second half of 18th century. Apart from these responsibilities of Delhi Safdarjung has not neglected the Oudh and its prosperity, which he considered as his family property. Due to corrupt policy of Delhi court and confrontation with Ahmad Shah, he came to Oudh in Dec' 1753 AD, where he died in Oct'1755 AD at the age of 46 years.

Tomb

The Safdarjung's Tomb, built in 1754 is now situated on a road known as Safdarjung Road, in New Delhi.

There are several other structures that carry his name today in the area, like Safdarjung Airport, Safdarjang Hospital, Safdarjung Terminal, and a nearby residential neighbourhood of Safdarjung (colony).

Shuja-ud-Daula

Shuja-ud-Daula (b.January 19, 1732 (1732-01-19)-d.January 26, 1775) was the Subedar Nawab of Oudh from 05 October 1754 to 26 January 1775, and the son of Muhammad Nasir.

Though a minor royal, he is best known for his key roles in two definitive battles in Indian history-the Third Battle of Panipat which ended Maratha domination of India, and the Battle of Buxar that definitively established British domination.

The Third Battle of Panipat

Shuja's decision about whom to join as an ally in the Third Battle of Panipat was one of the decisive factors that determined the outcome of the war as lack of food due to the Afghans cutting the supply lines of Marathas was one of the reasons that Marathas could not sustain the day long battle. Their forces were weak due to starvation and also fighting facing the sun.

Shuja was earlier not very sure about whose side should he take before the Third Battle of Panipat. Marathas were still further south then and it would have taken them considerable time to reach Shuja's province. Considering the risk he had with upsetting Abdali with his huge army on his soil he took (albeit hesitatingly) the decision to join the Afghans and Najib (Najib-ud-Daula). His mother was of the opinion that he should join the Marathas as they had helped his father previously on numerous occasions. Eventually he was forced to join the Afghans that were led by Ahmad Shah Durrani, whose troops crossed the flooded Ganga river into his province.

The Battle of Buxar

Shuja is also known for his role in the Battle of Buxar, a battle that was no less definite in Indian history. He along with the forces of Shah Alam II and Mir Qasim were defeated by the British forces in one of the key battles in the history of British rule in India.

Treaty of Allahabad

The Treaty of Allahabad was signed on August 16, 1765 between Mughal Emperor Shah Alam II of Bengal and Lord Clive of the British East India Company after the Battle of Buxar (1764). Based on the terms of the agreement, Shah Alam II granted Diwani rights to the East India Company. These rights allowed the Company to collect revenue from the people of Bengal, Bihar, and Orissa. In return, the Company gave an annual tribute of 2.6 million rupees (260,000 British pounds) while securing for Shah Alam II the districts of Kora and Allahabad. The tribute money paid to the emperor was for the maintenance of the court of Allahabad. The accord also dictated that Shah Alam II restore to Balwant Singh the province of Varanasi as long as Balwant Singh continued to pay revenue to the Company.— Excerpted from Treaty of Allahabad on Wikipedia, the free encyclopedia.

Whereas the Right Honourable Robert Lord Clive, baron Clive of Plassey, Companion on the most Honourable Order of the Bath, Major General and Commander of the Forces, President of the council and Governor of Fort-William, and of all the settlements belonging to the united Company of Merchants of England trading to the East Indies in the provinces of Bengal, Behar, and Orissa ; and John Carnac Esquire, Brigadier General, Colonel in the service of the said Company, and commanding officer of their forces upon the Bengal establishment, *are invested with full and ample powers,* on the behalf of his Excellency the Nabob Najim al Dowlah, Subahdar of Bengal, Bahar, and Orissa, and likewise on behalf of the united Company of Merchants of England trading to the East Indies, to negotiate, settle, and finally to conclude a firm and lasting peace with his Highness the Nabob Sujah al Dowlah, Vizier of the Empire : Be it known to all those to whom it may or shall in any manner belong, that the above-named plenipotentiaries have agreed upon the following articles with his Highness.

1st. A perpetual and universal peace, sincere friendship, and firm union shall be established between his Highness Sujah al Dowlah and his heirs, on the one part, and his Excellency Najim al Dowlah, and the English East India Company, on the other, so that the said contracting powers shall give their greatest attention to maintain between themselves, their dominions, and their subjects, this reciprocal friendship, without permitting, on either side, any kind of hostilities to be committed from henceforth for any cause, or under any pretence whatsoever ; and every thing shall be carefully avoided, which might hereafter prejudice the union now happily established.

2nd. In case the dominions of his Highness Sujah al Dowlah shall at any time hereafter by attacked, his Excellency Najim al Dowlah and the Englsih Company, shall assist him with a part or the whole of their forces, according to the exigency of his affairs, and so far as may be consistent with their own security ; and if the dominions of his Excellency Najim al Dowlah, or the English Company, shall be attaked, his Highness shall in like maner assist them with a part or the whole of his forces ; in the case of the English Company's forces being employed in his Highness's service, the extraordinary expense of the same is to be defrayed by him.

3rd. His Highness solemnly engages never to entertain Coffim Aly khawn, the late Subahdar of Bengal, &c. Sumroo the assassin of the English, nor any of the European deserters within his dominions, nor to give the least countenance, support, or protection to them : he likewise solemnly engages to deliver up to the English whatever Europeans may in future desert from this into his country.

4th. The King, Shah Allum, shall remain in full possession of Cora, and such part of the province of Illahabad as he now possesses, *which are ceded to his Majesty* as a royal demesne for the support of his dignity and expences.

5th. His Highness Sujah al Dowlah engaged, in the most solemn manner, to continue Bulwant Sing in the Zemindaries of Banaras, Ghazipoew, and all those districts he possessed at the time he came over to the late Nabob Jaffier Ally Khawn and the English, on condition of his paying the same revenue as heretofore.

6th. In consideration of the great expense incurred by the English Company in carrying on the late war, his Highness agrees to pay them (fifty) 50 lacks of rupees, in the following manner, viz. (twelve) 12 lacks in money, and a deposit of jewels, to the amountof eight lacks, upon the signing of this treaty ; (five) 5 lacks one month after, and the remaining (twenty-five) 25 lacks by monthly payments, so as that the whole may be discharged in (thirteen) 13 monts from the date hereof.

7th. It being firmly resolved to restore his Highness the country of Banaras, and the other districts now rented by Bulwant Sing, notwithstanding *the grant of the same from* THE KING to the English Company ; it is therefore agreed that they shall be ceded to His Highness in manner following, viz. They shall remain in the hands of the English Company with their revenues, till the expiration of the agreement between the Rajah Bulwant Sing and the Company, being on the 27th November next ; after which his Highness shall enter into possession, the fort of Chunar excepted, which is not to be evacuated until the 6th article of this treaty be fully complied with.

8th. His Highness shall allow the English Company to carry on trade, duty free, throughout the whole of his dominions.

9th. All the relations and subjects of his Highness, who in any manner assissted the English during the course of the late war, shall be forgiven, and no ways molested for the same.

10th. As soon as this treaty is executed, the English forces shall be withdrawn from the dominions of his Highness, excepting such as may be necessary for the garrison of Chunar, or for *the defence and protection of* THE KING in the city of Allahabad, if his Majesty should require a force for that purpose.

11th. His Highness the Nabob Sujah al Dowlah, his Excellency the Nabob Najim al Dowlah, and the English Company, promise to observe sincerely all the articles contained and settled in the present treaty ; and they will not suffer the same to be infringed, directly or indirectly, by their respective subjects ; and the said contracting powers generally and reciprocally guarantee to each other all the stipulations of the present treaty.

Clive, John Carnac, Sujah al Dowlah's seal and ratification, Mirza Qasim Khan, rajah shettabroy, meer masha allah, signed, sealed, and solemnly sworn to, according to their respective faiths, by the contracting parties at Allahabad, this 16th day of August, in the year of our Lord 1765, in the presence of us,— — edmund maskelyne, archib. Swinton, george vansittart.

Asaf-ud-Dowlah

Asaf-ud-Daula (birth:23 September 1748-death:21 September 1797) was the nawab wazir of Oudh from 26 January 1775 to 21 September 1797, and the son of Shuja-ud-Dowlah, his mother and grandmother being the begums of Oudh, whose spoliation formed one of the chief counts in the charges against Warren Hastings.

Life

A contemporary chronicler describes the person of Asafuddaula as follows:

"His features bore a general resemblance to his father's. The upper part of his body was rather long, but the lower part from waist downwards was very short. From his childhood he was obese ; his fat ears, neck and double chin were one fleshy mass. His fingers and palm were short and plump. From his boyhood he was addicted to frivolities and his natural inclinations and attachments were for low, ill-born and base-minded associates. He used to laugh unseasonably, fling derisive abuse at others and desire derisive abuse in return. He delighted in meaningless amusements and was immensely pleased with anyone who indulged in filthy language; and the more obscene the conversation was in any company the better he was pleased."

John Bristow, Resident in Oudh when Asafuddaula ascended the masnad, wrote of him: "His Excellency is juvenile in his amusements, volatile, injudicious in the choice of his confidants, and so familiar in his conversation as to throw aside the sovereign and admit his favourites to a freedom destructive to all subordination and a cause for the inattention paid by them to his commands. He frequently passes whole days in dissipation and is of late much given to liquor, for I have known him to make himself and his favourites and even his menial servants indecently drunk. By this mode of passing his time he can have little leisure for business and indeed he hardly attends to any excepting when I wait upon him on the Company's affairs, and then I am generally referred to his minister, to whom and other favourites he confides the entire charge of this government."

Shujauddaula had made all possible effort to make his eldest son and heir-apparent in every way a worthy successor to himself. The best of tutors were engaged to impart princely qualities to Asafuddaula, but all that he added to his native generosity was skill in archery. Of his generosity tales are still heard in Lucknow and elsewhere in Oudh, and shopkeepers in Lucknow even today open their shops with his name on their lips. Perhaps some vanity was mixed with his generosity, and many a foreign adventurer made fortunes by playing upon this trait of his character. He readily bought from them worthless tinsels for lakhs of rupees and when reprimanded by his ministers, confessed that he did so with his eyes open, but how could he refuse one who had taken the trouble of travelling all the way to Oudh having heard of his generosity!

When of marriageable age, Asafuddaula was married to the daughter of Imtiazuddaula, a nobleman who wielded considerable influence in the Court of the Emperor at Delhi. But the nawab was an invert and the marriage never seems to have been consummated.

Days in Reign

Asafuddaula became nawab at the age of 26, on the death of his father, Shujauddaula, on 28 January 1775.

When Shuja-ud-Daulah died he left two million pounds sterling buried in the vaults of the zenana. The widow and mother of the deceased prince claimed the whole of this treasure under the terms of a will which was never produced. When Warren Hastings pressed the nawab for the payment of debt due to the British East India Company, he obtained from his mother a loan of 26 lakh (2.6 million) rupees, for which he gave her a jagir (land) of four times the value; of subsequently obtained 30 lakh (3 million) more in return for a full acquittal, and the recognition of her jagirs without interference for life by the Company. These jagirs were afterwards confiscated on the ground of the begum's complicity in the rising of Chai Singh, which was attested by documentary evidence, as the evidence now available seems to show that Warren Hastings did his best throughout to rescue the nawab from his own incapacity, and was inclined to be lenient to the begums.

Towards the beginning of Asafuddaula's rule, men of learning and art avoided Lucknow because Asafuddaula had no regard for such people and gathered round the Begams and their eunuchs Court at Fyzabad, but later on Asafuddaula took greater interest in such people and induced most of them to attach themselves to his Court at Lucknow.

Faiz Bakhsh makes repeated references to the nawab's indifference to civil and military affairs and to his lack of ambition. Shujauddaula died in the month of Shaban. Four months after came the Muharram celebrations and taziadari was observed by Asafuddaula at Fyzabad. After that he spent four or five months on the banks of the Ghagra in the sand and dust without any reason, and he did not evince the slightest inclination to undertake the discipline of the troops or civil administration, to know the leading military officers or inspect the manoeuvres of the regiments, to examine the ammunition and equipment of tho artillery or hear the items of negligence in reports. In all these Shujauddaula had been unremittingly employed.

Asafuddaula left the entire work of administration in the hands of Mukhtaruddaula. In 1776 there occurred a serious mutiny among the nawab's regulars at Fyzabad, and although the nawab's and the English intelligencers had dispatched to the sarkar full accounts of the outrages and disturbances during two days and nights, the nawab was so indifferent to public affairs that he remained uninformed. After Mukhtaruddaula's death, Asafuddaula found a new minister in the person of Haidar Beg Khan in whose hands he left all power and authority. Faiz Bakhsh tells of an amusing incident which brings out the difference between Asafuddaula and his father. Referring to Asafuddaula's practice of annually visiting the hill resort of Bitul, he says, "Shujauddaula had once proposed to go to the foot of the hills. The people of the hills, knowing that he was an intrepid soldier and had an army and artillery, and fearing that he might become acquainted with the mountain paths and annex their country, became greatly alarmed, and they opened an embankment which confined the water in a certain place, and let it flow, so that his tents could not be pitched. He turned back quickly. The mountaineers, however, knew that Asafuddaula did not trouble himself about his dominions, that he had readily given up Benares, a rich province [to the British], and this was a gauge of his greed for territory, so they freely allowed him access."

Movement of Capital

In 1775 he moved the capital of Oudh from Faizabad to Lucknow and built various monuments in and around Lucknow, including the Bara Imambara.

Architectural & other Contribution

Nawab Asaf-ud-Dowlah is considered the Architect General of Lucknow. With the ambition to outshine the splendour of Mughal architecture, he built a number of monuments and developed the city of Lucknow into an architectural marvel. Several of the buildings survive today, including the famed Asafi Imambara which attracts tourits even today, and the Qaisar Bagh area of downtown Lucknow where thousands live in resurrected buildings.

The Asafi Imambara is a famed vaulted structure surrounded by beautiful gardens, which the Nawab started as a charitable project to generate employment during the famine of 1784. In that famine even the nobles were reduced to penury. It is said that Nawab Asaf employed over 20,000 people for the project (including commoners and noblemen), which was neither a masjid nor a mousoleum (contrary to the popular contemporary norms of buildings). The Nawab's sensitivity towards preserving the reputation of the upper class is demonstrated in the story of the construction of Imambara. During daytime, common citizens employed on the project would construct the building. On the night of every fourth day, the noble and upper class people were employed in secret to demolish the structure built, an effort for which they received payment. Thus their dignity was preserved.

The Nawab became so famous for his generosity that it is still a well-known saying in Lucknow that "he who does not receive (livelihood) from the Lord, will receive it from Asaf-ud-Dowlah" (*Jisko de na Moula, usko de Asaf-ud-Doula*).

One of his many acts of generosity was the digging of a canal known as Nahar-i-Asafi in Najaf Ashraf, where the prophet Ali's tomb is, at a cost of about 7 lakhs of rupees.

Death

The nawab died of dropsy on 21 September 1797 (28 Rabi I, 1212 A.H.) at the age of 48/51 in Lucknow and is buried at Bara Imambara, Lucknow.

His Durbar

Chief Minister (Diwan)

- Mukhtaruddaula Murtaza Khan (In office from 28 January 1775 to March 1776 (7 Safar 1190 A.H.))
- Muhammad Ilich Khan (In office from March 1776 to August 1776)
- Hasan Raza Khan (In office from August 1776 to June 1796)
- Jhao Lal (In office from June 1796 to early 1797)
- Almas All Khan (In office for a day, 1797)
- Tafazzul Hussain Khan (In office from early 1797 to 1800).

Assistant Minster to Chief Minister

- Haidar Beg Khan (In office from August 1776 to 5 June 1792)
- Raja Tikait Rai (In office from June 1792 to June 1796).

Other Durbaris

It will suffice to mention here only the names of some of the lesser personalities in the nawab's durbar who during the period under review had had a share in the government of Oudh.

They were :

- Surat Singh,
- Raja Jagannath,
- Hulas Rai,
- Buchhraj,

- Tahsin Ali Khan,
- Balakram,
- Bhagwan Das,
- Dhanpat Rai,
- Bhawani Mahra,
- Zainulabdin,
- Mirza Hasan,
- Mehdi Ali,
- Govindram,
- Ratan Chand,
- Abu Talib, etc.

They possessed varying degrees of ability and power, the two not always proportionate to each other because they were employed either haphazardly or deliberately with corrupt intentions.

Wazir Ali Khan

Wazir Ali Khan (b.c. 1780-d.c. 1817) was fourth nawab wazir of Oudh from 21 September 1797 to 21 January 1798, and the son of Muhammad Nasir.

Life

He was adopted the son of Asaf-Ud-Dowlah, who although keeping a Harem of 500 women had no legitimate son. He purchased the pregnant daughter of a servant. Enchanted by the boy he adopted and pampered him. At 13 years of age Ali, who was known to have a cruel streak, was married at the cost of £ 300000 in Lucknow.

After the death of his "father" he ascended to the throne (*musnud*), with support of the British. Within four month they accused him of being unfaithful. Sir John Shore (1751-1834) moved in with 12 battalions and replaced him with his uncle Saadat Ali Khan II.

Attack on Davis' House (14. Feb. 1799)

Ali was granted a pension of 20000 Rupies and removed to Benares. Government in Calcutta decided that he should be removed further from his former realm. Mr. Cherry, British resident, relayed this order to him on Feb. 14th during a breakfast invitation to which Ali had appeared with an armed guard. During the ensuing argument he struck Cherry a blow with his sabre, whereupon the guards killed the resident and two more Europeans. They then set out attack the house of Mr.Davis, another colonial officer. He defended himself on the staircase of his house until rescued by British troops.

Subsequently Ali assembled an rebellious army of svereal thousand men. A quickly assembled force commanded by Gen. Erskine moved into Benares and "restored order" by the 21st. Ali fled into Rajputana and was granted asylum by the Raja of Jeypore. On request of Arthur Wellesley, Earl of Mornington, the raja turned Ali over to the British on the condition that he neither be hanged nor be put in fetters.

The colonial government complied with this: Ali spent the rest of life-17 years-in an iron cage in Ft. Williams of Calcutta. He was buried in the Muslim graveyard of *Casia Baguan*.

Saadat Ali Khan II

Saadat Ali Khan (b.bf. 1752-d.c. 11 July 1814) was fifth nawab wazir of Oudh from 21 January 1798 to 11 July 1814, and the son of Muhammad Nasir.

Life

He was the second son of Nawab Shuja-ud-daula. Saadat Ali Khan succeeded his half-nephew, Mirza Wazir 'Ali Khan, to the throne of Oudh in 1798 after.

Succession to Throne

Saadat Ali Khan was crowned on 21 January 1798 at Bibiyapur Palace in Lucknow, by Sir John Shore after the assurance from Sadat Ali Khan for acquiescence to the company and to carry out its orders.

Reduction in Power

He was to sign another treaty by which the annual amount to be paid to the Company was increased by 20 lakhs to 76 lakhs. Fort of Allahabad and Fatehgarh along with 12 lakhs were given to Company for putting him on the throne. Governor asked him to reduce the force of Oudh (Which was 80,000 at the time of Asaf-ud-daula). His powers got reduced very much within three years of his reign. He became unable to pay the duesto the Company.

On Nov 10, 1801 AD Company has taken half of the Oudh after his signature. Company got the area of Rohilkhand, Farukhabad, Mainpuri, Etawah, Kanpur, Fatehgarh, Allahabad, Azamgarh, Basti and Gorakhpur, from where Oudh was getting an income of Rs. 3 crores, after the assurance from Sadat Ali Khan for acquiescence to the company and to carry out its orders.

Construction

Most of the buildings between the Kaiserbagh and Dilkusha were constructed by him.

He had a palace called Dilkusha Kothi designed and built by Sir Gore Ouseley in 1805.

Death

Nawab Saadat Ali Khan died in 1814 and he was buried with his wife 'Khursheed Zadi' in the twin Tombs of Qaiserbagh.

Ghazi-ud-Din Hyder

Ghazi-ud-Din Hyder was fifth nawab wazir of Oudh from 11 July 1814 to 19 October 1818 and first King of Oudh from 19 October 1818 to 19 October 1827.

Life

He was the third son of Nawab Saadat Ali Khan and Mushir Zadi was his mother. He became *Nawab Wazir* of Oudh on July 11, 1814 after the death of his father. In 1819, under the influence of Lord Hastings, the British Governor General, he declared himself as the independent *Padshah-i-Avadh* (King of Oudh). He died in the *Farhat Bakhsh* palace in Lucknow in 1827. He was succeeded by his son Nasir-ud-Din Hyder after his death.

Patron of art and Culture

Several monuments in Lucknow were constructed by Ghazi-ud-Din Hyder. He built the Chattar Manzil palace and added the *Mubarak Manzil* and the *Shah Manzil* in the Moti Mahal complex for better viewing of the animal fights. He also constructed the tombs of his parents, Sadat Ali Khan and Mushir Zadi Begum. For his European wife, he constructed a European style building known as the *Vilayati Bagh*. Another creation, the *Shah Najaf Imambara* (1816), his mausoleum, on the bank of the Gomti is a copy of the fourth Caliph Ali's burial place in Najaf, Iraq. His three wives,

Sarfaraz Mahal, Mubarak Mahal and Mumtaz Mahal were also buried here.

Ghazi-ud-Din first appointed a British artist, Robert Home (1752 – 1834) as his court artist and after his retirement in 1828, he appointed another British, George Duncan Beechey (1798 – 1852) as his court artist. In 1815, Raja Ratan Singh (1782-1851), a noted astronomer, poet and scholar of Arabic, Persian, Turkish, Sanskrit and English joined his court. Because of his initiative, a royal litho printing press in Lucknow was set up in 1821 and the *Haft Qulzum*, a dictionary and grammar of the Persian language in two volumes was published from this press in the same year.

Coins of Ghazi-ud-Din

After declaring himself as King, Ghazi-ud-Din Hyder issued coins on his name instead of the Mughal emperor, Shah Alam II from AH 1234 (1819). His coins were completely different from his predecessors. The most important feature of his coinage was the introduction of his coat of arms on the reverse of coin, consisting of two fish facing each other, two tigers each holding a pennon for support and a *Katar* (a small dagger) surmounted by a crown symbolizing the king.

Nasiruddin Hyder

Nasir-ud-din Haidar was second King of Oudh from 19 October 1827 to 7 July 1837.

Life

He was the son of Ghaziuddin Hyder..

After the death of Ghazi-ud-din Hyder his son Nasir-ud-din Hyder ascende the throne on October 20, 1827 at the age of 25 years.

He was fond of woman & wine and had a strong belief in Astrology & Astronomy.

He sat up an observatory at Lucknow *The Tarunwali Kothi* which was bedecked with exceptionally good astronomical instruments.

He made additions of *Darshan Vilas*, an european style Kothi, to Claude Martin's house-Farhat Buksh in 1832.

He reproduced a Karbala at lradatnagar for his place of burial.

Administration

By the time of Nasir-ud-din Hyder the Oudh government had started deteriorating. The administration of the kingdom was left to the hands of Wazir Hakim Mahdi and later to Raushan-ud-Daula.

Death

He was poisoned by his own friends & favourites.

Succession

Nasir-ud-din Hyder died without an offspring and Ghazi-ud-din Hyder's queen 'Padshah Begum' put forward Munna Jan, as a claimant to the throne though both Ghazi-ud-din Hyder and Nasir-ud-din Hyder had refused to acknowledge him as belonging to the royal family. The begum forcibly enthroned Munna Jan at Lalbaradari. The British intervened and exploited the situation to their interest. They arrested both the begum and Munna Jan and arranged for the accession of late Nawab Saadat Ali Khan's son, Nasir-ud-daula, under title of 'Muhammad Ali Shah', who promised to pay a large sum of money to the British for this.

Muhammad Ali Shah

Muhammad Ali Shah (b.c. 1777-d. 17 May 1842) was third King of Oudh from 7 July 1837 to 17 May 1842.

Life

Muhammad Ali Shah was son of Saadat Ali brother of Ghaziuddin Hyder and uncle of Nasiruddin Hyder.

Succession

Nasir-ud-din Hyder died without an offspring and Ghazi-ud-din Hyder's queen 'Padshah Begum' put forward Munna Jan, as a claimant to the throne though both Ghazi-ud-din Hyder and Nasir-ud-din Hyder had refused to acknowledge him as belonging to the royal family. The begum forcibly enthroned Munna Jan at Lalbaradari. The British intervened and exploited the situation to their interest. There was first battle between Oudh and British forces. They arrested both the begum and Munna Jan and arranged for the accession of late Nawab Saadat Ali Khan's son, Nasir-ud-daula, under title of 'Muhammad Ali Shah', after getting a written assurance that he will accept any new treaty put up by Governor

General. He promised to pay a large sum of money to the British for this.

Administration

Muhammad Ali Shah was 63 years of age when he ascended the throne. But he was an experienced man and had seen the glorious days of his father. He started to economize and set right the administration. His administrative, financial and defence powers were reduced very much.

Construction Work

He built the Husainabad (Chhota) Imambara in 1838 and created Huseinabad Endowment Fund (now Husainabad Trust) to support it.

He also built Husainabad Picture Gallery which is adjacent to the Clock Tower, this Gallery contains the life-size portraits of the Nawabs of Oudh.

He also started to build an edifice similar to Babylon's minaret or floating garden and named it Satkhanda, but it reached only its fifth storey in 1842 when he died.

Construction of great Jama Masjid situated to west of the Hussainabad Imambara was also started by him but completed after his death.

Nawab Mohammad Ali Shah of Oudh also built the Shrine of Hurr at Karbala.

Death

He died on May 16, 1842 AD.

Amjad Ali Shah

Amjad Ali Shah (b.c. 1801-d. 13 February 1847) was fourth King of Oudh from 17 May 1842 to 13 February 1847.

Life

He was son of Muhammad Ali Shah. Muhammad Ali Shah had made every effort to ensure that the heir apparent received an excellent education & had therefore entrusted him to the company of religious scholars, which instead of making him an intelligent ruler made him a devout muslim. Thus, he became the most deeply religious, circumspect and abstinent ruler of Oudh.

Administration

Amjad Ali Shah tooked rein in May 1842.

By this time British Government have become so powerfull in Oudh that it was searching a way to grab it. He was of helping nature, very polite and well mannered.

Due to his abstainism, the system of administration set up by Muhammad Ali Shah became completely disorganized, while the vicious officers had their day.

Constructions

He constructed Iron Bridge over river Gomti and constructed metal road from Lucknow to Kanpur which still follows the same route.

He also built Hazratganj, the great European style market.

The great Aminabad Bazar and a Serai at Kanpur road were constructed by his minister Amin-ud-Daula.

Nawab Amjad Ali Shah also to build the Shrines of Syedna Muslim and Hani, at Kufah.

Death

He died due to cancer on February 13, 1847 at the age of 47 years. He is buried at Imambara Sibtainabad in the western part of Hazratganj, Lucknow.

He was succeeded by his son Wajid Ali Shah.

Wajid Ali Shah

Wajid Ali Shah (b. 30 July 1822-d. 1 September 1887) was fifth King of Oudh from 13 February 1847 to 7 February 1856.

He was the tenth and last nawab of the princely kingdom of Oudh in present day Uttar Pradesh in India. He ascended the throne of Awadh in 1847 and ruled for nine years. His kingdom, long protected by the British under treaty, was eventually annexed peacefully on February 7, 1856-days before the ninth anniversary of his coronation. The Nawab was exiled to Garden Reach in Metiabruz, then a suburb of Kolkata, where he lived out the rest of his life off a generous pension. He was a poet, playwright, dancer and great patron of the arts. He is widely credited with the revival of Kathak as a major form of classical Indian dance.

As a Nawab

Wajid Ali Shah succeeded to the throne of Oudh when its glory days were already past it. The British had annexed much of the kingdom under the treaty of 1801, and had impoverished Oudh by imposing a hugely expensive, British-run army and repeated demands for loans. The independence of Oudh in name was tolerated by the British only because they still needed a buffer state between their presence in the East and South, and the remnants of the Mughal Empire to the North.

Wajid Ali Shah was most unfortunate to have ascended the throne of Oudh at a time when the British East India Company was determined to grab the coveted throne of prosperous Oudh, which was "the garden, granary, and queen-province of India."

In different circumstances perhaps, he might have succeeded as a ruler because he had many qualities that make a good administrator. He was generous, kind and compassionate towards his subjects, besides being one of the most magnanimous and passionate patrons of the Fine Arts. When he ascended the throne, he took keen interest in the administration of justice, introduced reforms, and reorganised the military department, but gradually sank into a life of pleasures surrounded by courtesans, singers, dancers, and eunuchs.

Wajid Ali Shah was widely regarded as a debauched and detached ruler, but some of his notoriety seems to have been misplaced. The main case for condemnation comes from the British Resident of Lucknow, General Sleeman who submitted a report highlighting maladministration and lawlessness supposed to be prevailing there. This proved to be the trigger the British were looking for, and formed the official basis for their annexation. Recent studies have, however, suggested that Oudh was neither as bankrupt nor as lawless as the British had claimed. In fact, Oudh was for all practical purposes under British rule well before the annexation, with the Nawab playing little more than a titular role. The army was composed mostly of British officers, while the purse strings were firmly under the control of the East India Company.

In his book "Awadh Under Wajid Ali Shah", Dr. G.D. Bhatnagar gives the following assessment of this ill-starred prince: "Cast by providence for the role of an accomplished dilettante, he found himself a misfit for the high office to which he was elevated by chance. Wajid Ali Shah's character was complex. Though he was a man of pleasure, he was neither an unscrupulous knave nor a brainless libertine. He was a lovable and generous gentleman. He was a voluptuary, still he never touched wine, and though sunk in pleasure, he never missed his five daily prayers. It was the literary and artistic attainments of Wajid Ali Shah which distinguished him from his contemporaries."

Patron of the Arts

Contribution to Music

A large number of composers who thrived under the lavish patronage of the Nawab rulers of Lucknow enriched the light classical form of thumri; most prominent among these was Wajid Ali Shah. He was not only a munificent patron of music, dance, drama, and poetry, but was himself a gifted composer. He had received vocal training under great Ustads like Basit Khan, Pyar Khan and Jaffar Khan. Although his pen-name was Qaisar, he used the pseudonym "Akhtarpiya" for his numerous compositions. Under this pen name, he wrote over forty works-poems, prose and Thumris. "Diwani-Akhtar", "Husn-i-Akhtar" contain his Ghazals. He is said to have composed many new ragas and named them Jogi, Juhi, Shah-Pasand, etc.

Revival of Kathak

Kathak dance attained new heights of popularity and glory under his expert guidance and lavish patronage. Thakur Prasadji was his Kathak guru, and the unforgettable Kalka-Binda brothers performed in his court. What with the grand pageantry of the Rahas, Jogiya Jashan, Dance dramas, and Kathak performances, Lucknow became the magnetic cultural centre where the most reputed musicians, dancers and poets of the time flourished. The greatest musicians, dancers and instrumentalists of the time enjoyed his munificent patronage and hospitality.

Hindustani Theatre

When Wajid Ali Shah was a young boy, some astrologers warned his parents that he would become a Yogi, and advised them that the boy should be dressed up as a Yogi on each birthday of his so as to counteract the effect of the evil stars. He established his famous Parikhaana (abode of fairies) in which hundreds of beautiful and talented girls were taught music and dancing by expert-teachers engaged by the royal patron. These girls were known as *Paris* (fairies) with names such as *Sultan pari, Mahrukh pari* and so on. On each birthday, the Nawab would dress up as a Yogi with saffron robes, ash of pearls smeared on his face and body, necklaces of pearls around his neck, and a rosary in his hand, and walk pompously into the court with two of his '*paris* dressed up as Jogans. Gradually he made it into a spectacular pageant or Mela known as Jogia Jashan, in which all citizens of Lucknow could participate, dressed as Yogis, irrespective of caste and creed. Later on, when his favourite venue, the Qaisarbagh Baradari was built, he began to stage his magnificent Rahas (obviously a Persianised name for Rasleela) full of sensuous poetry, his own lyrical compositions and glamorous Kathak dances.

Ranbir Singh gives details of Wajid Ali Shah's book entitled *Bani* in which the author mentions 36 types of Rahas all set in Kathak style (with colourful names like *Mor-Chchatr, Ghunghat, Salami, Mor Pankhi* and *Mujra*), and gives exhaustive notes about the costumes, jewellery, and stage-craft. Rahas, prepared at a fabulous cost of several lakhs (hundred thousands) of rupees, became very popular, and was performed at the Kaisarbagh-Rahas Manzil, (most probably the first Hindustani Theatre Hall). Many have regarded Wajid Ali Shah as "the first playwright of the Hindustani theatre", because his "Radha Kanhaiya Ka Kissa" staged in the Rahas Manzil was the first play of its kind. It featured Radha, Krishna, several sakhis, and a vidushaka-like character called "Ramchera". Songs, dances, mime, and drama were all delightfully synthesised in these Rahas performances. He dramatised many other poems such as Darya-i-Tashsq, Afsane-i-Isbaq, and Bhahar-i-Ulfat. It is said that Amanat's *Inder Sabha* was inspired by these dance-dramas, written, produced and staged by Nawab Wajid Ali Shah.

His Exile Years

In his exile in Metiabruz, he tried to keep the sweet memories of his Lucknow era alive by recreating the musical environments of his Kaisarbagh Baradari. The banished king had been given a number of fine houses with vast grounds stretching along the banks of the River Hooghly 3 or 4 miles south of Kolkata. Because of an Earthen Dome (raised platform), people called it "Matiya Burj". The king spent lavishly out of his income of 12 lakh (1.2 million) rupees per annum and before long a Second Lucknow arose in this area. "There was the same bustle and activity, same language, art, poetry, style of conversation-the same pomp and splendour, the same opulent style of living. Taking advantage of the Shia Law of Muta, he contracted temporary legal marriages with as many good-looking and talented girls as he fancied. Troupes of artistes congregated in his court, the best singers were enlisted into his service and there was a larger concourse of musicians in Matiyaburj than could be found anywhere else in India".

His legacy: "Babul Mora" Thumri

His Bhairavi thumri "Babul mora Naihar chhooto jaay" has been sung by several prominent singers, but the version most remembered is by Kundan Lal Saigal for the 1930s movie Street Singer.

In a strange manner this sad song epitomises the pain and agony of the poet king himself when he was exiled from his beloved Lucknow.

In Popular Culture

In Satyajit Ray's Shatranj Ke Khilari, Wajid Ali Shah is shown as very enuthusiatic patron of dance and music etc. He is proud of the fact that songs and poems composed by him are favourite of his subjects. When it is revealed that the British are about to annex his throne, his chief-minister breaks down, but he himself maintains his calm because, according to him *only music and poetry can bring a real man to tears*. The memorable role was played by Amjad Khan.

A new novel Recalcitrance throws new light on Waji Ali Shah's character. The author uses the "mutiny of 1857" as backdrop and describes the event from the viewpoint of contemporary Indians. It was published in 2008 on 150 anniversary year of The Great Uprising of 1857.

Birjis Qadra

Berjis Qadr was the son of Wajid Ali Shah and was last, Padshah-e Awadh, Shah-e Zaman.

Begum Hazrat Mahal

Begum Hazrat Mahal, also known as Begum of Awadh, was the first wife of Nawab Wajid Ali Shah.

Queen of Awadh

Her maiden name was Muhammadi Khanum and she was born at Faizabad, Awadh, India. She was a courtesan by profession and had been taken into the royal harem as a Khawasin, after being sold by her parents to Royal agents. Then promoted to a Pari. She became a Begum after being accepted as a royal concubine of the King of Oudh., and she was bestowed the title 'Hazrat Mahal' after the birth of their son, Birjis Qadra. Begum Hazrat Mahal was endowed with great physical charm and grace as well as organizational skills. She was a junior wife of the last Tajdaar-e-Awadh, Wajid Ali Shah. The British had annexed Oudh in 1856 and Wajid Ali Shah was exiled to Calcutta. After, her husband was exiled to Calcutta, she took charge of the affairs of the state of Awadh despite her divorce from the Nawab, which then was a large part of the current state of Uttar Pradesh, India.

First War of Independence

During India's First War of independence (1857-58), she led a band of her supporters against the British, and was even able to seize the control of Lucknow. She declared her son Birjis Qadra as the king of Oudh. She is believed to have worked in close association with other leaders of the India's First War of Independence, including Nana Sahib. When the forces under the command of the British re-captured Lucknow and most of Oudh, she was forced to retreat. She turned down all offers of amnesty and allowances by the British rulers. Begum was not only a strategist but also fought on the battlefield. She had rejected the offer to accept a pension of Rs 12 lakh by British. When her forces lost ground, she fled Oudh and tried to organise soldiers again in other places.

After War

Ultimately, she had to retreat to Nepal, where she was initially refused asylum by the Rana prime minister Jang Bahadur but was later allowed to stay. She died there in 1879 and was buried in a nameless grave on the grounds of Kathmandu's Jama Masjid.

Begum Hazrat Mahal Park

On 15 August 1962, she was honoured at a simple yet serious ceremony in the old Victoria Park. A marble memorial was announced as open that was built by the state Government in the memory of the Begum as she played a very crucial role during the era of the first freedom movement in 1857. This memorial was adorned with strings of flowers and brightened by multi-coloured bulbs and neon tubes. There is also a marble tablet that has four round brass plaques that bear the Coat of Arms of Awadh Royal Family.

It is located in the heart of the city, Begum Hazrat Mahal Park once used to be a rally ground. It's been witness many Ravanas go up in fire during Dusshera and numerous Lucknow Mahotsavas have been hosted here. But what you see today is a totally different landmark, a walker's paradise. With pathways that are interwoven into the beautiful, green landscaping in the Park, it's also a visual delight of sorts. While the mornings are marked by scores of people walking at different paces, the evenings are relatively inactive at the park. But when the fountains go up and the lights turn on, it's a sight most of can feast our eyes on. And one which comes as a relief from the mundane sight of the traffic zipping past it. It is on the crossing of B.H.M and opposite to hotel Clarks Avadh.

Commemorative Stamp

Government of India issued a commemorative stamp in the honour of Begum Hazrat Mahal on 10 May 1984.

3

Nawabs of the Carnatic

Nawabs of the Carnatic (also referred to as the Nawabs of Arcot), ruled the Carnatic region of South India between about 1690 and 1801. They initially had their capital at the town of Arcot near Chennai. Their rule is an important period in the history of Tamil Nadu, in which the Mughal Empire gave way to the rising influence of the European powers, eventually culminating in the British Raj.

Carnatic

The old province known as the Carnatic, in which Madras (Chennai) was situated, extended from the Krishna river to the Coleroon, and was bounded on the West by Cuddapah, Salem and Dindigul, all of which formed part of the State of Mysore. The Northern portion was known as the Mughal Carnatic, the Southern the Maharatta Carnatic with the Maharatta frontier fortress being Gingee. Carnatic, the name commonly given to the region of Southern India between the Eastern Ghats and the Coromandel Coast and the Western Ghats, extends from Palghat to Bidar and stretches from the Guntur district of Andhra Pradesh in the North, to Cape Comorin at the Southern-most tip of Tamil Nadu State.

History

The Nawabs of the Carnatic trace their origin back to second Caliph Umar ibn al-Khattab. The Nawabdom of the Carnatic was established by the Mughal emperor Aurangzeb, who in 1692 appointed Zulfikar Ali Nawab of the Carnatic, with his seat at Arcot as a reward for his victory over the Marathas. With the Vijayanagara Empire in serious decline, the Nawabdom of the

Carnatic controlled a vast territory south of the Krishna river. The Nawab Saadetullah of (1710-1732) moved his court from Gingee to Arcot. His successor Dost Ali (1732-1740) conquered and annexed Madurai in 1736.

Muhammad Ali Wallajah (1749-1795) was freed from his suzerainty and made the independent ruler of the Carnatic by the Mughal emperor in 1765. His rule was long and mostly peaceful. He donated generously to Churches, Temples and Mosques. The temple at Sri Rangam was one which benefited from his generosity.

The growing influences of the English and the French and their colonial wars had a huge impact on the Carnatic. Wallajah supported the English against the French and Hyder Ali, placing him heavily in debt. As a result he had to surrender much of his territory to the East India Company.

The thirteenth Nawab, Ghulam Muhammad Ghouse Khan (1825–1855), died without issue and the British annexed the Carnatic Nawabdom applying the doctrine of lapse. Ghouse Khan's uncle Azim Jah was created the first Prince of Arcot (Amir-E-Arcot) in 1867 by Queen Victoria, and was given a tax free pension *in perpetuity*. This privilege continues to be honoured by the Government of India. This status is protected by the Indian Constitution and the family continues to retain its privileges and titles. The current Prince of Arcot Abdul Ali came to the title in July 1994.

First Dynasty

Muhammed Saadatullah Khan I

Muhammed Saiyid was the Dewan to Daud Khan till 1710, when he was himself appointed as the Nawab of the Carnatic. Moved the capital from Gingee to Arcot.

The honorific title of Saadatullah Khan was given to him by the Emperor Aurangzeb. He was generally known as the *First Nawab of Arcot*. Like his predecessors, he also enjoyed control over all the territories of the Emperor, in the South. He also carried his contribution wars to the gates of Srirangapatnam and collected "peshkash" or tribute from its rulers.

In 1711, he started demanding the five villages granted in 1708 to the East India Company on the basis of insufficient grants. The

English resisted and even prepared for a war. Saadatullah Khan demanded Egmore, Tondiarpet and Purasawalkam also. But the matter was settled amicably by the good offices of Sunkurama and Rayasam Papaiya, the Company's Chief Merchants.

After the death of Aurangzeb, due to the inability of his successor, the control of Delhi became weak. Having no children, Saadatullah Khan adopted his brother Ghulam Ali's son Dost Ali as his own and nominated him as successor. He had obtained the private consent of the Mughal Emperor for this step even without communicating his desire to the Nizam of Deccan.

Though the Nizam claimed supremacy over the Nawab, his control became very weak and he could not prevent the office of the Nawab from becoming hereditary and so he wisely restricted himself to claiming the right of giving his formal approval to their appointment. Thus Saadatullah Khan became a senior and independent ruler of the Carnatic extending from the River Godicame on the North to the borders of Travancore on the South and enclosed between the Eastern Ghats and the Sea.

Governor Collect, obtained from him in 1717, the firman for Tiruvottiyur, Sattangadu, Kathiwakam, Vysarpady and Nungambakkam.

Dost Ali Khan

Ali Dost Khan, often referred to as Dost Ali Khan by most historians, was Nawab of the Carnatic from 1732 to 1740. He was the son of Ghulam Ali Khan, brother of the Nawab Saadatullah Khan. His childless uncle adopted him as heir, and he succeeded his uncle in 1732.

Dost Ali Khan had two sons, Safdar Ali Khan, Hasan Ali Khan, and several daughters. He gave one daughter in marriage to Chanda Sahib whom he appointed as his Dewan, and another to Murtuza Ali. (Murtuza Ali assassinated Safdar Ali Khan in 1742.)

The Rajah of Tirusivapuram, a vassal of the Nawab, refused to pay his tribute. Dost Ali Khan ordered Chanda Sahib to march against the Rajah. Thereupon the Rajah invited the assistance of the Marathas. At the same time, the Nizam, unhappy with the succession of Dost Ali Khan as Nawab, also incited the Marathas to invade. The Marathas responded to the double invitation. They sent a large army to invade Carnatic.

Dost Ali Khan and Chanda Sahib met the Maratha army under Chattrapati Shahu at Ambur, on 20 May 1740. The Marathas won the battle. Dost Ali Khan was killed and Chanda Sahib was captured

Safdar Ali Khan

Safdar Ali Khan was the son of Dost Ali Khan. After the death of his father in the battlefield at Ambur in 1740, he escaped to Vellore. In the same year, he was recognised as the Nawab of the Carnatic by the British.

There was total insecurity in the country during this period and Safdar Ali Khan took every possible measure to save his country and his family. He sent his son's wife to Madras for safety under the protection of the British, who securely lodged them in the Black Town.

But unfortunately he was murdered by his brother-in-law, Murthuza Ali in 1742.

Muhammed Saadatullah Khan II

Muhammad Sa'id Sa'adatullah Khan II was *Sahib Zada* (heir apparent) of Safdar Ali Khan, Nawab of Arcot. After the assassination of Safdar Ali Khan in 1742, Murtaza Ali claimed for himself the Nawabship of the Arcot (Carnatic), Chanda Sahib who was taken prisoner to Satara by Maratha leader Raghoji Bhonsle had managed to obtain his freedom after rigorous negotiations, also supported the claims of Murtaza Ali.

However, the British East India Company at Madras firmly supported Muhammad Sa'id and proclaimed him as the Nawab of Arcot. At the same time, Nizam ul Mulk Asaf Jah I came with a strong force and settled the claim in favour of Muhammad Sa'id.

But as he was a minor, he placed Anwaruddin Muhammed Khan as Regent. During this period, Benson, the Governor of Fort St. George obtained the Nawab's firman in 1743 granting the villages of Perambur, Sadiankuppam, Ernavore, Pudubakkam and Vepery.

However, Muhammad Sa'id, was as unfortunate as his father.He was murdered in 1744 at Arcot. So with him the first dynasty of the Nawabs of Arcot came to an end and as a result Anwaruddin Muhammed Khan was confirmed in his position as Nawab by Nizam ul Mulk Asaf Jah I.

Second Dynasty

Anwaruddin Muhammed Khan

Muhammad Anwaruddin (1672–1749) was the 1st Nawab of Arcot of the second Dynasty. He was a major figure during the Second Carnatic War.

He was a direct descendant of Hazarath Omar, the Second Caliph of Islam. Nawab Anwaruddin Khan was born at Gopamau, a place in Hardoi District, United Provinces, India in 1674. He was the son of Haji Muhammad Anwar. His official name was *Amin us-Sultanat, Siraj ud-Daula, Nawab Haji Muhammad Jan-i-Jahan Anwar ud-din Khan Bahadur, Shahamat Jang, Subadar of the Carnatic.*

He went to Delhi and enlisted in the imperial army and soon rose to a high position. The Emperor Aurangzeb was very pleased with him on account of his faithful work. He served as Governor of Surat. Also he was posted to Rajahmundry, where he served for several years as Governor. He was the Yameen-us-Sultanat (right hand man) of Nizam-ul-Mulk, the founder of Hyderabad State in India. He was also the ruler of Rajamundry.

Muhammad Anwaruddin was first appointed as the Regent during the minority of Muhammad Sa'id. After the death of Muhammad Sa'id, Anwaruddin was appointed by the Nizam as his representative and Nawab of the Carnatic on 28 March 1744. Thus he became the founder of the Second Dynasty of the Nawab of the Carnatic. Anwaruddin maintaining a cordial relationship with the East India Company would come into conflict with the French after the death of Nizam-ul-Mulk in 1748.

In 1746, the French and the English fought and achieve their supremacy in India, each over the other. The soil of the Carnatic became the arena of their action. In 1746, the French captured the English possessions at Madras and Cuddalore.

Muhammad Anwaruddin fought against the French on the banks of the Adyar and won a decisive victory, recaptured the two towns and restored them to the English. Thus, he maintained the honour of his administration and established the power of his "Nizamath" or government.

Muhammad Anwaruddin received overtures for support from both from the English and the French, but supported the English. The French wanted to reduce the growing influence of the English in the Carnatic. So they supported *Husayn Dost Khan,* alias Chanda Sahib as the rightful Nawab of the Carnatic against Muhammad Anwaruddin, who was supported by the British.

As the British and the French supported their respective candidates for the Nawabship, they took sides in the case of the successors of the Nizam also. After the death of the Nizam in 1748, there arose a rivalry between Nasir Jung, the second son of Nizam-ul-Mulk and Muzaffar Jang, the grandson of Nizam-ul-Mulk. Muzaffar Jang came to the South with a strong force and allied himself with Chanda Sahib and the French. The ageing Nawab Muhammad Anwaruddin, supported by the English, met the French army at Ambur in August 1749 and was killed in the battle.

Chanda Shahib

Chanda Shahib (died 1752) was the Nawab of the Carnatic between 1749 and 1752. His birth name is Husayn Dost Khan. He was the son-in-law of the Nawab of Carnatic Dost Ali Khan, under whom he worked as a Dewan. He came from the Nait community which had ruled the Carnatic under Aurangzeb. Chanda was an ally of the French and annexed the Madurai Nayak kingdom by treason, but was later captured and beheaded by Tanjore army.

Role in Ending Rule of Nayaks

Vijaya Ranga Chokkanatha died in 1731, and was succeeded by his widow Meenakshi, who acted as Queen-Regent on behalf of a young boy she had adopted as the heir of her dead husband. She had only ruled a year or two when an insurrection was raised against her by Vangaru Tirumala, the father of her adopted son, who pretended to have claims of his own to the throne of Madurai. At this juncture representatives of the Mughals appeared on the scene and took an important part in the struggle.

Since 1693, Madurai nominally had been the feudatory of the emperor of Delhi, and since 1698 the Carnatic region north of the Coleroon (Kollidam) river had been under direct Muslim rule. The local representative of the Mughal was the Nawab of Arcot, Dost Ali Khan and an intermediate authority was held by the Nizam of Hyderabad, who was in theory both a subordinate of the emperor, and the superior of the Nawab.

How regularly the kings of Tanjore and Madura paid their tribute is not clear, but in 1734 — about the time, in fact, that

Meenakshi and Vangaru Tirumala were fighting for the crown — an expedition was sent by the then Nawab of Arcot to exact tribute and submission from the kingdoms of the south. The leaders of this expedition were the Nawab Dost Ali khan's son, Safdar Ali Khan, and his nephew and confidential adviser, the well-known Chanda Sahib.

The invaders took Tanjore by storm and, leaving the stronghold of Trichinopoly untouched, swept across Madurai and Tinnevelly and into Travancore. On their return from this expedition they took part in the quarrel between Meenakshi and Vangaru Tirumala. The latter approached Safdar Ali Khan with an offer of three million rupees if he would oust the queen in favour of himself. Unwilling to attack Trichinopoly, the Muslim prince contented himself with solemnly declaring Vangaru Tirumala to be king and taking the bond for the three millions. He then marched away, leaving Chanda Sahib to enforce his award as best he could. The queen, alarmed at the turn affairs now had taken, had little difficulty in persuading that facile politician to accept her bond for a crore of rupees (ten million) and declare her duly entitled to the throne.

Queen Meenakshi required Chanda Sahib to swear on the Koran that he would adhere faithfully to his engagement, and he accordingly took an oath on a brick wrapped up in the spledid covering usually reserved for that holy book. He was admitted into the Trichinopoly fort and Vangaru Tirumala — apparently with the good will of the queen, who, strangely enough, does not seem to have wished him any harm — went off to Madurai, to rule over that country and Tinnevelly.

Chanda Sahib accepted the crore of rupees and departed to Arcot. Two years later 1736 he returned, again was admitted into the fort, and proceeded to make himself master of the kingdom. Meenakshi soon was little but a puppet: she had fallen in love with Chanda Sahib and so let him have his own way unhindered.

Chanda Sahib eventually marched against Vangaru Tirumala, who still was ruling in the south, defeated him at Ammaya Nayakkanur and Dindigul, drove him to take refuge in Sivaganga, and occupied the southern provinces of the Madurai kingdom. Having now made himself master of all of the unfortunate Meenakshi's realms, he threw off the mask, ceased to treat her with the consideration he hitherto had extended to her, locked her up in her palace, and proclaimed himself ruler of her kingdom. The hapless lady took poison and ended her life shortly afterwards.

Muslim Domination under Chanda Sahib (1736—1740)

For a time, Chanda Sahib had his own way. His success was regarded with suspicion and even hostility by the Nawab of Arcot. But family loyalties prevented a rupture and Chanda Sahib was left undisturbed, while he strengthened the fortifications of Trichinopoly and appointed his two brothers as governors of the strongholds of Dindigul and Madurai. It was at this period that he subjugated the king of Tanjore, although he did not annex his territory, and he compelled them to cede *Karaikal* (Pondicherry) to the French. In 14 February 1739, Karaikal became a French colony.

Chanda Sahib and the Maratha interlude (1740—1743)

Unable to help themselves, the king of Tanjore and Vangaru Tirumala called for the assistance of the Marathas of Satara in Maharashtra. These people had their own grievance against the Muslims of Arcot, with whom Chanda Sahib still was identified, because of long-delayed payment of the *chouth*, or one-fourth of their revenues, which they had promised in return for the withdrawal of the Marathas from their country and the discontinuation of their incursions.

They also were encouraged to attempt reprisals by the Nizam of Hyderabad, who — jealous of the increasing power of the Nawab and careless of the loyalty due to co-religionists — gladly would have seen his dangerous subordinate brought to the ground.

Early in 1740, therefore, the Marathas appeared in the south with a vast army, and defeated and killed the Nawab of Arcot (Dost Ali Khan) in the pass of Damalcheruvu in North Arcot. Then they came to an understanding with his son, the Safdar Ali Khan, recognised him as Nawab, and retired for a time.

The Second Carnatic War (1749-1754)

After the death of the Nizam of Hyderabad, a civil war for succession broke out in south between Nasir Jung and Muzaffar Jung. Also, Chanda Sahib began to conspire against the Nawab Anwaruddin Muhammed Khan in Carnatic. This led to the Second Carnatic War.

Defeat at Arcot

In 1751, there was an ongoing scuffle between Muhammad Ali, (who was the son of the previous Nawab of Arcot, Anwaruddin Muhammed Khan and hence the rightful claimant) and Chanda Sahib. Dupleix sided with Chanda sahib and Muzaffar Jung to bring them into power in their respective states. But soon the English intervened. To offset the French influence, they began supporting Nasir Jung and Muhammad Ali (son of deposed Nawab Anwaruddin Muhammed Khan). Chanda Sahib initially succeeded and became the Nawab, forcing Muhammed Ali to escape to the rock-fort in Tiruchirapalli. Chanda Sahib followed and with the help of the French, besieged Tiruchirapalli. Muhammed Ali and the English force supporting him were in a grim position. Ensign Robert Clive, (who had earlier joined the East India Company as a writer) with a small English force of 300 soldiers made a diversionary attack on Arcot to draw away Chanda Sahib's army from Trichy. Chanda Sahib dispatched a 10,000 strong force under his son Raza Sahib to retake Arcot. Raza Sahib was aided by the Nellore Army and Muhammed Yusuf Khan as a Subedar may have been in this force. There he was defeated by English forces.

Death

At Arcot, and later at Kaveripakkam, Chanda Sahib's son was badly defeated by Robert Clive and was later killed by the British. Following this Chanda Sahib escaped to Tanjore, only to be captured by the Tanjore army and was beheaded by a Tanjore General. The English quickly installed Muhammed Ali as the Nawab of Arcot and most of Chanda Sahib's native forces defected to the English.

Muhammed Ali Khan Wallajah

Mohamed Ali Khan Wala jah (1717 – 1795) was the Nawab of Arcot in India and an ally of the British East India Company.

Muhammad Ali was born to Anwaruddin Muhammed Khan, by his second wife, Nawab Fakhr un-nisa Begum Sahiba, a niece of Sayyid 'Ali Khan Safawi ul-Musawi, of Persia, sometime Naib suba of Trichonopoly on 7 July 1723 at Delhi.

Official Name

His official name was *Amir ul Hind, Wala Jah, 'Umdaṭ ul-Mulk, Asaf ud-Daula, Nawab Muhammad 'Ali Anwar ud-din Khan Bahadur,*

Zafar Jang, Sipah-Salar, Sahib us-Saif wal-qalam Mudabbir-i-Umur-i-'Alam Farzand-i-'Aziz-az Jan, Biradarbi Jan-barabar [Nawab Jannat Aramgah], Subadar of the Carnatic.

Life

It was said of Mohammad Ali, that he could be courteous, immensely hospitable, always emulating English customs and manners, such as taking breakfast and tea, and sitting on chairs rather than cushions-he even held two investitures, bestowing the KB upon Sir John Lindsay and Sir Hector Munro, in 1771 and 1779, respectively..

Sir John Macpherson, writing to Lord Macartney in November 1781 declared,

"I love the old man...mind me to my old Nabob. I have been sending him sheep and bags of rice by every ship. It is more than he did for me when I was fighting his battles."

The Nawab was an ally of the British East India Company, but still harboured great ambitions of power in the South Indian arena, where Haidar Ali of Mysore, the Marathas and the Nizam of Hyderabad were constant rivals.

The Nawab could also be unpredictable and devious, and his breach of promise in failing to surrender Tiruchirappalli to Haidar Ali in 1751 was at the root of so many confrontations between Hyder Ali and the British.

When Haidar swept into the Carnatic towards Arcot on 23 July 1781, with a terrifying army estimated at 86-100,000 men, it was not Mohammad Ali, however but the British who provoked Haidar's wrath, after seizing the French port of Mahe, which was under Haidar's protection. Much of the ensuing war was fought on the Nawab's territory.

For the defence of his territory, he paid the British 400,000 pagodas per annum (about £160,000) and 10 out of the 21 battalions of the Madras army were posted to garrison his forts. The British derived income from his jagirs (land grants).

Death

He died from gangrene poisoning, at Madras on 13 October 1795. He was buried outside the gate of the Gunbad of Shah Chand Mastan, Trichinopoly.

Umdat Ul-Umra

Ghulam Hussainy Umdat-Ul-Umra (died 1801) was the Nawab of the Carnatic region of India from 1795 to 1801.

Early Life

Umdat-Ul-Umra was the son of Mohamed Ali Khan Walajan. He was actually named by his grandfather Anwaruddin Khan as "Abdul Wali". But he was subsequently renamed as "Umdat-Ul-Umra" after the name of the court of the Mughal Emperor.

Reign

Umdat-Ul-Umra ruled from 1795 to 1801. During his reign, the British East India Company demanded pieces of land as gift. On the fall of Tippu Sultan in 1799, the British accused the Nawab of collaborating with Tippu Sultan and demanded the entire administration of the kingdom as indemnity. Umdat-Ul-Umra vehemently protested but was powerlesss. Umdat-Ul-Umra, however, died soon afterwards and the takeover was effected during the reign of his successor.

Azim-ud-Daula

Azim-ud-Daula was the Nawab of Carnatic from 1801 to 1819. He was the son of Umdat Ul-Umra and ascended the throne on his father's death in 1801.

Treaty of 1801

As soon as Azim-ud-Daula ascended the throne, he was compelled to sign a treaty handing over the civil and municipal administration of the Carnatic to the British East India Company. Azim-ud-Daula was, therefore, reduced to the position of a mere titular ruler. In return, Azim-ud-Daula was entitled to one-fifth of the total revenue of the state and the honour of a 21-gun salute.

Azam Jah of the Carnatic

Azam Jah (died 1825) was the Nawab of the Carnatic region of India from 1819 to 1825.

- Azam Jah ascended the throne on the death of his father Azim-ud-Daula in 1819. He ruled for a short period of time and died in 1825. Azam Jah was succeeded by his minor son Ghulam Muhammad Ghouse Khan.

Ghulam Muhammad Ghouse Khan

Ghulam Muhammad Ghouse Khan (c. 1824-1855) was the twelfth and last Nawab of the Carnatic. He reigned from 1825 to 1855. He belonged to the Second Dynasty.

Early life

Ghouse Khan was born to the Azam Jah, the eleventh Nawab of the Carnatic in about 1824. His father died when he was one year old. In 1825, Ghouse Khan was proclaimed king with his uncle Azim Jah as regent.

Reign

In 1825, Ghouse Khan was proclaimed king with Azim Jah as regent. He ruled from 1825 to 1842. Azim Jah served as regent to the young king from 1825 till 1842 when Ghouse Khan was formally installed as the Nawab of the Carnatic by Viceroy Lord Elphinstone.

During his reign, the Ghouse Khan established the Muhammadan Public Library in Madras and a choultry called Langar Khana. The Langar Khana now houses the Muslim Widows Association.

Death

Ghouse Khan died in 1855 at the age of 31. He did not leave behind any male issue. The candidatures of Ghouse Khan's uncle Azim Jah, the only possible successor to the throne were set aside and the kingdom was formally annexed by the British East India Company as per the Doctrine of Lapse.

Azim Jah of Arcot

Azim Jah (died 1874) was the brother of Azam Jah, the eleventh Nawab of the Carnatic and uncle of Ghulam Muhammad Ghouse Khan, the twelfth and last Nawab of the Carnatic. He held the title Nawab of Arcot from 1867 to 1874.

Early Life

Azim Jah was the younger brother of Azam Jah, the eleventh Nawab of the Carnatic. He became the heir-apparent and regent when Ghulam Muhammad Ghouse Khan succeeded Azam Jah on the former's death in 1825. Azim Jah served as the regent from 1825 to 1842 during Ghouse Khan's minority. In 1842, Ghouse Khan was formally installed as the monarch.

Claim to the Throne

Ghouse Khan ruled as the Nawab of the Carnatic from 1825 to 1855. On his death in 1855, the throne became vacant and in the absence of a legitimate male heir to Ghouse Khan, the state was formally annexed by the British according to the Doctrine of Lapse.

Azim Jah protested claiming that he was the legitimate successor to the throne but met with little success.

Assumption of the Title "Amir-i-Arcot"

After protracted negotiations and court cases, finally, in 1867, Azim Jah was granted the title of Nawab of Arcot or Amir-i-Arcot by Queen Victoria and given a political pension. The Letters Patent issued by the Queen was formally presented to Azim Jah at a banquet held by the Governor of Madras on April 12, 1871.

As Kalas Mahal or the Chepauk Palace, the official residence of the princes of the Carnatic had been taken over by the British in 1859, Azim Jahn constructed a new residence, the Amir Mahal, in Royapettah.

Zahir-ud-Daula

Sir Zahir-ud-Daula Bahadur GCSI (died 1879) was the titular Nawab of Arcot from 1874 to 1879.

Early Life

Zahir-ud-Daula was the son of Azim Jah, the first Nawab of Arcot and cousin to Ghulam Muhammad Ghouse Khan, the twelfth and last Nawab of the Carnatic.

Reign

Zahir-ud-Daula was recognized as the titular Nawab of Arcot or Amir-i-Arcot on the death of his father Azim Jah in 1874. In 1876, he moved the official residence to the Amir Mahal. He also participated in the Delhi Durbar of January 1877, during which the proclamation of Queen Victoria as the Empress of India was made. Zahir-ud-Daula was awarded the GCSI and the honour of a 15-gun salute.

Death

Zahir-ud-Daula died in 1879 and was buried with state honours.

Muhammad Munawar Khan

Sir Muhammad Munawar Khan KCIE (died 1903) was the Prince of Arcot from 1889 to 1903. Muhammad Munawar Khan was the nephew of Intizam-ul-Mulk, the third Prince of Arcot. He was made a Knight Commander of the Order of the Indian Empire during the reign of his uncle. He was exempted from appearing in civil courts. Khan succeeded his uncle Intizam-ul-Mulk and ruled till his death in 1903, in Delhi while attending Edward VII's coronation.

Ghulam Muhammad Ali Khan

Khan Bahadur Sir Ghulam Muhammad Ali Khan GCIE (1882-1952) was the fifth Prince of Arcot and ruled from 1903 to 1952.

Early Life

Ghulam Muhammad Ali Khan was born on February 26, 1882 to Muhammad Munawar Khan. He was educated at the Newington Court of Wards Institution.

Reign

Ghulam Muhammad Ali Khan succeeded to the throne on the death of his father Muhammad Munawar Khan in 1903. The next year he was nominated to the Madras Legislative Council and served from 1904 to 1906. In 1910, he was nominated to the Imperial Legislative Council of India representing the Muslims of Madras Presidency. He served as a member of the Imperial Legislative Council from 1910 to 1913. In 1916 has was re-nominated to the Madras Legislative Council and served a second term lasting from 1916 to 1919.

He also served as the President of the All India Muslim League and the South India Islamic League. He was the principal nobleman and the chief representative of Muslims in Madras Presidency.

Ghulam Muhammad Ali Khan died in 1952 and was buried with full state honours.

4

Nizam of Hyderabad

Nizam, a shortened version of Nizam-ul-Mulk, meaning *Administrator of the Realm,* was the title of the native sovereigns of Hyderabad State, India, since 1719, belonging to the Asaf Jah dynasty. The dynasty was founded by Mir Qamar-ud-Din Siddiqi, a viceroy of the Deccan under the Mughal emperors from 1713 to 1721 and who intermittently ruled under the title Asaf Jah in 1724, and After Aurangzeb's death in 1707, the Mughal Empire crumbled and the viceroy in Hyderabad, the young Asaf Jah, declared himself independent.

By the middle of 18th century, the scions, known as *The Nizams,* had quickly surpassed the Mughals ruling a vast dominion of about 125,000,000 acres (510,000 km) in south India. They were among the wealthiest people in the world. Seven Nizams ruled Hyderabad for two centuries until Indian independence in 1947.

The Asaf Jahi rulers were great patrons of literature, art, architecture, culture, jewellery collection and rich food. The Nizams ruled the state until its integration into the Indian Union in September 1948 after independence from the British.

The Asif Jahis were lineal descendants of the first Khalifa of Islam Hazrat Abu Bakar Siddiq (R.A) and they were fourteenth in direct male descent from Shaikh Shihab ud-din Suhrawardy a acclaimed sufi from Kurdistan. Even though they were staunch sunnis, they had a very liberal approach towards shia muslims and non-muslims.

Family Origins

The Asaf Jahi dynasty originated in the region around Samarkand, but the family came to India from Baghdad in the late

17th century. Shaikh Mir Ismail (Alam Shaikh Siddiqi) Alam ul-Ulema,son of Ayub younus Salim, son of Abdul Rehman Shaikh Azizan Siddiqi, fourteenth in direct decent from Sheikh Shihab-ud-din Siddiqi Suhrawardy, of Suharwada in Kurdistan, a celebrated [Sufi] mystic, or dervish, maternal (first), a lady of the family of Mir Hamadan (a descendant of the Prophet Mohammed)(SW), a distinguished Sayyid of Samarkand.

Origin of the Nizam Title

Nizam-ul-mulk was a title first used in Urdu around 1600 to mean *Governor of the realm* or *Deputy for the Whole Empire*. The word is derived from the Arabic word, nizam, meaning *order, arrangement*. The Nizam was referred to as Ala Hadrat/Ala Hazrat or *Nizam Sarkar*, meaning His Exalted Highness (The last Nizam was awarded this title. It is a heredity title).

Rise of the Nizams

The first Nizams ruled on behalf of the Mughal emperors. But, after the death of Aurangazeb, the Nizams split away from the Mughals to form their kingdom. When the British achieved paramountcy over India, the Nizams were allowed to continue to rule their princely states. The Nizams retained power over Hyderabad State until September 1948 when it was integrated into the Indian Union. The Asaf Jah dynasty had only seven rulers; however there was a period of 13 years after the rule of the first Nizam when three of his sons (Nasir Jung, Muzafar Jung and Salabath Jung) ruled. They were not officially recognized as the rulers. A legend about the first Nizam states that, on one of his hunting trips he was offered some kulchas (an Indian bread) by a holy man and was asked to eat as many as he could. The Nizam could eat seven kulchas and the holy man then prophesied that seven generations of his family would rule the state.

The Nizams, by an honoured Hyderabad tradition that no Nizam has ever left India no matter how good a reason might exist for doing so, they believed, "the Sovereign is too precious to his people ever to leave India.".

Ever since Hyderabad stood aloof from the great first war of Indian Independence of 1857 while betraying many Indians and also at time acting against those who opposed the British such as Haidar Ali and Tipu Sultan, its Royal Family had been accorded by British Royalty special honours and the Nizam was given the official status of *Faithful Ally.*

Lineage

1. Qamar-ud-din Khan, Asaf Jah I (1720-1748)
2. Mir Ahmed Ali Khan Siddiqi, Nizam-ud-Dowlah Nasir Jang (1748-1750)
3. Nawab Hidayat Mohi-ud-din Sa'adu'llah Khan Bahadur, Muzaffar Jang (1750-1751)
4. Nawab Syed Mohammed Khan Siddiqi, Amir ul Mulk, Salabat Jang (1751-1762)
5. Nawab Mir Nizam Ali Khan Siddiqi Bahadur, Nizam ul Mulk, Asaf Jah II (1762-1803)
6. Nawab Mir Akbar Ali Khan Sikandar Jah Siddiqi, Asaf Jah III (1803-1829)
7. Nawab Mir Farkhonda Ali Khan Siddiqi Nasir-ud-Daulah, Asaf Jah IV (1829-1857)
8. Nawab Mir Tahniat Ali Khan Siddiqi Afzal ud Daulah, Asaf Jah V (1857-1869)
9. Fateh Jang Nawab Mir Mahboob Ali Khan Siddiqi, Asaf Jah VI (1869-1911)
10. Fateh Jang Nawab Mir Osman Ali Khan Siddiqi, Asaf Jah VII (1911-1967)
11. Barkat Ali Khan Mukarram Jah Asaf Jah VIII (1967-present).

Qamar-ud-din Khan, Asaf Jah I

Qamar-ud-din Khan, *Chin Kilij (Kilich) Khan, Nizam-ul-Mulk, Asaf Jah I* (20 August 1671 – 1 June 1748), later known simply as "Nizam-ul-Mulk", was the founder of the Asaf Jahi dynasty which ruled the Hyderabad state from 1720 to 1948.

Birth

He was born to Ghazi ud-Din Khan Feroze Jung and his first wife Wazir un-nisa Begum at Agra, 20 August 1671 as Mir Qamar ud-din Khan. The name was given to him by the Mughal Emperor Aurangazeb. His Paternal grandfathers were both important Mughal Generals and courtiers namely; Kilich Khan II (Paternal) and *Jumlat-ul-Mulk* Allami Sa'adullah Khan (Maternal), the Prime Minister of Emperor Shah Jahan.

Early Life

He was educated privately.

At the age of six, Mir Qumaruddin Siddiqi accompanied his father to the Mughal court in 1677. Aurangzeb awarded him a Mansab. Mir Qumaruddin Siddiqi displayed considerable skill as a warrior and before he reached his teens began acompanying his father into battle. In 1688 aged 17 he joined his father in the successful assault on the fort of Adoni and was promoted to the rank of 2000 zat and 500 horse and presented with the finest Arab steed with gold trappings and a pastille perfumed with ambergris from the Mughal court.

At the age of nineteen, the Emperor bestowed on him the title "Chin Fateh Khan". He was also gifted a female elephant and now aged 20 he was bestowed with the title of "Chin Qilich Khan" (boy swordsman) for surviving an attack that blew off three of his horse's legs during the siege of Wakinhera Fort. For fighting on and capturing the fort he was raised to rank of 5000 horse and awarded 15 million dams, a jewelled sabre and a third elephant. At 26, he was appointed Commander in Chief and Viceroy, first at Bijapur, then Malwa and later of the Deccan.

He inherited his grandfather's piety and his fathers military prowess. Henry George Briggs (a historian) wrote "If Moosulman were accustomed to perpetuate the memory of their heroes by posthumous ovations, India might have seen a hundred statues of her greatest mohammedan hero of the eighteenth century".

Second Only to The Emperor

After Aurangzeb's death he was appointed Governor of Oudh, but after Bahadur Shahs death he opted for a private life in Delhi. His sabbatical was cut short when in 1712 the sixth of Aurangzeb's successors, Farrukhsiyar convinced him to take up the post of Viceroy of the Deccan with the title of Nizam ul-Mulk (Regulator of the Realm) Fateh Jung.

Diwan

Nizam ul-Mulk began building up his own power-base independently of the Mughals in Delhi, while continuing to give obeisance to the throne and even remitting money to the centre. He was then called upon by Farrukhsiyar to help fight off the Saiyid brothers. Farrukhsiyar was found and killed but Nizam ul-

Mulk was rewarded for defeating the Saiyids with the post of *Diwan* (Prime minister) in the court of Muhammad Shah, Farrukhsiyar's 18 year old successor.

But all did not work as well as planned. Nizam ul-Mulk's attempts to reform the corrupt Mughal administration with its cliques of concubines and eunuchs created many enemies. According to his biographer, Yusuf Husain, he grew to hate the "harlots and jesters" who were the Emperor's constant companions and greeted all great nobles of the realm with lewd gestures and offensive epithets. Nizam ul-Mulk's desire to restore the etiquette of the Court and the discipline of the State to the standard of Shah Jahan's time earned him few friends. By envious malicious insinuations (the courtiers) poisoned the mind of the Emperor against his devoted servant.

Viceroy of the Deccan

In 1724 Nizam ul-Mulk resigned his post in disgust and set off for the Deccan to resume the Vice-royalty, only to find Mubariz Khan, who had been appointed governor by Emperor Farrukhsiyar nine years earlier, refusing to vacate the post. Mubariz Khan had successfully restored law and order in the Deccan but he was also paying lip service to the Mughal throne making only token payments and dividing plum administrative posts among his sons, his uncle and his favourite slave eunuchs. Unimpressed by the upstart occupying what he considered to be his rightfull place, Nizam ul-Mulk gathered his forces at Shakarkhelda in Berar for a showdown with Mubariz Khan's army. The encounter was short but decisive. Wrapped in his bloodsoaked shawl, Mubariz Khan drove his war elephant into battle until he died from his wounds. His severed head was then sent to Delhi as proof of Nizam ul-Mulk's determination to annihilate anyone who stood in his way.

Now there came from the Emperor an elephant, jewels and the title of Asaf Jah, with directions to settle the country, repress the turbulent, punish the rebels and cherish the people. Asaf Jah or the equal to Asaf, the Grand Vazir in the court of the biblical ruler King Solomon, was the highest title that could be awarded to a subject of the Mughal Empire. There were no lavish ceremonies to mark the establishment of the Asaf Jahi dynasty in 1724. The inauguration of the first Nizam took place behind closed doors in a private ceremony attended by the new ruler's closest advisors.

Nizam ul-Mulk never formally declared his independence and insisted that his rule was entirely based on the trust reposed in him by the Mughal Emperor.

The Nizams has no throne, no crown and no symbol of sovereignty. Coins were still minted with the Emperor's name until 1858. It was in the name of the Mughal ruler and not the Nizam that prayers were read out in the Friday Sermon. Qamaruddin Khan was essentially the servant of the Mughal Emperor.

As the Viceroy of the Deccan, the Nizam was the head of the executive and judicial departments and the source of all civil and military authority of the Mughal empire in the Deccan. All officials were appointed by him directly or in his name. Assisted by a Diwan the Nizam drafted his own laws, raised his own armies, flew his own flag and formed his own government.

Acknowledging Muhammad Shah's farman, Nizam ul-mulk had good reason to be grateful. Alongside his own personal wealth came the spoils of war and status, he was also entitled to the lions share of gold unearthed in his dominions, the finest diamonds and gems from Golconda mines and the income from his vast personal estates.

He then divided his newly acquired kingdom into three parts. One third became his own private estate known as the Sarf-i-Khas, one third was allotted for the expenses of the government and was known as the Diwans territory, and the remainder was distributed to muslim nobles (Jagirdar, Zamindars, Deshmukh), who in return paid nazars (gifts) to the Nizam for the privilege of collecting revenue from the villages under their suzerainty. The most important of these were the Paigah estates. The Paigah's doubled up as generals, making it easy to raise an army should the Nizams Dominions come under attack. They were the equivalent to the Barmakids for the Abbasid Caliphate. Only second to the Nizams family, they were very important in the running of the government and even today their legacy lingers on with ruined palaces and tombs doted around the once very feudal city of Hyderabad. On the sanads (scrolls) granting them their lands, inscribed in Persian were the words "as long as the Sun and the Moon are in rotation". The owners of the estates were mostly absentee landlords who cared little for the condition of the lands under their control. Jagirs were usually split into numerous pieces in order to prevent the most powerful of the nobles from entertaining any thought of carving out an empire for themselves. The system, which continued relatively unchanged until 1950, ensured a steady source of income for the state treasury and the Nizam himself.

Clash with the Marathas

In 1725, the Marathas clashed with the Nizam, who refused to pay Chauth and Sardeshmukhi to the Marathas. The war began in August 1727 and ended in March 1728. The Nizam was given a crushing defeat at Palkhed near Daulatabad. By the treaty of Munji Shivagaon, the Nizam was forced to abide by the following terms:

- Chhatrapati Shahu was recognised as the only Maratha ruler.
- Marathas were given the right to collect Chauth and Sardeshmukhi of Deccan.
- Those revenue collectors driven out would be reappointed.
- The balance revenue was to be paid to Chhatrapati Shahu.

Nadir Shah

In 1738, from beyond the Hindu kush, Nadir Shah started advancing towards Delhi through Afghanistan and the Punjab.

Nizam ul-Mulk sent his troops to Karnal, where Mughal Emperor Muhammed Shah's forces had gathered to turn back the Persian army. But the combined forces were cannon fodder for the Persian cavalry and its superior weaponry and tactics. Nadir Shah defeated the combined armies of Muhammed Shah and the Nizam.

Nadir Shah entered Delhi and ordered it to be ransacked. Unable to prevent his capital being destroyed, Muhammed Shah again summoned Nizam ul-Mulk for help. Accordingly, Nizam negotiated with Nadir Shah to stop the ransacking.

Later Life

The Nizam was not so well suited to ruling his own territory. The Feudal Lords had the power of life and death and exercised a kind of "imperium-in-imperio". His territory was almost depopulated in some areas and chaos reigned almost everywhere.

In March 1742, the British who were based in Fort St. George in Madras sent a modest hamper to Nizam ul-mulk in recognition of his leadership of the most important of the Mughal successor states. Its contents included a gold throne, gold and silver threaded silk from Europe, two pairs of large painted looking glasses, and equipage for coffee cups, 163.75 yards of green and 73.5 yards of crimson velvet, brocades, Persian carpets, a gold ceremonial cloth, two Arab horses, half a dozen ornate rose-water bottles and 39.75 chests of rose water-enough to keep the Nizam and his entire darbar fragrant for the rest of his reign. In return, the Nizam sent one horse, a piece of jewellery and a note warning the British that they had no right to mint their own currency, to which they complied.

It was after Nizam ul-mulks death that his son and grandson sought help from the British and French in order to win the throne. Just days before he died in 1748, Asaf Jah dictated his last will and testament. The 17 clause document was a blueprint for governance and personal conduct that ranged from advice on how to keep the troops happy and well fed to an apology for neglecting his wife. He then reminded his successors to remain subservient to the Mughal Emperor who had granted them their office and rank. He warned against declaring war unnecessarily, but if forced to do so to seek the help of elders and saints and follow the sayings and practices of the Prophet. Finally, he insisted to his sons that "you must not lend your ears to tittle-tattle of the backbiters and slanderers, nor suffer the riff-raff to approach your presence.

Legacy

Nizam-ul-Mulk is remembered as laying the foundation for what would become the one of the most important Muslim states outside the Middle East by the first half of the twentieth century. Hyderabad state survived right through the period of British rule up to the time of Indian independence 1947, and was indeed the largest-the state covered an extensive 95,337 sq. miles, An area larger than Mysore or Gwalior and the size of Nepal and Kashmir put together (although it was the size of France when the first Nizam held reign)-and one of the most prosperous, among the princely states of the British Raj.

Death

Nizam ul-mulk died aged 76. He had four sons and a daughter, Mir Ahmed Ali Khan Nasir Jung, Mir Ghazi uddin Khan Bahadur Firuz jung, Nawab Syed Mohammed Khan Salabath Jung, Nawab

Mir Nizam Ali Khan Bahadur Nizam Ul Mulk Azaf Jah II, Sahibzadi Khair unisa Begum.

He died at Burhanpur, 1 June 1748 and was buried at *mazaar* of Shaikh Burhan ud-din Gharib Chisti, Khuldabad, near Aurangabad.

Titles

- 1685 : Khan
- 1691 : Khan Bahadur
- 1697 : Chin Qilich Khan (by Emperor Aurangazeb)
- 9 December 1707 : Khan-i-Dauran Bahadur
- 1712 : Ghazi ud-din Khan Bahadur and Firuz Jang
- 12 January 1713 : Khan-i-Khanan, Nizam ul-Mulk and Fateh Jang (by Emperor Farukh Siar)
- 12 July 1737 : Asaf Jah (by Emperor Muhammad Shah)
- 26 February 1739 : Amir ul-Umara and Bakshi ul-Mamaluk (Paymaster-General).

Positions

- 1701-1705 : Faujdar of the Carnatic and Talikota
- 1705-1706 : Faujdar of the Bijapur, Azamnagar and Belgaum
- 1706-1707 : Faujdar of Raichur, Talikota, Sakkhar and Badkal
- 1707 : Faujdar of Firoznagar and Balkona
- 9 December 1707-6 February 1711 : Subedar of Oudh and Faujdar of Gorakhpur
- 12 January 1713-April 1715 : Subedar of the Deccan and Faujdar of the Carnatic
- April 1717-7 January 1719 : Faujdar of Moradabad
- 7 February-15 March 1719: Subedar of Patna
- 15 March 1719-1724 : Subedar of Malwa
- 1722-1724 : Subedar of Gujarat.

Nasir Jang Mir Ahmad

Nasir Jang Mir Ahmad (February 26, 1712 – December 16, 1750) was the Nizam, or ruler, of the Hyderabad State from 1748 to 1750.

Official Name

His official name was *Humayun Jah, Nizam ud-Daula, Nawab Mir Ahmad Ali Khan Siddqi Bahadur, Nasir Jang, Nawab Subadar of the Deccan.*

Life

He ruled Hyderabad State in India from June 1, 1748 to 1750. He was appointed as his father's Deputy during his absence in Delhi from 1737–1741. He attempted to seize power, but was defeated by his father at the Eid Gah Maidan in Aurangabad, on July 23, 1741. After his father's death, he ascended the throne on June 2, 1748 at Burhanpur.

Death

He was killed at Dupleix-Fathabad (Sarasangupettai), near Gingee, by the Pathan Himmat Khan, Nawab of Kadapa, on December 16, 1750 and was buried at the Mausoleum of Hazrat Burhan ud-Din Gharib, Khuldabad.

Positions Held

- Subedar of Aurangabad 1745–1746.

Muhyi ad-Din Muzaffar Jang Hidayat

Muhyi ad-Din Muzaffar Jang Hidayat (died February 13, 1751) was the ruler of Hyderabad briefly, from 1750 to his death in battle in 1751.

Birth

He was born to Nawab Talib Muhi ud-din Mutawassil Khan Bahadur (Naib Subedar of Bijapur) and his wife Sahibzadi Khair un-nisa Begum who was the daughter of Asaf Jah I. His official name was *Nawab Hidayat Muhi ud-din Sa'adu'llah Khan Bahadur, Muzaffar Jang, Nawab Subadar of the Deccan.*

Life

Initially he was appointed to an Imperial mansab of 3,000 zat and 2,000 sowar and later promoted to 4,000 zat on his appointment to Bijapur. He was Subadar of Bijapur after the death of his father. Assumed the Viceroyalty of the Deccan on the death of his uncle, 16 December 1750. He installed at Pondicherry, where he granted territories and titles to Dupleix and the French, 31 December 1750.

He was granted the titles of Muzaffar Jang and Sa'adu'llah Khan. He was invested with the Mahi-o-Maratib 3 April 1751.

The Nizam approached the French for help against the Marathas. French agreed to help. Accordingly, Nizam marched against the Marathas. However, the Nizam was defeated and had to pay 6 million rupees.

Death

He was killed in battle at the Lakkireddipalli Pass, in the Rayachoti taluka, when the Nawab of Kurnool struck him in the head with a spear, 13 February 1751,

Family

Muzaffar Jang had only one son named, Nawab Muhammad Sa'ad ud-din Khan Bahadur who was a minor at the death of his father in February 1751. He became Subedar of Bijapur in 1751. But died later from smallpox.

Positions Held

- Subadar of Bijapur.

Asaf ad-Dawlah Mir Ali Salabat Jang

Asaf ad-Dawlah Mir Ali Salabat Jang (November 24, 1718-September 16, 1763 in Bidar) was the Nizam (ruler) of Hyderabad. He was the third son of H.H. Asaf Jah I Nayab, Subedar of the Deccan. He was appointed as Deputy Viceroy to his elder brother, Ghazi Uddin, in 1751. He was proclaimed at the camp near Luckridpalli, at French instigation.

Birth

Nawab Sa'id Muhammad Khan Siddiqi Bahadur was born in Hyderabad as the third son of Asaf Jah I before 24 November 1718.

Official Name

His official name is *Amir ul-Mamalik, Asaf ud-Daula, Nawab Said Muhammad Khan Siddiqi Bahadur, Zaffar Jang, Nawab Subadar of the Deccan.*

Life

Asaf ad-Dawlah Mir Ali Salabat Jang succeeded as Nizam of Hyderabad after the death of his predecessor and nephew, *Nizam*

Muzaffar Jang. Muzaffar Jang was killed in the Battle of Lakkireddipalli Pass, when the Nawab of Kurnool struck him in the head with a spear on February 13, 1751.

Again the eldest brother of the Nizam, Ghazi ud-Din Khan Feroze Jung II, was ignored while he was at Delhi serving the Mughal Emperor Ahmad Shah Bahadur. But he would not wait long to contest this supercession. This supercession took place right after the Battle of Lakkireddipalli Pass by the help of French commander Marquis de Bussy-Castelnau.

Salabat Jang was invested by Imperial *firman*, at Aurangabad, Maharashtra, September 12, 1749. He was granted the titles of *Khan Bahadur* and *Salabat Jang* during his father's lifetime and was promoted to *Asaf ud-Daula* and *Zafar Jang* in 1751 and *Amir ul-Mamalik* by the Emperor Alamgir II. He was the ruler of the Hyderabad State in India from 1751 until 1762. Khilwath palace of Hyderabad was built by him.

Death

He was deposed by his brother, Asaf Jah II, on July 8, 1762 and ordered held in Bidar Fort prison where he was killed on September 16, 1763. He was buried at Mecca Masjid, Hyderabad. Having had issue two sons at Chow Mahala Palace one in March 12, 1756 and other on March 27, 1759.

Ali Khan Asaf Jah II

Nawab Mir Nizam Ali Khan Siddiqi Bahadur Asaf Jah II (7 March 1734 – 6 August 1803) was the Nizam of Hyderabad State in South India between 1762 and 1803.

Birth

He was born on March 7, 1734 as fourth son to Asaf Jah I and Unda Begum.

Official Name

His official name is *Asaf Jah II, Nizam ul-Mulk, Nizam ud-Daula, Nawab Mir Nizam 'Ali Khan Siddiqi Bahadur, Fath Jang, Sipah Salar, Nawab Subedar of the Deccan.*

Life

Asaf Jah II became the subahdar of the Deccan on July 8, 1762. He transferred his capital from Aurangabad to Hyderabad in 1763 as Aurangabad was very close to Maratha Territory and therefore prone to aggression.

In 1762, Raghunathrao allied with the Nizam due to mutual distrust and differences with Madhavrao Peshwa. The Nizam marched towards Poona. In 1763, Madhavrao defeated Nizam at Rakshabhuvan and signed a treaty with the Marathas. In 1795, he was defeated by the Marathas and was forced to cede Daulatabad, Aurangabad and Sholapur and pay an indemnity of Rs. 30 million. The following year, judging himself menaced by Tipu Sultan of Mysore, he entered into Subsidiary Alliance with the British East India Company. Thus Hyderabad, which is in both area and population comparable to the United Kingdom, became a princely state within the British Raj.

A French general, Monsieur Raymond, served as his military leader, strategist and advisor.

Death

Asaf Jah II died at Chowmahalla, Hyderabad at the age of 69 on August 6, 1803.

Mir Akbar Ali Khan Sikander Jah, Asaf Jah III

Mir Akbar Ali Khan Siddiqi Sikander Jah Asaf Jah III (11 November 1768 – 21 May 1829), Nizam of Hyderabad, was the ruler of Hyderabad state in India from 1803 to 1829. He was born in Chow Mahalla in the Khilwath palace. He was married with Jahan Parwar Begum Sahiba (Haji Begum)d/o Nawab Saif Ul Mulk)Maali Mian)s/o Moin un Daula Nawab Gulam Said Khan Bahadir Surab Jang in May 1800.

Birth

Shazada Nawab Mir Tafazul Ali Khan Mir Badesha (Saif-ul-mulk) only son of Sikander Jah Nizam III born with married wife Jahan Parwar Begum Sahiba (Haji Begum)d/o Nawab Saif Ul Mulk) Maali Mian) s/o Arastu Jah (was the prime minister during the Asaf Jah III).

Official Name

His original names were Sikandar Jah, Asaf ul-Mulk, Asad ud-Daula, Nawab Mir Akbar 'Ali Khan Siddiqi Bahadur, Asad Jang. He was officially known as *Asaf Jah III, Nizam ul-Mulk, Nizam ud-*

Daula, Mir Akbar 'Ali Khan Siddiqi Bahadur, Fulad Jang, Nizam of Hyderabad.

Reign

During his reign, a British cantonment was established in Hyderabad and the area was christened after him as Secunderabad. His son Samsamadaula (Mir Basheeruddin Ali Khan) was Defence Adviser to his brother, Nasir ud Daula, and nephew, Afzal ud daula. But he did not have any pact with the British for maintaining the contingent. The state was in a financial mess during his reign.

Nasir-ud-dawlah, Asaf Jah IV

Nasir ad-Dawlah Mir Farqunda Ali Khan Siddiqi, Asaf Jah IV, Nizam of Hyderabad (25 April 1794-16 May 1857), was the ruler of Hyderabad state in India from 1829 to 1857. He was the eldest son of Asaf Jah III.

Reign

During his reign General C.B. Low took over as the Resident, he received a message from Lord Dalhousie to pay sixty-four lakh rupees which were due to the British for maintaining the Contingent. On 20 May 1853 a new treaty was concluded by which the strength of the Contingent force was settled for its payments.

The Contingent ceased to be a part of the Nizam's Army and became a force kept by the British Government for the benefit of Hyderabad State.

Afzal ad-Dawlah, Asaf Jah V

Afzal ad-Dawlah, Asaf Jah V (11 October 1827 – 26 February 1869) was the ruling Nizam of Hyderabad from 1857 to 1869.

A progressive ruler, Asaf Jah V reformed the Hyderabad revenue and judicial systems, instituted a postal service and constructed the first rail and telegraph networks in the state.

On 31 August 1861, the Order of the Star of India was conferred on Asaf Jah V. His dominion was divided into five Subas and sixteen districts. Each Suba was headed by a Subedar and each district was under a Taluqdar. During his reign, the reforms carried out by Sir Salar Jung included the establishment of a Government central treasury in 1855.

He died 26 February 1869.

Mahbub Ali Khan, Asaf Jah VI

Asaf Jah VI (August 17, 1866-August 31, 1911) was the sixth Nizam of Hyderabad. He ruled Hyderabad state, one of the Princely states in India between 1869 and 1911.

Official full Name and Style

Lieutenant-General *His Highness Rustam-i-Dauran, Arustu-i-Zaman, Wal Mamaluk, Asaf Jah VI, Muzaffar ul-Mamaluk, Nizam ul-Mulk, Nizam ud-Daula, Nawab Mir Sir Mahbub 'Ali Khan Bahadur, Sipah Salar, Fath Jang, Nizam of Hyderabad, Knight Grand Cross of the Most Honourable Order of the Bath, Knight Grand Commander of the Most Exalted Order of the Star of India, Kaiser-i-Hind, Honourable Lieutenant-General in the Army.*

Personal Life

Mahbub Ali Khan was born on August 17, 1866. He was the only son of Nawab Afzal-ud-Daula. When his father died he was two years and seven months old, and thus became the Sixth Nizam of the Asaf Jahi dynasty in 1869. He was installed as Nizam by Mir Turab Ali Khan, Salar Jung I the Great, Nawab Rasheeduddin Khan Shams-ul-Umra III who functioned as the Regent. Shams-ul-Umra III died on December 12, 1881 and Salar Jung become the sole regent.He remained administrator and Regent until his death.

Special attention was paid to the education of Mahboob Ali Khan who was tutored by the English. With the concurrence of Salar Jung, Capt. John Clerk was appointed tutor to His Highness and scholars well versed in Persian, Arabic and Urdu were also engaged as tutors. The personality and noble life of Sir Salar Jung had a great influence on His Highness's Life. He was a respected and dignified personality and was popularly know as *Mahboob Ali Pasha*. He was retained as administrator and regent until his death on Tuesday, August 31, 1911.

Dr. Abdul Husain, later given the title Arastu Yar Jung, was physician to Mahbub Ali Khan. As such, Mahbub Ali Khan often sought counsel for matters concerning the Bubonic plague epidemic that worried Hyderabad, and other matters as well.

Mahbub Ali Khan was well known for lavish lifestyle and luxuries, and had an enormous fascination for clothes and cars. His collection of garments was one of the most extensive in the world at the time, with sherwanis, shirts, coats, collars, socks, shoes, headgear, walking sticks, perfumes-not one each, but dozens of almost each item. He devoted a whole wing of his palace to his wardrobe and would never wear the same dress twice.

He bought the Jacob Diamond, which stands out among the Jewels of The Nizams now owned by the Government of India.

Titles

- 1866-1869: Sahibzada Mir Mahbub Ali Khan Bahadur
- 1869-1877: His Highness Rustam-i-Dauran, Arustu-i-Zaman, Wal Mamaluk, Asaf Jah VI, Muzaffar ul-Mamaluk, Nizam ul-Mulk, Nizam ud-Daula, Nawab Mir Mahbub 'Ali Khan Bahadur, Sipah Salar, Fath Jang, Nizam of Hyderabad
- 1877-1884: His Highness Rustam-i-Dauran, Arustu-i-Zaman, Wal Mamaluk, Asaf Jah VI, Muzaffar ul-Mamaluk, Nizam ul-Mulk, Nizam ud-Daula, Nawab Mir Mahbub 'Ali Khan Bahadur, Sipah Salar, Fath Jang, Nizam of Hyderabad, KIH
- 1884-1902: His Highness Rustam-i-Dauran, Arustu-i-Zaman, Wal Mamaluk, Asaf Jah VI, Muzaffar ul-Mamaluk, Nizam ul-Mulk, Nizam ud-Daula, Nawab Mir Sir Mahbub 'Ali Khan Bahadur, Sipah Salar, Fath Jang, Nizam of Hyderabad, GCSI, KIH
- 1902-1910: His Highness Rustam-i-Dauran, Arustu-i-Zaman, Wal Mamaluk, Asaf Jah VI, Muzaffar ul-Mamaluk, Nizam ul-Mulk, Nizam ud-Daula, Nawab Mir Sir Mahbub 'Ali Khan Bahadur, Sipah Salar, Fath Jang, Nizam of Hyderabad, GCB, GCSI, KIH
- 1910-1911: Lieutenant-General His Highness Rustam-i-Dauran, Arustu-i-Zaman, Wal Mamaluk, Asaf Jah VI, Muzaffar ul-Mamaluk, Nizam ul-Mulk, Nizam ud-Daula, Nawab Mir Sir Mahbub 'Ali Khan Bahadur, Sipah Salar, Fath Jang, Nizam of Hyderabad, GCB, GCSI, KIH.

Honours

- Kaiser-i-Hind Gold Medal (KIH)-1877
- Knight Grand Commander of the Order of the Star of India (GCSI)-1884
- Knight Grand Cross of the Order of the Bath (GCB)-1902

- Delhi Durbar Gold Medal-1903
- Grand Cross of the Order of the Red Eagle of Prussia-1911.

Osman Ali Khan, Asaf Jah VII

Asaf Jah VII, born Osman Ali Khan Bahadur (April 6, 1886 – February 24, 1967), was the last Nizam (or ruler) of the Princely State of Hyderabad and of Berar, a state with majority of Hindu population. He ruled Hyderabad between 1911 and 1948, until it was merged into India. He was styled *His Exalted Highness The Nizam of Hyderabad.*

During his days as Nizam, he was reputed to be the richest man in the world, having a fortune estimated at US$2 billion in the early 1940s. He was featured on the cover of TIME magazine, portrayed as such. In 1950, the treasury of the newly independent Union government of India reported annual revenue of US$1 billion. The Nizam is widely believed to have remained as the richest man in South Asia until his death in 1967, though his fortunes fell to US$1 billion by then and became a subject of multiple legal disputes between bitterly fighting rival descendants. Adjusting for inflation, his fortune may be valued around $225 billion in 2008 U.S. dollars.

He built the Hyderabad House in Delhi, now used for diplomatic meetings by the Government of India.

Early Life and Education

Osman Ali was born on April 6, 1886, at Purani Haveli in Hyderabad state, the second son of Mir Mahboob Ali Khan,Asaf Jah VI, by his first wife Amat-uz-Zahrunnisa Begum. The death of his elder brother in 1887, rendered Osman Ali the heir apparent of Hyderabad.

Great attention was paid to his education, and eminent scholars were engaged to teach Osman Ali English, Urdu and Persian. He was also tutored in Islamic studies by Hafiz Anwarullah Faruqi of the Jami'ah Nizamiyyah of Hyderabad. Mir Osman Ali Khan was a great scholar and wrote poetry in Urdu and Persian.

Marriages and Children

On April 14, 1906, Osman Ali married Dulhan Pasha Begum (1889-1955), daughter of Nawab Jahangir Jung, at Eden Bagh at the age 21. She was the first of his seven wives and 42 concubines, and the mother of two eldest of his sons Azam Jah and Moazzam Jah. His second wife was Iqbal Begum daughter of Nawab Nazir Jung Bahadur (Mirza Nazir Beg).

The first brother-in-law of Osman Ali Khan was Nawab Khudrath Nawaz Jung son of Nawab Jahangir Jung and elder brother of Dulhan Pasha Begum first wife of Osman Ali Khan

Their eldest son, Azam Jah, was married to Durru Shehvar, daughter of Abdul Mejid II (the last Ottoman Caliph and cousin and heir of the last Sultan of the Ottoman Empire). Moazzam Jah married Princess Niloufer, a princess of the Ottoman empire.

It has been suggested that through these dynastic marriages, Osman Ali hoped to acquire the Caliphate for his descendants.

In total, Osman Ali Khan sired at least 40 children, including:

- Yawar un-nisa Begum Sahiba (d. in childhood)
- Hidayat un-nisa Begum Sahiba (1901-1925)
- His Highness Azam Jah (1907-1970)
- His Highness Muazzam Jah (1907-1987)
- Osman 'Ali Khan Bahadur (29 February-30 June 1908)
- Ahmad un-nisa Begum Sahiba (1910-1985)
- Ahmad 'Ali Khan Bahadur (1912-)
- Kazim Jah (1912-1952)
- Abid Jah (1913-1983)
- Hashmat Jah (1913-1988)
- Hashim Jah (1913-1991)
- Taqi Jah (1913-1985)
- Hurmat un-nisa Begum Sahiba (1913-)
- Karim un-nisa Begum (1913-)
- Jamal un-nisa Begum Sahiba (1913-1973)
- Behbood un-nisa Begum Sahiba (1914-)
- Mahmood un-nisa Begum Sahiba (1914-1984)
- Basharat Jah (1915-1991)
- Mehar un-nisa Begum Sahiba (1915-1964)
- Ghaffoor un-nisa Begum Sahiba (1915-)
- Aleem un-nisa Begum Sahiba (1915-)
- Nazeer un-nisa Begum Sahiba (1916-1975)

- Rajjab Jah (1917-1968)
- Sa'adat Jah (1917-1988)
- Faruq un-nisa Begum Sahiba (1918-)
- Kabir un-nisa Begum Sahiba (1920-)
- Masud un-nisa Begum Sahiba (1923-1980)
- Asmat un-nisa Begum Sahiba (1924-1979)
- Bashir un-nisa Begum Sahiba (1927-)
- Ramzani Begum Sahiba (1931-1974)
- Jawad Jah (d. 1936)
- stillborn son (1938)
- Mashadi Begum Sahiba (1939-)
- Zulfiqar Jah (1943-)
- Imdad Jah (1944-)
- Nawazish Jah (1944-)
- Fazal Jah (1946-)
- Bhojat Jah (1947-1982)
- Sabir Jah (1948-1985)
- Sayida Begum Sahiba (1949-).

Reign

On February 22, 1937, Time magazine called the Nizam the richest man in the world. Osman Ali acceded as Nizam of Hyderabad upon the death of his father in 1911. The state of Hyderabad was the largest of the princely states in pre-independence India. With an area of 86,000 square miles (223,000 km^2), it was roughly the size of present-day United Kingdom. Its ruler was the highest-ranking prince in India, was one of only five princes entitled to a 21-gun salute, held the unique title of "Nizam", and was created "His Exalted Highness" and "Faithful Ally of the British Crown" after World War One due to his financial contribution to the British Empire's war effort. (For example, No. 110 Squadron RAFs original complement of DH.9As were Osman Ali's gift. Each aircraft bore an inscription to that effect, and the unit became known as the Hyderabad Squadron.

Osman Ali was the absolute ruler of this principality. In some accounts, he is held to have been a benevolent ruler who patronized education, science and development. His 37-year rule witnessed the introduction of electricity, railways, roads and airways were developed, the Nizamsagar lake in Hyderabad city was excavated and some irrigation projects on the Tungabhadra river were undertaken.

In 1941, Mir Osman Ali Khan started his own bank, the *Hyderabad State Bank* (now State Bank of Hyderabad) as the state's central bank, which managed the *Osmania sikka,* the currency of the Hyderabad state. It was the only state which had its own currency, the Hyderabadi rupee, which was different from the rest of India. Banknotes of Hyderabad gives a good reference of the banking of that period.

Nearly all the major public buildings in Hyderabad city, such as the Osmania General Hospital, Andhra Pradesh High Court, Asafiya Library now known as *State Central Library,* Town Hall now known as *Assembly Hall,* Jubilee Hall, Hyderabad Museum, now known as *State Museum,* Nizamia Observatory and many other monuments were built during his reign. Up to 11% of the Nizam's budget was spent on education. Osmania University was founded while schools and colleges and even a "Department for Translation" were set up. Primary education was made compulsory and provided free for the poor. The Nizam (as well as his predecessors) have been criticised for largely ignoring the native languages in favour of Urdu.

Osman Ali donated to many institutions in India and abroad. Recipients included educational institutions such as the Jamia Nizamia, the Darul Uloom Deoband and the Banaras Hindu University.

Hyderabad was the only state in British India where the ruler was allowed to issue currency notes. A 100 rupee note was introduced in 1918.

He also paid for a Royal Australian Navy vessel, N-class destroyer, HMAS Nizam (G38) in.

Osman Ali lived at King Kothi Palace—bought from a nobleman— during his entire life, after age 13. He never moved to Chowmahalla Palace not even after his accession to the throne.

Abdication

After Indian independence in 1947, the country was partitioned on communal lines and Pakistan was established as a Muslim nation. The princely states were left free to make whatever arrangement they wished with either India or Pakistan. The Nizam ruled over more than 16 million people and 82,698 square miles (214,190 km) of territory when the British withdrew from the subcontinent in 1947. The Nizam refused to join either India or Pakistan, preferring to form a separate kingdom within the British Commonwealth of nations.

The proposal for independent state was rejected unambiguously by the British government. The Nizam then resolved upon exploring the possibility of independence. Towards this end, he kept up open negotiations with the Government of India regarding the modalities of a future relationship while opening covert negotiations with Pakistan on a similar vein. He also concurrently encouraged the activities of the Razakars. The Nizam cited the Razakars as evidence that the people of the state were opposed to any agreement with India.

Many peasants of the Hyderabad state revolted against the Nizam under the leadership of Communist Party of India. The Telangana peasant armed struggle was successful in driving out local landlords (zamindars), and distributing their land to the landless. Nizam was able to suppress the armed struggle.

However, majority of his subjects were Hindus and his territory was surrounded on all sides by Indian territory. The resulting violence and exodus of people outside of Hyderabad state prompted the new Indian government to invade and annex Hyderabad in 1948. The Nizam then acceded to the Dominion of India and received the ceremonial post of Rajpramukh in 1950. But he resigned from this office when the states were re-organised in 1956. Hyderabad was then split along linguistic lines.

Later Life

Osman Ali Khan was elected to the Indian Parliament twice from Kurnool and Anantapur Lok Sabha constituencies in 1957 and 1962 respectively and was member of various parliamentary committees.

Mir Osman Ali Khan Bahadur died on Friday, February 24, 1967. It was the end of a princely era. His funeral procession was one of the largest in Indian history. He had willed that he be buried in the Judi Mosque that faced King Kothi Palace.

Official Name and Titles

His Exalted Highness Rustam-i-Dauran, Arustu-i-Zaman, Wal Mamalik, Asaf Jah VII, Muzaffar-ul-Mulk-Wal-Mamalik, Nizam ul-Mulk, Nizam ud-Daula Nawab Mir Sir Osman Ali Khan Bahadur, Sipah Saula, Fateh Jung, Nizam of Hyderabad and of Berar, Knight Grand Commander of The Most Exalted Order of the Star of India, Knight Grand Cross of the Most Excellent Order of the British Empire, Royal Victorian Chain, Honourable General in the Army, Faithful Ally of the British Government.

His Exalted Highness was the honorary Colonel of the 20 Deccan Horse. In 1918, Nawab Mir Osman Ali Khan was elevated by King George V from *His Highness* to *His Exalted Highness*. In a letter dated 24 January 1918, the title *Faithful Ally of the British Government* was conferred on him.

The titles during his life were:

- 1886-1911: Nawab Mir Osman Ali Khan Bahadur
- 1911-1912: *His Highness* Rustam-i-Dauran, Arustu-i-Zaman, Wal Mamaluk, Asaf Jah VII, Muzaffar ul-Mamaluk, Nizam ul-Mulk, Nizam ud-Daula, Nawab Mir Sir Osman 'Ali Khan Bahadur, Sipah Salar, Fath Jang, Nizam of Hyderabad, GCSI
- 1912-1917: Colonel *His Highness* Rustam-i-Dauran, Arustu-i-Zaman, Wal Mamaluk, Asaf Jah VII, Muzaffar ul-Mamaluk, Nizam ul-Mulk, Nizam ud-Daula, Nawab Mir Sir Osman 'Ali Khan Bahadur, Sipah Salar, Fath Jang, Nizam of Hyderabad, GCSI
- 1917-1918: Colonel ''*His Highness* Rustam-i-Dauran, Arustu-i-Zaman, Wal Mamaluk, Asaf Jah VII, Muzaffar ul-Mamaluk, Nizam ul-Mulk, Nizam ud-Daula, Nawab Mir Sir Osman 'Ali Khan Bahadur, Sipah Salar, Fath Jang, Nizam of Hyderabad, GCSI, GBE
- 1918-1936: Lieutenant-General *His Exalted Highness* Rustam-i-Dauran, Arustu-i-Zaman, Wal Mamaluk, Asaf Jah VII, Muzaffar ul-Mamaluk, Nizam ul-Mulk, Nizam ud-Daula, Nawab Mir Sir Osman 'Ali Khan Bahadur, Sipah Salar, Fath Jang, Faithful Ally of the British Government, Nizam of Hyderabad, GCSI, GBE
- 1936-1941: Lieutenant-General *His Exalted Highness* Rustam-i-Dauran, Arustu-i-Zaman, Wal Mamaluk, Asaf

Jah VII, Muzaffar ul-Mamaluk, Nizam ul-Mulk, Nizam ud-Daula, Nawab Mir Sir Osman 'Ali Khan Bahadur, Sipah Salar, Fath Jang, Faithful Ally of the British Government, Nizam of Hyderabad and Berar, GCSI, GBE

- 1941-1967: General *His Exalted Highness* Rustam-i-Dauran, Arustu-i-Zaman, Wal Mamaluk, Asaf Jah VII, Muzaffar ul-Mamaluk, Nizam ul-Mulk, Nizam ud-Daula, Nawab Mir Sir Osman 'Ali Khan Bahadur, Sipah Salar, Fath Jang, Faithful Ally of the British Government, Nizam of Hyderabad and Berar, GCSI, GBE

Honours

- Delhi Durbar Gold Medal-1911
- Knight Grand Commander of the Order of the Star of India (GCSI)-1911
- Bailiff Grand Cross of the Order of St. John (GCStJ)-1911
- Knight Grand Cross of the Order of the British Empire (GBE)-1917
- King George V Silver Jubilee Medal-1935
- King George VI Coronation Medal-1937
- Royal Victorian Chain (RVC)-1946.

Line of Succession

The Asaf Jah dynasty followed the policy of male primogeniture during their long rule, regardless of the mother's marital status or rank. Currently, the line of succession to the Hyderabad throne is as follows:

- 1. His Highness Azmet Jah, the Prince of Berar (1960-). Eldest son of Asaf Jah VIII.
- 2. Azam Jah (1979-). Second son of Asaf Jah VIII.
- 3. Muffakham Jah (1939-). Younger brother of Asaf Jah VIII.
- 4. Rafat Jah (1966-). Elder son of Muffakham Jah.
- 5. Farhad Jah. Younger son of Muffakham Jah.
- 6. Shahamat Jah (1957-). Son of His Highness Moazzam Jah, the paternal uncle of Asaf Jah VIII.
- 7. Mir Ahmad 'Ali Khan Bahadur (1912-). Paternal uncle of Asaf Jah VIII.

- 8. Ahmad Jah. Paternal first cousin of Asaf Jah VIII through his uncle Kasim Jah (1912-1952).
- 9. Baqir Jah. Paternal first cousin of Asaf Jah VIII through his uncle Kasim Jah (1912-1952).
- 10. Mir Arshad 'Ali Khan. Son of Ahmad Jah.
- 11. Muhammed Shaik aijamal waheed Ali.

Palaces of the Nizams

The Asaf Jahis were prolific builders. Several palaces of the Nizams were:

- Chowmahalla Palace
- Purani Haveli
- King Kothi Palace
- Hyderabad House, New Delhi.
- Mahboob Mansion
- Falaknuma Palace
- Bella Vista
- Hill Fort Palace
- Chiran Palace.

Chowmahalla Palace

Chowmahalla Palace or Chowmahallat (4 Palaces), was a palace belonging to the Nizams of Hyderabad state. It was the seat of the Asaf Jahi dynasty and was the official residence of the Nizam.

In Urdu, Chow means four and Mahalat (plural of Mahel) means palaces, hence the name Chowmahallat/four palaces.

All ceremonial functions including the accession of the Nizams and receptions for the Governor-General were held at this palace.

History

While Salabat Jung initiated its construction in 1750, it was completed by the period of Afzal ad-Dawlah, Asaf Jah V, the V Nizam ensured its completion between 1857 and 1869.

It is believed to be modelled on Shah of Iran's palace in Tehran.

The palace is unique for its style and elegance. Building of the palace began in the late 18th century and over the decades a synthesis of many architectural styles and influences emerged.

This palace consists of two courtyards, southern courtyard and northern courtyard. They have elegant palaces, the grand Khilwat (the Durbar Hall), fountains and gardens.

The palace originally covered 45 acres (180,000 m), but only 14 acres (57,000 m) remain today.

Southern Courtyard

This is the oldest part of the palace, and has four palaces Afzal Mahal, Mahtab Mahal, Tahniyat Mahal and Aftab Mahal.

It was build in the neo-classical style

Northern Courtyard

This part has *Bara Imam,* A long corridor of rooms on the east side face the central fountain and pool that, once housed the administrative wing. and *Shishe-Alat* meaning mirror image.

It has Mughal domes and arches and many Persian elements like the ornate stucco work that adorn the Khilwat Mubarak. These were characteristic of buildings built in Hyderabad at the time.

As you enter it you will see historic buildings around the central pool.

Opposite to the Bara Imam is a building that is its shishe or mirror image. The rooms were once the used as guest rooms for officials accompanying visiting dignitaries.

Khilwat Mubarak

This is heart of Chowmahalla Palace. It is held in high esteem by the people of Hyderabad, as it was the seat of the Asaf Jahi dynasty. The grand pillared Durbar Hall has a pure marble platform on which the Takht-e-Nishan or the royal seat was laid. Here the Nizams held their durbar and other religious and symbolic ceremonies. The 19 spectacular Chandeliers of Belgian crystal recently reinstalled to recreate the lost splendour of this regal hall.

Clock Tower

The clock above the main gate to Chowmahalla Palace is affectionately called as Khilwat Clock. It has been ticking away for around 250 years. An expert family of clock repairers winds the mechanical clock every week. The name of the clock repairer is Mohammed Khasim and his shop is located in Lad Bazaar. Now his son, Mohammed Hussain, is the proprietor and the people of the locality wait for its chime.

Council Hall

This building housed a rare collection of manuscripts and priceless books.The Nizam often met important officials and dignitaries here. Today it is venue for temporary exhibitions from the treasures of the Chowmahalla Palace Collection that offer a glimpse of a bygone era.

Roshan Bangla

The sixth Nizam is believed to have lived here and the building was named after his mother Roshan Begum.

Purani Haveli

Purani Haveli is a palace located in Hyderabad, India. It was the official residence of the Nizam. It was also known as *Haveli Khadeem*, which means old mansion, was constructed for Sikander Jah, Asaf Jah III (1803-1829) by his father Ali Khan Bahadur, Asaf Jah II.

The Haveli is "U" shaped in plan, with two oblong wings running parallel to each other and the residential palace located perpendicularly in the middle. The main building resembles 18th-century European palaces. A unique feature of this palace is the world's longest wardrode, built in two levels with a hand-cranked wooden lift (elevator) in place. This occupies the entire length of one wing of the palace.

The palace also houses the Nizam's museum, which is dedicated to the last Nizam of Hyderabad state.

King Kothi Palace

King Kothi Palace is a royal palace located in Hyderabad, India. It was the palace where the erstwhile ruler, the Seventh Nizam, Osman Ali Khan, Asaf Jah VII, of Hyderabad state lived here.

History

The palace was not purchased but instead given by Kamal Khan, and the young Nizam moved in when he was only 13.Fact pertaining to The nizam purchasing King Kothi is still under question by people from that era. The Nizam was famous for either taking what he wanted as a "nazr"(present) or by force. After his accession to the throne in 1911, he continued to stay at the palace and did not move to Chowmahalla Palace where his father lived.

In his sprawling King Kothi palace, diamonds, rubies, sapphires, pearls and lesser gems were stored in 3 steel trunks fastened with English-made padlocks.

The Palace has three main buildings, divided into two groups.

The Eastern Half

The eastern half, now occupied by a state government hospital, was used by the Nizam for official and ceremonial purposes.

The Western Half

The western half which is now walled, has the main residential buildings known as Nazri Bagh or Mubarak Mansion and is still belongs to the Nizam's private estate.

The main entrance to Nazri Bagh always had a curtain draped across it, so it has come to be known as the *purdah gate*. When Nizam went out of the Palace, the purdah was lifted up which indicated the king was not home.

The gate was guarded by Maisaram Regiment, police and Sarf-e-Khas Army with lances in their hands..

Present Status

Of the three principal buildings of the King Kothi Complex, the main building, now houses a hospital, and the Mubarak Mansion (Nazri Bagh) accommodating the offices of the Nizam's Private Estates (Sarf E Khas) only survive.

The third building, Osman Mansion, was demolished in the early eighties and in its place a new hospital building is constructed by the State Government. Originally built by an architect Kamal Khan, the complex was acquired by the Nizam VII. Both the surviving buildings in King Kothi are in European style. Nizam VII, the last ruling Nizam (1911-1948) lived here and died in this building on February 24, 1967.

The VI Nizam, Osman Ali Khan had willed that he be buried in the Judi Mosque that faced his fabulous residence, as his final resting place.

Ghadial Gate-the gate with a clock.

The King Kothi complex has various European styles. The canopies over windows, the intricate woodwork, the sloping tiled roofs in octagonal pyramid shapes of the Ghadial Gate complex, and the classical semicircular arches are among the characteristic features of King Kothi.

Hyderabad House

Hyderabad House earlier known as Palace of the Nizam of Hyderabad is a former princely residence of Osman Ali Khan, Nizam VII located at New Delhi. This house was built in 1926 by eminent architect Edwin Lutyens. It was the Delhi palace for the last Nizam of Hyderabad state.

It is currently used by the Government of India for banquets and meetings for visiting foreign dignitaries. It has also been a venue for joint press conferences and major government events.

History

Hyderabad House was designed by Edwin Lutyens, the principal architect of New Delhi, as a residence for the Nizam of the erstwhile kingdom of Hyderabad. The need for a residence in Delhi arose because the most important traditional rulers (maharajas) of Indian states were inducted in 1919 into a Chamber of Princes and, therefore, had to come to Delhi to attend the Chambers meetings of the British.

The Nizam's sons disliked the building, finding it too western in style for their taste. Consequently, the building was seldom used. After Indian independence in 1947, the palace came under the Government of India.

Building

Osman Ali Khan, Asaf Jah VII appointed then famous architect, Edwin Lutyens, to build the Palace. It was completed in 1928.

Hyderabad House was built in the shape of a butterfly. It was the largest and most expensive palace at that time. The entrance hall of the palace, a domed roof is the outstanding feature. It is located to the northwest of the India Gate.

The Hyderabad House is an amalgam of the Mughal and European styles of architecture.

It is the largest and grandest of all palaces that were built during the period 1921-1931, to house various state rulers and it is the biggest and grandest of all princely houses built in New Delhi by this renowned British architect.

Hyderabad House has 36 rooms, four of which have now been converted into dining rooms.

Mahboob Mansion

Mahboob Mansion is a palace, named after Mahbub Ali Khan, Asaf Jah VI, the With Nizam who lived here occasionally, though his permanent residence was the Purani Haveli. It is located in the Malakpet district of Hyderabad.

Built in the late nineteenth century, this is a large palace in architecture of classical European and Mughal style. It is similar to the eastern blocks of Mubarak Mansion Nazri Bagh of King Kothi Palace.

The palace is abandoned and in very poor condition, and the surrounding estates have been entirely taken over by housing and commercial developments.

Falaknuma Palace

Falaknuma Palace is one of the finest palaces in Hyderabad, India. It is located in Falaknuma, 5 km. from Charminar was built by Nawab Vikar-ul-Umra, the then Prime Minister of Hyderabad. Falaknuma literally means "Star of Heaven" in Urdu.

Design

An Italian architect designed this palace and the foundation for the construction was laid by H.E. Sir Vicar Ul Umra Bahadur on 3 March 1884. It took 9 years to complete the construction and furnishing the Palace (Sir Vicar moved into the Gol Bangla and Zanana Mahel of The Falaknuma Palace in December 1889 and closely monitered the finishing work at the Mardana Portion of Falaknuma). It was totally made with Italian marble and it covers a total area of 9,39,712-sq-metre.

The palace is laid out in the shape of a scorpion with two stings spread out as wings on the north. The middle part is occupied by the main building and the kitchen Gol Bangla, Zenana mehal and harem quarters stretch to the south. The Nawab being an avid traveller, various influences show on the palace architecture. The Falaknuma palace is a rare blend of Italian and Tudor architecture. Its glass stained windows throw a spectrum of colours into the rooms.

History

The Nizam VI in 1898 used the palace as a royal guest house as it had a commanding view of the entire city. As the Nizam liked the guest house, the Falaknuma palace was gifted to the sixth Nizam of Hyderabad, Mehboob Ali Khan by the generous Nawab Sir Vicar Ul Umra. Amir e Paigah Sir Vicar Ul Umra (prime minister of Hyderabad and Berar) used this palace as his private residence till it changed owners and the palace was handed over to H.H. The 6th Nizam of Hyderabad in 1897-1898.

The Palace

One of the highlight's of the palace is the state reception room, whose ceiling is decorated with frescoes and gilded relief's. The ballroom contains a two-ton manually operated organ said to be the only one of its kind in the world.

The palace has as many as 220 lavishly decorated rooms and 22 spacious halls. It has some of the finest treasures collections of the Nizam. Falaknuma houses a large collection of rare treasures including paintings, statues, furniture, manuscripts and books.

The Jade collection of the Palace is considered to be unique in the world.

The famed dining hall of the palace could seat 100 guests on its dining table. The furniture was very aesthetic. The chairs were made of carved rosewood with green leather upholstery. The tableware was made of gold and crystal to which fluted music was added.

The palace has a library with a walnut carved roof, a replica of the one at Windsor Castle. The library had one of the finest collections of the Quran in India.

The ground floor of the palace housed the living quarters. A marbled staircase leads to the upper floor. It has carved balustrades, which supports marble figurines with candelabra at intervals.

On the walls of the landing are excellent oil paintings of the Asaf Jahi family, past ministers and notable personages, the whole forming a very interesting historical picture gallery which adds greatly to the imposing effect of the staircase.

The Falaknuma palace has other unique things to its credit. It includes the largest collection of Venetian chandeliers. It is said that it took six months to clean a 138-arm Osler chandelier and the palace has 40 such chandeliers adorning the halls.

The telephone and electrical system was introduced in 1883 by Osler and the palace has one of the largest electrical switchboards in India.

Bella Vista, Hyderabad

Bella Vista, Hyderabad is a royal palace of the Nizam built in the year 1910.

Bella Vista is the Indo-European building standing on a 10-acre (40,000 m) verdant campus. The building's French architect christened it as Bella Vista, meaning *beautiful sight,* since it overlooks the Hussain sagar lake.

It is located at Saifabad suburb. It was modelled on the Henley-on-Thames of England.

History

It was in this palace that the heir apparent to the masnad (throne) of Hyderabad, Prince of Berar, Nawab Mir Himayat Ali Khan, Azam Jah Bahadur, the elder son of the Seventh Nizam, Mir Osman Ali Khan, stayed.

It now houses the Administrative staff college of India.

The princely state had one of the finest palaces in India with rich adornments. Fine objects of art and furnishings in the palaces reflect the grandeur.

End of the Dynasty and Removal of the Last Nizam

The liberation of Hyderabad in September 1948 by "Hyderabad Police Action" (code-named "Operation Polo") was the operation by the Indian armed forces that ended the rule of the Nizam of Hyderabad and led to the integration of the princely state of Hyderabad into the Indian Union.

The operation was necessitated as the princely State of Hyderabad under Nizam Osman Ali Khan, Asif Jah VII, decided to not join either India or Pakistan after the partition of India. The

Nisam's defiance was backed by Qasim Razvi's armed militias, known as *Razakars* and had the moral support of Pakistan,. When all attempts to persuade the Nizam to act friendly towards India failed, and wary of a hostile independent state right in the middle of India, Deputy Prime Minister Sardar Patel decided to annex the state of Hyderabad. He sent the Indian army and the Hyderabad State Forces were defeated within five days.

At that time, Hyderabad state had some 17 polo grounds, the largest number in India. Hence the name "Operation Polo".

Background

The State of Hyderabad, located over most of the Deccan Plateau in southern India, was established in 1724 by Nizam-ul-Mulk Asif Jha after the collapse of the Mughal Indian Empire.

As was the case in several Indian royal states, the Nizam was a Muslim, while a majority of the subject population was Hindu. In 1798, Hyderabad became the first Indian royal state to accede to British protection under the policy of Subsidiary Alliances instituted by Arthur Wellesley.

When the British finally departed from the Indian subcontinent in 1947, they offered the various princely states in the subcontinent the option of assimilating into either India or Pakistan, or staying on as an independent state.

The State of Hyderabad under the leadership of its 7th Nizam, Mir Osman Ali, was the largest and most prosperous of all princely states in India.

It covered 82,698 square miles (214,190 km) of fairly homogenous territory and comprised a population of roughly 16.34 million people (as per the 1941 census) of which a majority (85%) was Hindu. Hyderabad State had its own army, as well as its own airline, telecommunication system, railway network, postal system, currency and radio broadcasting service, with a GDP larger than that of Belgium.

It was in this context that the Nizam, then the richest man in the world, desired to retain independence for his state. The Indians however, were wary of having an independent-and possibly hostile in the heart of its territory, and were determined to assimilate Hyderabad into the Indian Union, in the same manner as the other five hundred and sixty five royal states that had already acceded.

Events Preceding Hostilities

Political and Diplomatic Negotiations

The Nizam of Hyderabad initially approached the British government with a request to take on the status of an independent constitutional monarchy under the British Commonwealth of Nations. This request was however rejected.

When Indian Home Minister Sardar Vallabhai Patel requested the Hyderabad Government to sign the instrument of accession, the Nizam refused and instead declared Hyderabad as an independent nation on 15 August 1947, the same day that India became independent. Alarmed at the idea of an independent Hyderabad in the heart of Indian territory, Sardar Patel approached the governor general of India, Lord Mountbatten who advised him to resolve the issue without the use of force.

Accordingly, the Indian government offered Hyderabad a 'Standstill Agreement' which made an assurance that the status quo would be maintained and no military action would be taken. Unlike in the case of other royal states, instead of an explicit guarantee of eventual accession to India, only a guarantee stating that Hyderabad would not join Pakistan was given. Negotiations were opened through K.M. Munshi, India's envoy and agent general to Hyderabad, and the Nizam's envoys, Laik Ali and Sir Walter Monckton. Lord Mountbatten, who presided over the negotiations, offered several possible deals to the Hyderabad government which were rejected. The Hyderabadi envoys accused India of setting up armed barricades on all land routes and of attempting to economically isolate their nation. The Indians retaliated by accusing the Hyderabad government of importing arms from Pakistan. Hyderabad had given Rupees 200 million to Pakistan, and had stationed a bomber squadron there.

In June 1948, Mountbatten prepared the 'Heads of Agreement' deal which offered Hyderabad the status of an autonomous dominion nation under India. The deal called for the restriction of the regular Hyderabadi armed forces along with a disbanding of its voluntary forces. While it allowed the Nizam to continue as the executive head of the state, it called for a plebiscite along with general democratic elections to set up a constituent assembly. The Hyderabad government would continue to administer its territory as before, leaving only foreign affairs to be handled by the Indian government. Although the plan was approved and signed by the Indians, it was rejected by the Nizam who demanded only complete independence or the status of a dominion under the British Commonwealth. The Nizam also made unsuccessful attempts to seek the arbitration of the President Harry S. Truman of the United States of America and intervention of the United Nations.

Civil Unrest in Hyderabad

The 1941 census had estimated the population of Hyderabad to be 16.34 million, over 85% of who were Hindus and with Muslims accounting for about 12%. It was also a multilingual state consisting of peoples speaking Telugu (48.2%), Marathi (26.4%), Kannada (12.3%) and Urdu (10.3%). In spite of the overwhelming Hindu majority, Hindus were severely under-represented in government, police and the military. Of 1765 officers in the State Army, 1268 were Muslims, 421 were Hindus, and 121 others were Christians, Parsis and Sikhs. Of the officials drawing a salary between Rs.600-1200 per month, 59 were Muslims, 5 were Hindus and 38 were of other religions. The Nizam and his nobles, who were mostly Muslims, owned 40% of the total land in the State.

Even as India and Hyderabad negotiated, most of the subcontinent had been thrown into chaos as a result of communal Hindu-Muslim riots pending the imminent partition of India. Fearing a Hindu civil uprising in his own kingdom, the Nizam allowed Qasim Razvi, a close advisor, and leader of the radical Majlis-e-Ittehadul Muslimeen (MIM) Party, to set up an voluntary militia of Muslims called the 'Razakars'. The Razakars-who numbered up to 200,000 at the height of the conflict-swore to uphold Islamic domination in Hyderabad and the Deccan plateau in the face of growing public opinion amongst the majority Hindu population favouring the accession of Hyderabad into the Indian Union.

As the manpower and arsenal of the Razakars grew, there was an escalation of violence between the Razakars and Hindu communities. In all, more than 150 villages (of which 70 were in Indian territory outside Hyderabad State) were pushed into violence. In Telengana, large groups of peasants, aided by the Communist Party of India revolted against local Muslim landlords, and also came into direct confrontation with the Razakars. Meanwhile, parties like the Hyderabad State Congress were involved in nonviolent protests against the Nizam's rule. On December 4, 1947, Narayan Rao Pawar, a member of a Hindu nationalist organisation called the Arya Samaj made a failed attempt to assassinate the Nizam outside his palace.

Hyderabadi Military Preparations

The Nizam of Hyderabad had a large army with a tradition of hiring mercenary forces. These included Arabs, Rohillas, North Indian Muslims and Pathans. The State Army consisted of three armoured regiments, a horse cavalry regiment, 11 infantry battalions and artillery. These were supplemented by irregular units with horse cavalry, four infantry battalions (termed as the Saraf-e-khas, paigah, Arab and Refugee) and a garrison battalion-all forming a total of 22,000 men. This army was commanded by Major General El Edroos, an Arab. 55 per cent of the Hyderabadi army was composed of Muslims, with 1,268 Muslims in a total of 1,765 officers as of 1941. In addition to these, there were about 200,000 irregular militia called the Razakars under the command of civilian leader Qasim Razvi. A quarter of these were armed with modern small firearms, while the rest were predominantly armed with muzzle-loaders and swords. It is reported that the Nizam received arms supplies from Pakistan and from the Portuguese administration based in Goa. In addition, additional arms supplies were received via airdrops from an Australian arms trader Sidney Cotton.

Breakdown of Negotiations

As the Indian government received information that Hyderabad was arming itself and was preparing to ally with Pakistan in any future war with India, Sardar Patel described the idea of an independent Hyderabad as an ulcer in the heart of India-which had to removed surgically. In response, Hyderabad's prime minister Laik Ali stated "India thinks that if Pakistan attacks her, Hyderabad will stab her in the back. I am not so sure we would not." Sardar Patel responded later by stating "If you threaten us with violence, swords will be met with swords".

In Hyderabad, militia leader Qasim Razwi told a crowd of Razakars, "Death with the sword in hand, is always preferable to extinction by a mere stroke of the pen.". Razwi was later described by Indian government officials as "The Nizam's Frankenstein Monster". In response to reports that India was planning to invade

Hyderabad Razwi stated, "If India attacks us I can and will create a turmoil throughout India. We will perish but India will perish also." The magazine "Time" pointed out that if India invaded Hyderabad, the Razakars would massacre Hindus, which would lead to retaliatory massacres of Muslims across India.

Skirmish at Kodar

On September 6 an Indian police post near Chillakallu village came under heavy fire from Razakar units. The Indian Army command sent a squadron of The Poona Horse led by Abhey Singh and a company of 2/5 Gurkha Rifles to investigate who were also fired upon by the Razakars. The tanks of the Poona Horse then chased the Razakars to Kodar, in Hyderabad territory. Here they were opposed by the armoured cars of 1 Hyderabad Lancers. In a brief action the Poona Horse destroyed one armoured car and forced the surrender of the state garrison at Kodar.

Indian Military Preparations

On receiving directions from the government to seize and annex Hyderabad, the Indian army came up with the Goddard Plan (laid out by Lt. Gen E.N. Goddard, the C-in-C of the Southern Command). The plan envisaged two main thrusts-from Vijayawada in the East and Solapur in the West-while smaller units pinned down the Hyderabadi army along the border. Overall command was placed in the hands of Lt. Gen. Rajendrasinghji, DSO.

The attack from Solapur was led by Major General J.N. Chaudhari and was composed of four task forces:

1. Strike Force comprising a mix of fast moving infantry, cavalry and light artillery,
2. Smash Force consisting of predominantly armoured units and artillery,
3. Kill Force composed of infantry and engineering units
4. Vir Force which comprised infantry, anti-tank and engineering units.

The attack from Vijaywada was led by Major General A.A. Rudra and comprised the 2/5 Gurkha Rifles, one squadron of the 17th (Poona) Horse, and a troop from the 19th Field Battery along with engineering and ancillary units. In addition, four infantry battalions were to neutralize and protect lines of communication. Two squadrons of Hawker Tempest aircraft were prepared for air support from the Pune base. The date for the attack was fixed as 13 September, even though General Sir Roy Bucher, the Indian chief of staff, had objected on grounds that Hyderabad would be an additional front for the Indian army after Kashmir.

Commencement of Hostilities

Day 1, September 13

The first battle was fought at Naldurg Fort on the Solapur Secundarabad Highway between a defending force of the 1st Hyderabad Infantry and the attacking force of the 7th Brigade. Using speed and surprise, the 7th Brigade managed to secure a vital bridge on the Bori river intact, following which an assault was made on the Hyderabadi positions at Naldurg by the 2nd Sikh Infantry. The bridge and road secured, an armoured column of the 1st Armoured Brigade-part of the Smash force-moved into the town of Jalkot, 8 km from Naldurg, at 0900 hours, paving the way for the Strike Force units under Lt. Col Ram Singh Commandant of 9 DOGRA (a motorised battalion) to pass through. This armoured column reached the town of Umarge, 61 km inside Hyderabad by 1515 hours, where it quickly overpowered resistance from Razakar units defending the town. Meanwhile, another column consisting of a squadron of 3rd Cavalry, a troop from 18th King Edward's Own Cavalry, a troop from 9 Para Field Regiment, 10 Field Company Engineers, 3/2 Punjab Regiment, 2/1 Gurkha Rifles, 1 Mewar Infantry, and ancillary units attacked the town of Tuljapur, about 34 km northwest of Naldurg. They reached Tuljapur at dawn, where they encountered resistance from a unit of the 1st Hyderabad Infantry and about 200 Razakars who fought for two hours before surrendering. Further advance towards the town of Lohara was stalled as the river had swollen. The first day on the Western front ended with the Indians inflicting heavy casualties on the Hyderabadis and capturing large tracts of territory. Amongst the captured defenders was a British mercenary who had been tasked with blowing up the bridge near Naldurg.

In the East, forces led by Lt. Gen A.A. Rudra met with fierce resistance from two armoured units of Humber armoured cars and Staghound armoured cars, but managed to reach the town of Kodar by 0830 hours. Pressing on, the force reached Mungala by the afternoon.

There were further incidents in Hospet-where the 1st Mysore assaulted and secured a sugar factory from units of Razakars and Pathans-and at Tungabhadra-where the 5/5 Gurkha attacked and secured a vital bridge from the Hyderabadi army.

Day 2, September 14

The force that had camped at Umarge proceeded to the town of Rajasur, 48 km east. As aerial reconnaissance had shown well entrenched ambush positions set up along the way, the air strikes from squadrons of Tempests were called in. These air strikes effectively cleared the route and allowed the land forces to reach and secure Rajasur by the afternoon. The Assault force from the East was meanwhile slowed down by an anti-tank ditch and later came under heavy fire from hillside positions of the 1st Lancers and 5th Infantry 6 km from Surriapet. The positions were assaulted by the 2/5 Gurkha-veterans of the Burma Campaign-and was neutralised with the Hyderabadis taking severe casualties. At the same time, the 3/11 Gurkha Rifles and a squadron of 8th Cavalry attacked Osmanabad and took the town after heavy street combat with the Razakars who determinedly resisted the Indians

A force under the command of Maj. Gen. D.S. Brar was tasked with capturing the city of Aurangabad. The city was attacked by six columns of infantry and cavalry, resulting in the civil administration emerging in the afternoon and offering a surrender to the Indians. There were further incidents in Jalna where 3 Sikh, a company of 2 Jodhpur infantry and some tanks from 18 Cavalry faced stubborn resistance from Hyderabadi forces.

Day 3, September 15

Leaving a company of 3/11 Gurkhas to occupy the town of Jalna, the remainder of the force moved to Latur, and later to Mominabad where they faced action against the 3 Golconda Lancers who gave token resistance before surrendering.

At the town of Surriapet, air strikes cleared most of the Hyderabadi defences, although some Razakar units still gave resistance to the 2/5 Gurkhas who occupied the town. The retreating Hyderabadi forces destroyed the bridge at Musi to delay the Indians but failed to offer covering fire, allowing the bridge to be quickly repaired. Another incident occurred at Narkatpalli where a Razakar unit was decimated by the Indians.

Day 4, September 16

The task force under Lt. Col. Ram Singh moved towards Zahirabad at dawn, but was slowed down by a minefield, which had to be cleared. On reaching the junction of the Bidar road with the Solapur-Hyderabad City Highway, the forces encountered gunfire from ambush positions. However, leaving some of the units to handle the ambush, the bulk of the force moved on to reach 15 kilometres beyond Zahirabad by nightfall in spite of sporadic resistance along the way. Most of the resistance was from Razakar units who ambushed the Indians as they passed through urban areas. The Razakars were able to use the terrain to their advantage until the Indians brought in their 75 mm guns.

Day 5, September 17

In the early hours of September 17, the Indian army entered Bidar. Meanwhile, forces led by the 1st Armoured regiment were at the town of Chityal about 60 km from the capital city, while another column took over the town of Hingoli. By the morning of the 5th day of hostilities, it had become clear that the Hyderabad army and the Razakars had been routed on all fronts and with extremely heavy casualties. The Nizam's defeat was now imminent.

Capitulation and Surrender

Consultations with Indian Envoy

On September 16, faced with imminent defeat, the Nizam summoned the Prime Minister Mir Laik Ali and requested his resignation by the morning of the following day. The resignation was delivered along with the resignations of the entire cabinet.

On the noon of September 17, a messenger brought a personal note from the Nizam to India's Agent General to Hyderabad, K.M. Munshi summoning him to the Nizam's office at 1600 hours. At the meeting, the Nizam stated "The vultures have resigned. I don't know what to do". Munshi advised the Nizam to secure the safety of the citizens of Hyderabad by issuing appropriate orders to the Commander of the Hyderabad State Army, Major General El Edroos. This was immediately done.

Radio Broadcast of Surrender Offer

Munshi also suggested that the Nizam might make a broadcast welcoming the Police Action and withdrawing his complaint to the Security Council. Munshi explained and offered to help draft the speech. It was the Nizam's first visit to the radio station. No red carpet was spread for him; no formalities were observed. No music, no anthem was played before or after the broadcast. The speech was in English. Nobody bothered to translate it into Urdu. After the broadcast the Nizam drove back to King Kothi Palace to brood.

The Surrender Ceremony

The surrender ceremony was fixed at 4 p.m. General Chaudhuri spoke gravely: "I have been ordered by Lt. General Maharaj Rajendrasinhji, General Officer Commanding-in-Chief, Southern Command to take the surrender of your army".

"You have it".

"You understand that this surrender is unconditional".

"Yes, I understand".

Chaudhuri smiled and shook hands with Edroos. Then he opened his cigarette case and offered him a cigarette. Edroos proffered a lighter. Chaudhuri's team joined them. The party drove to the residence of India's Agent General. A jubilant crowd cheered the victorious general there. He waved in return and then sat down to discuss the details with Munshi, Edroos and others.

The Aftermath

"Operation Polo" resulted in moderate casualties for Indian forces, with significantly higher losses for Hyderbadi forces. Indian losses were 32 killed and 97 wounded. Among the Indian units, the Punjab Regiment had by far suffered the greatest number of casualties, with 20 of its soldiers killed in action. The losses suffered by Hyderabad state forces and Irregular forces combined were 1,863 killed, 122 wounded, and 3,558 captured. In the following weeks the state erupted in widespread communal violence. 50,000 people may have died in the reprisals that followed the invasion. Most of the violence occurred in the state's rural districts, sparking large scale migration both to the capital at Hyderabad, and to Pakistan. The Nizam received the ceremonial post of Rajpramukh in 1950, but resigned from this office when the states were re-organized in 1956 on linguistic basis and large parts of Hyderabad state went to Bombay State. Many officials and members of the royal family fled and re-settled in Pakistan where they now live.

5

Rohilla

The Rohilla are a community of Urdu speaking Pashtun also known as Pathan, historically found in the state of Uttar Pradesh, in North India. Many are now also found in Pakistan. They form one of the largest Pashtun diaspora community in India, and have given their name to the Rohilkhand region. Many members of Rohilla community have migrated to Pakistan after independence have settled in Karachi, Sindh.

Origin

The Rohilla are descended from a number of Pashtun tribes that settled in the Rohilkhand region the 17th and 18th Centuries.They Rohillas belonged mainly to Yousafzai tribe of Pashtuns, of Mandanh sub-section but other Pashtuns also became part of the community. Rohilla's Sardar like Daud Khan, Ali Muhammad Khan, and legend Hafiz Rehmat Khan were from renowned Afghan Tribe Barech, originally from Kandahar Province. The term *Rohilla* was used for all Pashtuns, except for the Shia Bangashes who settled in the Rohilkhand region, or men serving under Rohilla chiefs. They were awarded the *Katehr* region in the then northern India by Mughal emperor Aurangzeb Alamgir (ruled 1658-1707) to suppress Rajput uprisings. Originally, some 20,000 Soldiers from Pashtun Tribes (Yusafzais, Ghoris, Lodis, Ghilzai, Barech, Marwat, Durrani, Tanoli, Tarin, Kakar, Khattak, Afridi and Baqarzai) were hired by Mughals to suppress Rajputs, Marathas and Sikhs but later, as their loyalty & bravery was appreciated by Aurangzeb Alamgir, an additional force of 25,000 men was given respected positions in Mughal Army. However most of them settled in the Katehar region during Nadir Shah's invasion of northern

India in 1739 increasing their population up to 100,0000. Due to the large settlement of Rohilla Afghans, the Katehar region gained fame as Rohilkhand. Bareilly was made the capital of the Rohilkhand state. Other important cities were Moradabad, Rampur, Shahjahanpur, Badaun, and others. According to 1901 census of India, the total Pathan population in Bareilly District was 40,779, out of a total population of 1,090,117. Their principal clans were the Yusafzais, Ghoris, Lodis, Ghilzai, Barech, Marwat, Durrani, Tanoli, Tarin, Kakar, Khattak, Afridi and Baqarzai.

This region is nowadays located in modern Uttar Pradesh state of India, and still home to a significant Rohilla population, although many Rohillas did emigrate to Pakistan, after the independence in 1947.

Rohillas were distinguished by their separate language and culture. They spoke Pashto among each other but gradually lost their language over time and now converse in Urdu. After independence of Pakistan in 1947, most Rohillas moved to Karachi in Pakistan with smaller scattered populations still to be found in Burma, Suriname and Guyana. A significant number of Urdu Speakers (Muhajir) in Pakistan are of Pashtun heritage.

History

The founders of the Pashtun state of Rohilkhand were Daud Khan and his adopted son Ali Mohammed Khan. Daud Khan arrived in 1705 in South Asia along with a band of his tribe namely Barech a Pushtoon tribe. He was succeeded in 1721 by Ali Mohammed Khan, who became so powerful that he refused to send tax revenues to the central governament. Safdar Jang, the Nawab of Oudh, warned Mughal emperor Mohammed Shah of the growing power of the Rohillas. This caused Mohammed Shah to send an expedition against him as a result of which he surrendered to imperial forces. He was taken to Delhi as a prisoner, but was later pardoned and appointed governor of Sirhind. In 1748, he returned to Rohilkhand and recovered his lost possessions. Later that year Ali Mohammed Ali Khan died, leaving six sons. However, two of his elder sons were in Afghanistan at the time of his death while the other four were too young to assume the leadership of Rohilkhand. As a result, power transferred to other Rohilla Sardars, the most important being Hafiz Rahmat Khan and Dundi Khan.

Following the Battle of Panipat in 1761

In the third battle of Panipat (1761) one of the Rohilla Sardars, Najib-ul-Daula, allied himself with Ahmad Shah Abdali against the Marathas. He not only provided 40,000 Rohilla troops but also 70 guns to combined forces. He also convinced Shuja-ul-Daula, the Nawab of Oudh, to join Ahmad Shah Abdali's forces against the Marathas. In this battle, the Maratha's were defeated and as a consequence Rohilla increased in power. Rohilkhand was invaded by the Marathas to retaliate against the Rohillas' participation in the Panipat war. The Marathas entered the *jagir* (land) of the late Sardar Najib-ud-Daula which was now held by his son Zabita Khan. Zabita Khan gave tough resistance but was defeated and forced to flee to the camp of Shuja-ud-Daula; and his country was ravaged by Marathas. The principal remaining Rohilla Sardar was Hafiz Rahmat Khan Barech and through him an agreement was formed with the Nawab of Oudh, Shuja-ud-Daula, by which they had to pay 4 million rupees in return to their military help against the Marathas. However after the war, the Rohillas refused to pay.

Subsequently the Rohillas were attacked by Oudh with help from British East India Company forces under Colonel Alexander Champion. When Hafiz Rahmat Khan was killed, in April 1774, they were defeated, and Rohilkhand was plundered.

Rohillas fled to jungles across the Ganges, and later began a guerilla war against the occupation. In response, the Rohillas were hunted down by the British and were subsequently scattered in the countryside, and settled in many small towns. Later charges of destroying a nation (ethnic cleansing or genocide) were brought against Warren Hastings of the East India Company, by Edmund Burke, later taken up by Thomas Babington Macaulay.

The Rohillas took an active part in War of Independence in 1857 against British imperial forces (referred to as the *Mutiny* by the British historians, or the War of Independence). The revolt was bitterly suppressed, and in its wake the British dramatically reorganized the government of South Asia, bringing an end to the British East India Company's regime and leading to almost a century of direct rule of the South Asia by Britain under the British Raj. A significant groups of Rohillas sought refuge in state of Tonk in Rajasthan, which was ruled by Pathan nawabs, and now form the core of the Tonkia Pathans.

Ali Mohammed Khan

Ali Muhammad Khan (bf.1706-September 15, 1748) was a rohilla (Pashtun highlanders) chief who founded the Pathan (Pashtun) state of Rohilkhand in the northwestern region of the Uttar Pradesh state of India. He succeeded *rohilla* Sardar Daud Khan and helped develop Rohilkhand into a powerful nation, which became independent in 1721.

Safdar Jang of Oudh informed the Mughal emperor of India Mohammed Shah (ruled 1719-1748) about Ali Mohammed Khan's supposed intentions to create his own Sultanate. Mohammed Shah sent an expedition against him, as a result of which he was imprisoned. Later he was pardoned and made governor of Sirhind. After Nadir Shah, the conqueror of Iran, took control of Kabul and sacked Delhi in 1739, Ali Mohammed Khan returned to his homeland and ruled the independent state of Rohilkhand until his death in 1748.

Descendants

Nawab Faizullah Khan (1730?-1793) was the second son of Ali Muhammad Khan. He assumed rule of the Rohillas after his father's death. In 1774, during the invasion of Rohilkhand by the united armies of the Vizier Sujah ul Dowlah and the British East India Company, Faizullah Khan led a resistance in which many of the Rohilla's principal chiefs were killed. Escaping from the slaughter, Faizullah Khan "made his retreat good towards the mountains, with all his treasure." He collected the scattered remains of his countrymen; and as he was the eldest surviving son of Ali Mohammed Khan, he seems at length to have been generally acknowledged by his natural subjects the undoubted heir of his father's authority.

Faizullah Khan

Faizullah Khan (c.1730-24 July 1793) was the first Nawab of Rampur. The princely state of Rampur was set up in 1774, after the First Rohilla War, by the dismemberment of the Rohilla state of Rohilkhand. Faizullah Khan, the surviving heir of Ali Mohammed Khan and opponent of the forces of Awadh and the British East India Company in the war, was installed as ruler of what was a puppet state. It bordered the Maratha Empire to the south, making it a strategic point.

Under tutelage of the East India Company, Faizullah Khan ruled peacefully for 20 years. The capital Rampur was founded, and the Raza Library collection gathered.

Hafiz Rahmat Khan

Hafiz Rahmat Khan (1708/9-23 April 1774) was Regent of Rohilkhand in North India, from 1749 to 1774. He was a Pashtun by background, ruling over Rohillas (Afghan highlanders).

In 1623 two Afghan brothers of the Baretz tribe, Shah Alam and Husain Khan, settled here and founded a small state of Rampur, bringing with them many other Pashtun settlers. Ali Muhammad Khan, grandson of Shah Alam, later united the Rohillas between 1707 and 1720, making Bareilly his capital. Hafiz Rahmat Khan, who was his uncle, succeeded him, extended his power from Almora in the North to Etawah in the South-West.

He played an important part in Indian warfare over several decades, being on the winning side at the Third Battle of Panipat of 1761, but was defeated and killed in the Rohilla War. In 1772 Rohilkhand was invaded by the Marathas; however the Nawabs of Awadh came to the aid of the Rohillas in repulsing the invasion. After the war Nawab Shuja-ud-Daula demanded payment for their help from the Rohilla chief, Hafiz Rahmat Khan. When the demand was refused the Nawab joined with the British under Governor Warren Hastings and his Commander-in-Chief, Alexander Champion, to invade Rohilkhand and Hafiz Rahmat Khan was killed in the ensuing battle at Miranpur Katra in 1774. The whole of Rohilkhand (including Bareilly, Pilibhit and Shahjanpur) was surrendered to the East India Company by the treaty of November 10, 1801. Later, Bareilly was a centre of disaffection for the entire area in the Indian Mutiny of 1857.

He also founded the town of Pilibhit, where he also built a Jama Masjid, a replica of the Jama Masjid, Delhi

Hafiz Rahmat Khan

Hafiz Rahmat Khan (1708/9-23 April 1774) was Regent of Rohilkhand in North India, from 1749 to 1774. He was a Pashtun by background, ruling over Rohillas (Afghan highlanders).

In 1623 two Afghan brothers of the Baretz tribe, Shah Alam and Husain Khan, settled here and founded a small state of Rampur, bringing with them many other Pashtun settlers. Ali Muhammad Khan, grandson of Shah Alam, later united the Rohillas between 1707 and 1720, making Bareilly his capital. Hafiz Rahmat Khan, who was his uncle, succeeded him, extended his power from Almora in the North to Etawah in the South-West.

He played an important part in Indian warfare over several decades, being on the winning side at the Third Battle of Panipat of 1761, but was defeated and killed in the Rohilla War. In 1772 Rohilkhand was invaded by the Marathas; however the Nawabs of Awadh came to the aid of the Rohillas in repulsing the invasion. After the war Nawab Shuja-ud-Daula demanded payment for their help from the Rohilla chief, Hafiz Rahmat Khan. When the demand was refused the Nawab joined with the British under Governor Warren Hastings and his Commander-in-Chief, Alexander Champion, to invade Rohilkhand and Hafiz Rahmat Khan was killed in the ensuing battle at Miranpur Katra in 1774. The whole of Rohilkhand (including Bareilly, Pilibhit and Shahjanpur) was surrendered to the East India Company by the treaty of November 10, 1801. Later, Bareilly was a centre of disaffection for the entire area in the Indian Mutiny of 1857.

He also founded the town of Pilibhit, where he also built a Jama Masjid, a replica of the Jama Masjid, Delhi

Ghulam Muhammad Khan Bahadur

Al-Haj Nawab Ghulam Muhammad Khan Bahadur (11 July 1763 – 1828) was briefly Nawab of Rampur from 1793 to 1794. The younger son of Faizullah Khan, Ghulam Muhammad became Nawab in 1793 after deposing his elder brother, Muhammad Ali Khan Bahadur. His reign quickly took on a tyrannical aspect, and he was soon deemed a danger to the region's stability. Thus, in 1794, he was himself deposed by troops of the East India Company and of the Nawab of Awadh, being succeeded as Nawab by his nephew, Ahmad Ali Khan Bahadur. Ghulam Muhammad then undertook the Hajj, after which he fled to Mysore and Tipu Sultan, later settling in the Emirate of Afghanistan. He died at Nadaun in 1828.

Ahmad Ali Khan Bahadur

Nawab Ahmad Ali Khan Bahadur (12 October 1787 – 5 July 1840) was Nawab of Rampur from 1794 to 1840, succeeding his brother Ghulam Muhammad Khan Bahadur. The only son of Muhammad Ali Khan Bahadur, Ahmad Ali was made Nawab following the deposition of his cousin Ghulam Muhammad by the British East India Company and the Nawab of Awadh. Ahmad Ali ruled for 46 years, although he reigned from 1794-1811 under a regency. He transformed the cultural fabric of Rampur and started a tradition of cultural involvement that has been maintained by his successors to the present day. In 1801, Rampur became a vassal of the HEIC following the cession of Rohilkand by the Nawab of Awadh. Ahmad Ali died on 5 July 1840, aged 52. As his only son had died young, he was succeeded as Nawab by his cousin, Muhammad Said Khan Bahadur.

Yusef Ali Khan Bahadur

Nawab Muhammad Yusef Ali Khan Bahadur, KSI, (5 March 1816-21 April 1865) was a Nawab of the princely state of Rampur from 1855 to 1865. During the First War of Independence, he rendered many useful services to the Government of India by keeping the British supply and communication lines to Naini Tal open, rescuing fugitives and securing the town of Moradabad. For his service, he was granted extensive lands in Bareilly by the Viceroy of India, Lord Canning, was knighted in 1861 and given a 13-gun salute along with the style of *His Highness*. Finally, he was made a member of the Viceroy's Council. Despite this multitude of honours, Sir Yusef continued to preserve the Mughal artistic tradition by inviting musicians, scholars and artists of Bahadur Shah Zafar II's court to resettle at Rampur, including the great poet Ghalib. Dying at 49 in 1865, he was succeeded by his son, Sir Kalb Ali Khan Bahadur.

Kalb Ali Khan of Rampur

Hajji Nawab Kalb Ali Khan Bahadur (1834-23 March 1887) was a Nawab of the princely state of Rampur from 1865 to 1887. Succeeding his father, Sir Yusef Ali Khan Bahadur, he continued his father's good works, expanding the Rampur library, constructing the Jama Masjid for Rs.3 lakhs and encouraging the spread of education, architecture, literature and art in general. A gifted ruler, Sir Kalb Ali Khan was highly literate in Arabic and Persian and patronised scholars from across India and the Islamic world. He was a member of John Lawrence's council from 1878 to his death, attended the Delhi Durbar of Queen Victoria and was granted a personal salute of 17-guns. He was succeeded at his death in 1887, aged 53, by his son, Muhammad Mushtaq Ali Khan Bahadur.

Rohilla War

The First Rohilla War of 1773-1774 was a punitive campaign by Shuja-ud-Daula, Nawab of Awadh, against the Rohillas, Afghan highlanders settled in Rohilkhand, northern India. The Nawab was supported by troops of the British East India Company, in a successful campaign brought about by the Rohillas reneging on a debt to the Nawab.

Background

Having been driven into the mountains by the Marathas, a few years earlier, the Rohillas had appealed for aid to Shuja-ud-Daula, an ally at that time of the British. He promised to assist them in return for a sum of money; but when the Mahrattas were driven off the Rohilla chiefs refused to pay. The Nawab then decided to annex their country, and appealed to Warren Hastings for assistance, which was given in return for a sum of forty lakhs of rupees.

Hastings justified his action on the ground that the Rohillas were a danger to the British as uncovering the flank of Awadh.

Course of the War

The Rohillas under Hafiz Rahmat Ali Khan were defeated by Colonel Alexander Champion in April 1774. The decisive battle, in which Hafiz Rahmat Khan died, was at Miranpur Katra, on 23 April.

Consequences

Rohilkhand fell to Awadh, was plundered and occupied. The majority of the Rohillas left. They fled across the Ganges in numbers, to start a guerilla war; or emigrated. A Rohilla state under British protection was set up in Rampur.

There was a second Rohilla War, in 1794.

6

Kingdom of Mysore

The Kingdom of Mysore (1399–1947 AD) was a kingdom of southern India, traditionally believed to have been founded in 1399 in the vicinity of the modern city of Mysore. The kingdom, which was ruled by the Wodeyar family, initially served as a vassal state of the Vijayanagara Empire. With the decline of the Vijayanagara Empire (circa 1565), the kingdom became independent. The 17th century saw a steady expansion of its territory and, under Narasaraja Wodeyar I and Chikka Devaraja Wodeyar, the kingdom annexed large expanses of what is now southern Karnataka and parts of Tamil Nadu to become a powerful state in the southern Deccan.

The kingdom reached the height of its military power and dominion in the latter half of the 18th century under Hyder Ali and his son Tipu Sultan, who deposed the Wodeyars to take control of the kingdom. During this time, it came into conflict with the Marathas, the British and the Nizam of Golconda which culminated in the four Anglo-Mysore wars. Success in the first two Anglo-Mysore wars was followed by defeat in the third and fourth. Following Tipu's death in the fourth war of 1799, large parts of the kingdom were annexed by British which signalled the end of a period of Mysorean hegemony over southern Deccan. The British, however, restored the Wodeyars to the throne by way of a subsidiary alliance and a diminished Mysore was now transformed into a Princely state. The Wodeyars continued to rule the state until Indian independence in 1947, when Mysore acceded to the Union of India.

Even as a princely state, Mysore came to be counted among the more modern and urbanized regions of India. This period

(1799–1947) also saw Mysore emerge as one of the important centres of art and culture in India. The Mysore kings were not only accomplished exponents of the fine arts and men of letters, they were enthusiastic patrons as well and their legacies continue to influence music and art even today.

History

Early History

Sources for the history of the kingdom include numerous extant lithic and copper plate inscriptions, records from the Mysore palace and contemporary literary sources in Kannada, Persian and other languages. According to traditional accounts, the kingdom originated as a small state based in the modern city of Mysore and was founded by two brothers, Yaduraya (also known as Vijaya) and Krishnaraya. Their origins are mired in legend and are still a matter of debate; while some historians posit a northern origin at Dwaraka, others locate it in Karnataka. Yaduraya is said to have married Chikkadevarasi, the local princess and assumed the feudal title "Wodeyar" (*lit*, "Lord"), which the ensuing dynasty retained. The first unambiguous mention of the Wodeyar family is in 16th century Kannada literature from the reign of the Vijayanagara king Achyuta Deva Raya (1529–1542); the earliest available inscription, issued by the Wodeyars themselves, dates to the rule of the petty chief Timmaraja II in 1551.

Autonomy: Advances and Reversals

The kings who followed ruled as vassals of the Vijayanagara empire until the decline of the latter in 1565. By this time, the kingdom had expanded to thirty-three villages protected by a force of 300 soldiers. King Timmaraja II conquered some surrounding chiefdoms, and King *Bola* Chamaraja IV (*lit*, "Bald"), the first ruler of any political significance among them, withheld tribute to the nominal Vijayanagara monarch Aravidu Ramaraya. After the death of Aravidu Ramaraya, the Wodeyars began to assert themselves further and King Raja Wodeyar I wrested control of Srirangapatna from the Vijayanagara governor (*Mahamandaleshvara*) Aravidu Tirumalla – a development which elicited, if only *ex post facto*, the tacit approval of Venkatapati Raya, the incumbent king of the diminished Vijayanagar empire ruled from Chandragiri. Raja Wodeyar I's reign also saw territorial expansion with the annexation of Channapatna to the north from Jaggadeva Raya – a development which made Mysore a regional political factor to reckon with.

Consequently, by 1612–13, the Wodeyars exercised a great deal of autonomy and even though they acknowledged the nominal overlordship of the Aravidus, tributes and transfers of revenue to Chandragiri stopped. This was in marked contrast to the major chiefs (*Nayakas*) of Tamil country who continued to pay off Chandragiri well into the 1630s. Chamaraja V and Kanthirava Narasaraja I attempted to expand further northward but were thwarted by the Bijapur Sultanate and its Maratha subordinates, though the Bijapur armies under Ranadullah Khan were effectively repelled in their 1638 siege of Srirangapatna. Expansionist ambitions then turned southward into Tamil country where Narasaraja Wodeyar acquired Satyamangalam (in modern northern Coimbatore district) while his successor Dodda Devaraja Wodeyar expanded further to capture western Tamil regions of Erode and Dharmapuri, after successfully repulsing the chiefs of Madurai. The invasion of the Keladi Nayakas of Malnad was also dealt with successfully. This period was followed by one of complex geo-political changes, when in the 1670s, the Marathas and the Mughals pressed into the Deccan.

Chikka Devaraja (r. 1672–1704), the most notable of Mysore's early kings, who ruled during much of this period, managed to not only survive the exigencies but further expanded territory. He achieved this by forging strategic alliances with the Marathas and the Mughals. The kingdom soon grew to include Salem and Bangalore to the east, Hassan to the west, Chikkamagaluru and Tumkur to the north and the rest of Coimbatore to the south. Despite this expansion, the kingdom, which now accounted for a fair share of land in the southern Indian heartland, extending from the Western Ghats to the western boundaries of the Coromandel plain, remained landlocked without direct coastal access. Chikka Devaraja's attempts to remedy this brought Mysore into conflict with the *Nayaka* chiefs of Ikkeri and the kings (*Rajas*) of Kodagu (modern Coorg); who between them controlled the Kanara coast (coastal areas of modern Karnataka) and the intervening hill region respectively. The conflict brought mixed results with Mysore annexing Periyapatna but suffering a reversal at Palupare.

Nevertheless, from around 1704, when the kingdom passed on to "Muteking" (*Mukarasu*) Kanthirava Narasaraja II, the survival and expansion of the kingdom was achieved by playing a delicate game of alliance, negotiation, subordination on occasion, and annexation of territory in all directions. According to historians Sanjay Subrahmanyam and Sethu Madhava Rao, Mysore was now formally a tributary of the Mughal empire. Mughal records claim a regular tribute (*peshkash*) was payed by Mysore. However, historian Suryanath Kamath feels the Mughals may have considered Mysore an ally, a situation brought about by Mughal–Maratha competition for supremacy in southern India. By the 1720s, with the Mughal empire in decline, further complications arose with the Mughal residents at both Arcot and Sira claiming tribute. The years that followed saw Krishnaraja Wodeyar I tread cautiously on the matter while keeping the Kodagu chiefs and the Marathas at bay. He was followed by Chamaraja Wodeyar VI during whose reign power fell into the hands of prime minister (*Dalwai* or *Dalavoy*) Nanjarajiah (or Nanjaraja) and chief minister (*Sarvadhikari*) Devarajiah (or Devaraja), the influential brothers from Kalale town near Nanjangud who would rule for the next three decades with the Wodeyars relegated to being the titular heads. The latter part of the rule of Krishnaraja II saw the Deccan Sultanates being eclipsed by the Mughals and in the confusion that ensued, Hyder Ali, a captain in the army, rose to prominence. His victory against the Marathas at Bangalore in 1758, resulting in the annexation of their territory, made him an iconic figure. In honour of his achievements, the king gave him the title "Nawab Hyder Ali Khan Bahadur".

Under Hyder and Tipu

Vijayanagara feudatory	(1399-1565)
Yaduraya	(1399–1423)
Chamaraja Wodeyar I	(1423–1459)
Timmaraja Wodeyar I	(1459–1478)
Chamaraja Wodeyar II	(1478–1513)
Chamaraja Wodeyar III	(1513–1553)
Independent Wodeyar Kings	(1565-1761)
Timmaraja II	(1553–1572)

Contd...

Chamaraja Wodeyar IV	(1572–1576)
Bettada Wodeyar	(1576–1578)
Raja Wodeyar I	(1578–1617)
Chamaraja Wodeyar V	(1617–1637)
Raja Wodeyar II	(1637–1638)
Narasaraja Wodeyar I	(1638–1659)
Dodda Devaraja Wodeyar	(1659–1673)
Chikka Devaraja Wodeyar	(1673–1704)
Narasaraja Wodeyar II	(1704–1714)
Krishnaraja Wodeyar I	(1714–1732)
Chamaraja Wodeyar VI	(1732–1734)
Under Hyder Ali and Tipu Sultan	(1761-1799)
Krishnaraja Wodeyar II	(1734–1766)
Nanjaraja Wodeyar	(1766–1772)
Chamaraja Wodeyar VII	(1772–1776)
Chamaraja Wodeyar VIII	(1776–1796)
Under British Rule	(1799-1947)
Krishnaraja Wodeyar III	(1799–1868)
Chamaraja Wodeyar IX	(1881–1901)
Krishnaraja Wodeyar IV	(1901–1940)
Jayachamaraja Wodeyar	(1940–1947)

C Rajagopalachari

(*Governor-General-Republic of India*)

Though illiterate, Hyder Ali has earned an important place in the history of Karnataka for his fighting skills and administrative acumen. The rise of Haidar came at a time of important political developments in the subcontinent. While the European powers were busy transforming themselves from trading companies to political powers, the Nizam as the *subedar* of the Mughals pursued his ambitions in the Deccan, and the Marathas, following their defeat at Panipat, sought safe havens in the south. The period also saw the French vie with the British for control of the Carnatic – a contest in which the British would eventually prevail. Though the Wodeyars remained the nominal heads during this period, real power lay in the hands of Hyder Ali and his son Tipu.

By 1761, the Maratha menace had diminished and by 1763, Hyder Ali had captured the Keladi kingdom, defeated the rulers of Bilgi, Bednur and Gutti, invaded the Malabar in the south and conquered the Zamorin's capital Calicut with ease in 1766 and extended the Mysore kingdom up to Dharwad and Bellary in the north. Mysore was now a major political power in the subcontinent and Hyder's meteoric rise from relative obscurity and his defiance formed one of the last remaining challenges to complete British hegemony over the Indian subcontinent – a challenge which would take them more than three decades to overcome.

In a bid to stem Haidar's rise, the British formed an alliance with the Marathas and the Nizam of Golconda, culminating in the first Anglo-Mysore war in 1767. Despite early reverses, Hyder Ali drove the British out of most of their forts in the Carnatic and dictated peace terms at the very centre of its power – South Madras (modern Chennai). In 1770, when the Maratha armies of Madhavrao Peshwa invaded Mysore(three wars were fought between 1764-1772 by Madhavrao against Hyder, in which Hyder lost), Hyder expected British support as per the 1769 treaty but they betrayed him by staying out of the conflict. The British betrayal and Hyder's subsequent defeat reinforced Hyder's deep distrust of the British — a sentiment that would be shared by his son and one which would inform Anglo-Mysore rivalries of the next three decades.

By 1779, Hyder Ali had captured parts of modern Tamil Nadu and Kerala in the south, extending the Kingdom's area to about 80,000 mi² (205,000 km²). In 1780, he befriended the French and made peace with the Marathas and the Nizam. However, Hyder Ali was betrayed by the Marathas and the Nizam, who made treaties with the British as well. Between May 1780 and July 1781, the Mysorean army overran British territories, either killing or routing key British commanders, until the arrival of General Eyre Coote, when the fortunes of the British began to change. Hyder Ali died on 7 December 1782, even as fighting continued with the British. He was succeeded by his son Tipu Sultan who continued hostilities against the British by recapturing Baidanur and Mangalore.

In 1783, even as the Mysore armies stood on the verge of scoring a decisive victory against the British, the French withdrew their support following the peace settlement in Europe. Undaunted, Tipu, popularly known as the "Tiger of Mysore", defeated the British in Wandiwash in 1783, but lost some regions in modern coastal Karnataka to them. He later lost the Kittur, Nargund and

Badami territories to the Marathas. The treaty of Mangalore, which is known to have favoured Tipu, was signed in 1784 bringing hostilities with the British to a temporary and uneasy halt. A start of fresh hostilities between the British and French in Europe would have been sufficient reason for Tipu to abrogate his treaty and further his ambition of striking at the British. His attempts to lure the Nizam, the Marathas, the French and the King of Turkey failed to bring direct military aid.

Tipu's unsuccessful attack in 1790 on the Kingdom of Travancore, a British ally, resulted in the third Anglo-Mysore war. In the beginning, the British made little progress, winning some ground and losing some. By 1792, seeking aid from the Marathas who attacked from the northwest and the Nizam who moved in from the northeast, the British under Lord Cornwallis successfully besieged Srirangapatna, resulting in Tipu's defeat and the Treaty of Srirangapatna. Half of Tipu's kingdom were seized and distributed among the allies, and two of his sons were held to ransom. A humiliated but indomitable Tipu went about re-building his economic and military power. He attempted to covertly win over support from Revolutionary France, the Amir of Afghanistan, the Sultanate of Turkey and Arabia. However, these attempts to involve the French soon became known to the British, who found in it enough of an excuse for war and in this, were backed by the Marathas and the Nizam. In 1799, Tipu died fighting in the fourth Anglo-Mysore war, heralding the end of the Kingdom's independence. Modern Indian historians consider Tipu Sultan an inveterate enemy of the British, an able administrator and an innovator.

Princely State

Following Tipu's fall, a part of the kingdom of Mysore was annexed and divided between the Madras Presidency and the Nizam. The remaining territory was transformed into a Princely State; the five-year-old scion of the Wodeyar family, Krishnaraja III, was installed on the throne with chief minister (*Diwan*) Purniah, who had earlier served under Tipu, handling the reins as regent and Lt. Col. Barry Close taking charge as the British Resident. The British now took control of Mysore's foreign policy and also exacted an annual tribute and a subsidy for maintaining a standing British army at Mysore. As Diwan, Purniah distinguished himself with his progressive and innovative administration until he retired from service in 1811 (and died shortly thereafter) following the 16th birthday of the boy king.

The years that followed witnessed cordial relations between Mysore and the British until things began to sour in the 1820s. Even though the Governor of Madras, Thomas Munro determined after a personal investigation in 1825 that there was no substance to the allegations of financial impropriety made by A. H. Cole, the incumbent Resident of Mysore, the civil insurrection which broke out towards the end of the decade changed things considerably. In 1831, close on the heels of the insurrection and citing mal-administration, the British took direct control of the princely state. For the next fifty years, Mysore passed under the rule of successive British Commissioners; Sir Mark Cubbon, renowned for his statesmanship, served from 1834 until 1861 and put into place an efficient and successful administrative system which left Mysore a well developed state. In 1876–77, however, towards the end of the direct British rule, Mysore was struck by a devastating famine with estimated mortality figures which ranged between 700,000 and 1,100,000, or nearly a fifth of the population. Shortly thereafter, Maharaja Chamaraja IX, educated in the British system, took over the rule of Mysore in 1881, following the success of a lobby set up by the Wodeyar dynasty that was in favour of rendition. Accordingly, a resident British officer was appointed at the Mysore court and a Diwan was to handle the administration. From then onwards, until Indian independence in 1947, Mysore remained a Princely State under the British Raj with the Wodeyars continuing their rule.

After the demise of Maharaja Chamaraja IX, Krishnaraja IV, still a boy of eleven ascended the throne in 1895. His mother Maharani Kemparajammanniyavaru ruled as regent until Krishnaraja took over the reins on 8 February 1902. Under his rule, with Sir M. Vishweshwariah as his Diwan, the Maharaja set about transforming Mysore into a progressive and modern state, particularly in industry, education, agriculture and art. Such were the strides that Mysore made that Mahatma Gandhi called the Maharaja a "saintly king" (*Rajarishi*). Paul Brunton, the British philosopher and orientalist, John Gunther, the American author, and British statesman Lord Samuel praised the ruler's efforts. Much of the pioneering work in educational infrastructure that took place during this period would serve Karnataka invaluably in the coming decades. The Maharaja was an accomplished musician, and like his predecessors, avidly patronised the development of the fine arts. He was followed by his nephew Jayachamaraja whose rule came to an end when he signed the instrument of accession and Mysore joined the Indian Union on 9 August 1947.

Administration

Records pertaining to the administration of the Mysore territory during the overlordship of the Vijayanagara Empire (1399 to 1565) are not available. After the decline of the Vijayanagara Empire, King Raja Wodeyar gradually gained independence, eventually ousting the governor at Srirangapatna. The regional head of the diminished Empire now ruled from their new capital at Chandragiri (in modern Andhra Pradesh). During the rule of Narasaraja Wodeyar, the first gold coins were issued from Mysore. The position of the fledgling Mysore kingdom improved considerably during the rule of King Chikka Devaraja Wodeyar, who increased the value of the Treasury to 90,000,000 *pagoda* (a unit of currency). For his achievements, the king earned the title *Navakotinarayana* (literally 9 crore Narayana). Chikka Devaraja Wodeyar founded the *Attara Kacheri,* the central secretariat comprising of eighteen departments.

When Hyder Ali became the Kingdom's de-facto ruler in the later half of the eighteenth century, a large booty of gold coins usurped from the coffers of the Nizam of Golconda helped fund Mysore's expansionary policy. Hyder Ali's military success was due to his fast moving French trained cavalry. The Kingdom was divided into 5 provinces (*Asofis*) of unequal size, comprising 171 *Paraganas* (taluk) in total. The Sira province comprised 5 *Paraganas* that contributed 200,000 *varaha* (a unit of currency) and the Srirangapatna province contained 102 *Paraganas* and contributed 1,70,0000 *varaha.*

When Tipu Sultan became the de-facto ruler, the Kingdom, which encompassed 62,000 mi^2 (160,000 km^2), was divided into 37 *Asofi* and a total of 124 taluks (*Amil*). Each *Asofi* had a governor, or *Asof,* and one deputy *Asof.* The taluk was headed by an *Amildar* and a *Patel* was in charge of a group of villages. The central administration comprised six departments headed by ministers, each aided by an advisory council of up to four members; the military by Mir Miran, the revenue ministry by Mir Asaf, the navy by Mir Yem, the treasury, the commerce and the ordnance by Muluk-ut-Tufar. It has been noted that the policy of replacing Hindu governors with Muslim *Asofs* may have led to its revenue downfall. It is claimed that for a very brief period, the Kannada language was replaced by the Persian language in administration and accounting. The army consisted of infantry, cavalry, artillery and the navy. The navy had forty ships operating from Mangalore, Kundapura and Tadadi.

Following Tipu's death in 1799, the kingdom came under direct British rule in 1831. Lushington, Briggs and Morrison, the early commissioners, were followed by Mark Cubbon and Lewin Bowring. Mark Cubbon took charge in 1834 and is known for his excellent handling of the kingdom. He made Bangalore the capital and divided the princely state into 4 divisions, each under a British superintendent. The state was further divided into 120 taluks with 85 taluk courts, with all lower level administration in the Kannada language. The *Amildar* was in charge of a taluk to whom a *Hoblidar*, the caretaker of a *Hobli* comprising a few villages, reported. The office of the commissioner had eight departments; revenue, post, police, cavalry, public works, medical, the animal husbandry, judiciary and education. The judiciary was hierarchical with the commissioners' court at the apex, followed by the *Huzur Adalat*, four superintending courts and eight *Sadar Munsiff* courts at the lowest level. Mark Cubbon is credited with the construction of over one thousand miles of roads, hundreds of dams, coffee production and improvements in the tax and revenue systems.

Lewin Bowring became the chief commissioner in 1862 and held the position until 1870. Under Lewin Bowring, the state was divided into three divisions, each under a British commissioner. There were eight districts in all under these divisions, with each looked after by a deputy commissioner who was aided by the *Amildars* and *Hoblidars*. The property "Registration Act", the "Indian Penal code" and "Code of Criminal Procedure" came into effect and the judiciary was separated from the executive branch of the administration. Lewin Bowring expanded the education system with the formation of the Central Educational Agency, helping the kingdom modernize quickly. However, unlike Mark Cubbon, Lewin Bowring generally preferred to employ British officers. In 1881, following a strong lobby favouring rendition, the British handed back the administration of Mysore to King Chamaraja Wodeyar VIII. The post of commissioner was abolished and replaced by a Diwan, his two advisers and a British resident in the Mysore court.

Rangacharlu, a native of Chennai, became the Diwan, while the first ever Representative Assembly of British India, with 144 members consisting of prominent people from various fields was formed in 1881. Rangacharlu identified himself with the Kannada language and patronised it by establishing the Palace drama company. Rangacharlu started favourable economic policies such as public loans and public works as well as building the railway line from Bangalore to Mysore. He was followed by Sheshadri Iyer in 1883. During his time, gold mining at Kolar Gold Fields began and extensive coffee plantations and railway lines were laid. The Representative Assembly elections were held with a three year tenure for elected members. Taluk boards were formed giving decentralised authority at that level, the Mysore Civil Service Examinations were held for the first time in 1891 and the Department of Geology and the Department of Agriculture were founded in 1894 and 1898. Other notable achievements include the construction of the Vanivilas Sagar dam across Vedavati river, the initiation of the Shivanasamudra hydroelectric project in 1899 (the first such major attempt in India), electricity and drinking water (the latter through pipes) being supplied to Bangalore and the founding of the Archaeological Survey of Mysore (1890) and the Oriental Manuscripts Library.

P.N. Krishna Murthy, a descendant of the late Diwan Purnaih, took office in 1901. The founding of The Secretariat Manual to maintain records, the introduction of British administrative methods and the founding of the Cooperative Department in 1905 are credited to him. V.P. Madhava Rao, who became the Diwan in 1906, paid attention to conservation of forests. He started the Legislative Council in 1907, the Central Cooperative Bank in Bangalore, aided the Vokkaligara Sangha in 1906 and created the Mysore News Paper Regulation Act of 1908. He was followed by T. Ananda Rao, who inaugurated the Mysore Economic Conference, finalised the Kannambadi dam and completed the Mysore Palace in 1910.

The name Sir M. Visveshwarayya, popularly known as the "Maker of Modern Mysore" holds pride of place in the history of Karnataka. A visionary by any standard and an engineer by education, he wrote the book *A Vision of Prosperous Mysore* in 1902, stressing the need for technological and educational advancement as a catalyst to industry, commerce and agriculture. He became the Diwan in 1909. Membership of the Mysore Legislative Assembly was increased from 18 to 24 with powers to discuss the state budget. The Mysore Economic Conference was expanded into three committees; industry and commerce, education and agriculture, with publications in English and Kannada. Village panchayats, local boards and municipalities were headed by elected members. A long list of important projects were commissioned during his time including the construction of the Kannambadi dam, the Government Soap Factory and the Mysore Sandal Oil Factory and the founding of the Bhadravati Iron Works and the Mysore Bank in 1913. Sir M.V, as he was affectionately known, founded the Mysore University in 1916, the Mysore Chamber of Commerce and Industry, the Visveshwarayya College of Engineering in Bangalore and the Karnataka Sahitya Parishad. Sir M.V. was followed by Sir Sardar Kantaraj Urs in 1919 and Sir Albion Banerji in 1922.

Sir Mirza Ismail took office as Diwan in 1926 and built on the foundation laid by Sir. M. Visveshwarayya, making substantial progress in modernising the Kingdom of Mysore. Amongst his contributions were the expansion of the Bhadrawati Iron works, the founding of a cement and paper factory in Bhadrawati. Hindustan Aeronautics Limited, a porcelain factory and a glass factory were founded in Bangalore, the sugar factory at Mysore and the first fertilizer factory in Belgola were established. An able administrator with a penchant for gardens, he founded the Brindavan Gardens (Krishnaraja Sagar), the Mysore Medical College and the Kaveri high level canal to irrigate 120,000 acres (490 km) in modern Mandya district. Sir Mirza Ismail was followed by Sir N. Madhava Rao and Sir Arcot Ramaswamy Mudaliar before the Kingdom was incorporated into the newly independent India in 1947.

Economy

The economy of the Kingdom was based on agriculture, due to the majority of its people being villagers. Ownership of land was considered a prestige and people from all trades aimed to own a piece of land, whether they were directly involved in cultivation or not. The agrarian population consisted of landlords (gavunda, zamindar, heggadde) great and small who tilled the land by employing a number of landless labourers. Payments for services were in kind, usually grain, and even minor cultivators were willing to hire themselves out as labourers if the need arose. It was due to the availability of these landless labourers that kings and landlords were able to execute major projects such as palaces, temples, mosques, anicuts (chack dam) and tanks. Because land was abundant and the population relatively sparse, no rent was charged on land ownership. Instead, landowners paid tax for cultivation, normally amounting up to one half of all produce that was harvested.

Tipu Sultan, who ruled Mysore from 1782 to 1799 is credited with founding the state trading depots in various locations of his kingdom. In addition, he founded depots in foreign locations such as Karachi, Jeddah and Muscat, where Mysore products could be sold. It is to Tipu's credit that French technology was used for the first time in carpentry and smithy. Also, Tipu's rule saw Chinese technology used for the sugar production, while technology from Bengal helped improve the sericulture industry. State factories were established in Kanakapura and Taramandelpeth for producing cannons and gunpowder respectively. The state monopolised the production of essentials such as sugar, salt, iron, pepper, cardamom, betel nut, tobacco and sandalwood, as well as the extraction of incense oil from sandalwood and the mining of silver, gold and precious stones. Sandalwood was exported to China and the Persian gulf countries and sericulture was developed in twenty one centres within the kingdom.

A bond existed between the landlords and his labourers who were called *panial* or *padial*. In this system, when work ceased to exist in a land, the labourers were free to find employment elsewhere, but were bound to come back whenever required by the landlord. This had a mutual benefit in that it ensured regular employment to the landless and prevented their starvation. Landlords, however, were not required to increase labour rates during times when labour was in demand. Instead, they judiciously gave loans and presents to the labourer during times of need such as marriages and other family ceremonies. These loans bound the labourer to the estate who was not charged with interest on the loan. Instead, the labourer was required to pay back the principal amount only if he wished to free himself permanently from his bond to the landlord and seek employment elsewhere.

This system changed under the British, when tax payments were in cash, and were used for the maintenance of the army, police and other civil and public establishments. A portion of the tax was transferred to England and called "Indian tribute". Unhappy with the loss of their traditional revenue system and the problems they faced, peasants rose in rebellion in many parts of south India. The construction of anicuts and tanks helped alleviate problems in some areas of the peninsula, though there were variations in living conditions in different regions.

After 1800, the Cornwallis land reforms came into play. Reade, Munro, Graham and Thackeray were some administrators who improved the economic conditions of the masses. However, the home spun textile industry suffered during British rule, due to the manufacturing mills of Manchester, Liverpool and Scotland being more than a match for the traditional hand woven industry, especially spinning and weaving. Only weavers who produced the very finest cloth not manufacturable by machines survived the changing economy. Even here, the change in the dressing habits of the people, who adapted to English clothes, had an adverse impact. Only the agricultural and rural masses with their need for coarse cloth sustained the low quality home industry. Also, the British economic policies created a class structure consisting of a newly found middle class. This class consisted of four occupational groups; the trading and merchant class consisting of agents, brokers, shopkeepers; the landlords created under the Zamindar system and Janmi system of land tenure; the money lenders; and the white collared lawyers, teachers, civil servants, doctors, journalists and bankers. However, due to a more flexible caste hierarchy, this middle class consisted of a more heterogeneous mix of people from different castes.

The 19th century brought about the so called "backward classes movement", a direct result of the hegemony in employment (in educational and government sectors) by the wealthy few and the loss of jobs across southern India due to the Industrial Revolution in England. This movement was heralded first by the Lingayats followed by the Vokkaligas and the Kurubas. The economic revolution in England and the tariff policies of the British caused massive de-industrialization in India, especially in the textile sector. For example, Bangalore was known to have had a flourishing textile industry prior to 1800 and the gunny bag weaving business had been a monopoly of the Goniga people, a state of events that changed significantly when the British began ruling the area. The import of a chemical substitute of saltpetre (potassium nitrate) affected the Uppar community, the traditional makers of salt petre for use in gun powder. The import of kerosene affected the Ganiga community who supplied oils. Foreign enamel and crockery industries had an impact on the native pottery business and the mill made blankets replaced the country made *kambli*. This economic fallout led to the formation of community based social welfare organizations such as the *Lingayat Vidyavardhakara Sangha* in Dharwad in 1883, the *Vokkaligara Sanga* in Bangalore in 1906 and the *Praja Mitra Mandali* in Mysore in 1917. The goal of these organizations was to help those within the community to cope better with a new economic situation. Community based youth hostels sprang up to help students seeking education and shelter.

Culture

Religion

The early kings of the Wodeyar dynasty worshipped the Hindu god Shiva. The later kings, starting from the 17th century, took to Vaishnavism, the worship of the Hindu god Vishnu. According to musicologist Meera Rajaram Pranesh, King Raja Wodeyar I was a devotee of the god Vishnu, King Dodda Devaraja was honoured with the title "Protector of Brahmins" (*Deva Brahmana Paripalaka*) for his support to Brahmins, and Maharaja Krishnaraja III was devoted to the goddess Chamundeshwari (a form of Hindu goddess Durga). Wilks ("History of Mysore", 1800) wrote about a *Jangama* (Veerashaiva saint-devotee of Shiva) uprising, related to excessive taxation, which was put down firmly by Chikka Devaraja. Historian D.R. Nagaraj claims that four hundred *Jangamas* were murdered in the process but clarifies that Veerashiava literature itself is silent about the issue. Historian Suryanath Kamath claims King Chikka Devaraja was a Srivaishnava (follower of Sri Vaishnavism, a sect of Vaishnavism) but was not anti-Veerashaiva. Historian Aiyangar concurs that some of the kings including the celebrated Narasaraja I and Chikka Devaraja were Vaishnavas, but suggests this may not have been the case with all Wodeyar rulers. The rise of the modern day Mysore city as a centre of south Indian culture has been traced from the period of their sovereignty. Raja Wodeyar I initiated the celebration of the Dasara festival in Mysore, a proud tradition of the erstwhile Vijayanagara royal family.

Jainism, though in decline during the late medieval period, also enjoyed the patronage of the Mysore kings, who made munificent endowments to the Jain monastic order at the town of Shravanabelagola. Records indicate that some Wodeyar kings not only presided over the *Mahamastakabhisheka* ceremony, an important Jain religious event at Shravanabelagola.

The contact between South India and Islam goes back to the 7th century, when trade between Hindu kingdoms and Islamic caliphates thrived. These Muslim traders settled on the Malabar coast and married local Hindu women, and their descendants came to be known as *Mappillas*. By the 14th century, Muslims had become a significant minority in the south, though the advent of Portuguese missionaries checked their growth. Hyder Ali, though a devout Muslim, did not allow his faith to interfere with the administration of the predominantly Hindu kingdom. Historians are, however, divided on the intentions of Hyder Ali's son, Tipu Sultan. It has been claimed that Tipu raised Hindus to prominent positions in his administration, made generous grants to Hindu temples and brahmins, and generally respected other faiths, and that any religious conversions that Tipu undertook were as punishment to those who rebelled against his authority. However, this has been countered by other historians who claim that Tipu Sultan treated the non-Muslims of Mysore far better than those of the Malabar, Raichur and Kodagu regions. They opine that Tipu was responsible for mass conversions of Christians and Hindus in these regions, either by force or by offering them tax incentives and revenue benefits to convert. Society

The society in the Kingdom followed age old and deeply established norms of social interaction between people in the centuries prior to the 18th century. In the 18th century, fundamental changes occurred due to the struggle between native and foreign powers. Wars between Hindu kingdoms and Sultanates continued, though the battles between native rulers (including Muslims) and the new foreigners, the British, took centre stage. Social reforms in the 19th century ushered in a more flexible society which granted people of lower castes access to schools, public office and courts.

The spread of English education, the introduction of the printing press, and the criticism of the prevailing social system by Christian missionaries also had a positive influence. Literature became more secular, while the fine arts such as music, drama, dance and painting saw a renaissance. The rise of modern nationalism all over India had its impact on Mysore as well. This manifested itself in two ways-a longing to preserve all that was good in past tradition and an acceptance of western influence.

For centuries, primary education was imparted in *Agraharas* and *Pathashalas* where Sanskrit and the local vernacular was the medium of instruction. With the arrival of Islam, instruction to Muslims in the Arabic language was given in Madrasas. With the rise of British power, the English education gained prominence. These changes were orchestrated by Lord Elphinstone, the governor of the Madras Presidency. He developed his own method which had considerable influence on the status of education in the presidency. His plan became the constitution of the central collegiate institution or University Board, which gained fruition in 1841. Accordingly, a high school department of the university was established. For imparting education in the interior regions, schools were raised in principal towns which eventually were elevated to college level, with each college becoming central to many Zilla schools (local schools). The language of instruction in these schools was English. The earliest English medium schools appeared in 1833 in Mysore and spread across the region. In 1858, the department of education was founded in Mysore and it is estimated that by 1881, there may have been 2087 English medium schools in the Mysore Kingdom. Higher education became available with the formation of Bangalore Central College (1870) and Maharajas college in Mysore (1879). The Maharanis college in Mysore (1901) and the St. Agnes college in Mangalore (1921) served women. The Mysore University was founded in 1916.

Social reforms aimed at practices such as sati, untouchability and emancipation of the lower classes swept across India and had their positive influence on Mysore territory as well. Welfare organisations that were founded in Bangalore and Mangalore were the Brahmo Samaj (1866 and 1870), the Theosophical society (1886 and 1901) and the Arya Samaj (1894 and 1919). In 1894, the Mysore kingdom passed laws to abolish marriage of girls below the age of eight and in 1923 provided women the right to franchise.

Re-marriage of widowed women and marriage of destitute women was encouraged by enlightened men and women of Mysore. There were uprisings against British authority in India and in the Mysore region. The first unsuccessful revolt, aided by the French, came in the Malnad region in early 1800 by a Maratha called Dhondiya Wagh who was eventually killed. This event was followed by a revolt of a Zamindar Virappa in Koppal (1819), the rebellion of brave queen Rani Chennamma of Kittur in 1824, by her trusted aide Sangolli Rayanna in 1829, the Kodagu uprising in 1835 (after the British dethroned the local ruler Chikkaviraraja) and the Kanara uprising of 1837.

The era of printing heralded by the Christian missionaries resulted in the first Kannada book publication in 1817, followed by a Kannada Bible in 1820, an English-Kannada dictionary in 1824, a Kannada-English dictionary in 1832 and the first Kannada newspaper called *Mangaluru Samachara* in 1843 (later renamed *Kannada Samachara*). The Mysore Amba Vilas palace opened a press in 1840 followed by a government press in Bangalore (1842). Eighty six Kannada printing presses were operating by the end of 19th century. This popularised the publication of ancient Kannada classics such as *Pampa Bharata* by Adikavi Pampa in 1891, the *Jaimini Bharata* by Lakshmisa in 1848 and the *Basavapurana* in 1850. On the same lines as the English language historicals published by British and Indian historians recording the achievements of Karnataka Empires, Alur Venkata Rao published a consolidated Kannada version called *Karnataka Gatha Vaibhava* rekindling Kannada nationalism.

Modern Kannada stage was popularised by the Yakshagana, the founding of a stage in Chandrasala Totti in the Mysore palace and a drama troupe in 1881. Classical English and Sanskrit plays influenced Kannada stage and produced famous dramatists such as Shirahatti Venkoba Rao and Gubbi Veeranna. The public began to enjoy Carnatic music through its broadcast on public address systems set up in the palace grounds. Mysore paintings were inspired by the Bengal Renaissance paintings and produced such well known artists as Sundarayya, Tanjavur Kondayya, Ala Singarayya, B.Venkatappa, the Raju brothers, Keshavayya and others. Female poets such as Cheluvambe (the queen of Krishnaraja Wodeyar I), Haridasa Helavanakatte Giriyamma, Sri Rangamma (1685) and Sanchi Honnamma (author of *Hadibadeya Dharma*) wrote classics in Kannada language. The devadasi system that had existed in India for centuries was abolished in 1909, though a unique form of temple dancing was lost.

Literature

The era of the Kingdom of Mysore is considered an important age in the development of Kannada literature. Not only was the Mysore court adorned by famous Brahmin and Veerashaiva writers and composers, the kings themselves were accomplished in the fine arts. While conventional literature in philosophy and religion remained popular, writings in new genres such as chronicle, biography, history, encyclopedia, novel, drama, and musical treatise became popular. A native form of folk literature with dramatic representation called Yakshagana gained popularity. A remarkable development of the later period was the influence of English literature and classical Sanskrit literature on Kannada.

Govinda Vaidya, a native of Srirangapatna, wrote *Kanthirava Narasaraja Vijaya*, a eulogy of his patron King Narasaraja I. Written in *sangatya* metre (a composition meant to be rendered to the accompaniment of a musical instrument), the book describes the king's court, popular music and the types of musical compositions of the age in twenty-six chapters. King Chikka Devaraja was the earliest composer of the dynasty. To him is ascribed the famous treatise on music called *Geetha Gopala*. Though inspired by Jayadeva's Sanskrit writing *Geetha Govinda*, it had an originality of its own and was written in *saptapadi* metre. Contemporary poets who left their mark on the entire Kannada-speaking region include the Brahman poet Lakshmisa and the itinerant Veerashaiva poet Sarvajna. Female poets also played a role in literary developments, with Cheluvambe (the queen of Krishnaraja Wodeyar I), Helavanakatte Giriyamma, Sri Rangamma (1685) and Sanchi Honnamma (*Hadibadeya Dharma*, late 17th century) writing notable works.

A polyglot, King Narasaraja II authored fourteen Yakshaganas in various languages, though all are written in Kannada script. Maharaja Krishnaraja III was a prolific writer in Kannada for which he earned the honorific *Abhinava Bhoja* (a comparison to the medieval King Bhoja). Over forty writings are attributed to him, of which the musical treatise *Sri Tatwanidhi* and a poetical romance called *Saugandika Parinaya* written in two versions, a *sangatya* and a drama, are most well-known. Under the patronage of the Maharaja, Kannada literature began its slow and gradual change towards modernity. Kempu Narayana's *Mudramanjusha* ("The Seal Casket", 1823) is the earliest work that has touches of modern prose. However, the turning point came with the historically important *Adbhuta Ramayana* (1895) and *Ramaswamedham* (1898) by Muddanna, whom the Kannada scholar Narasimha Murthy considers "a Janus like figure" of modern Kannada literature. Muddanna has deftly handled an ancient epic from an entirely modern viewpoint.

Basavappa Shastry, a native of Mysore and a luminary in the court of Maharaja Krishnaraja III and Maharaja Chamaraja IX, is known as the "Father of Kannada theatre" (*Kannada Nataka Pitamaha*). He authored dramas in Kannada and translated William Shakespeare's "Othello" to *Shurasena Charite*. His well-known translations from Sanskrit to Kannada are many and include *Kalidasa, Abhignyana Shakuntala.*

Music

The Kingdom of Mysore (1399-1947) was founded by Yaduraya in 1399 as a feudatory of the Vijayanagara Empire and became an independent kingdom in the early 17th century, after the decline of the Vijayanagara Empire. Many musicians and composers have presumably adorned the courts of the Mysore kings from Yaduraya's time, furthering the *Dakshinadi* school (southern school) of music that had developed in earlier centuries. However, records are only available from the time of King Ranadheera Kanteerava Narasaraja Wodeyar (1638). Musical treatises surviving from this time, though, provide ample information on the music, musical instruments, the types of compositions, the *raga* (melodies) and the *tala* (rhythms) used. Though all the Mysore kings patronised music, the golden age of Carnatic music was considered to be during the reigns of Kings Krishnaraja Wodeyar III (1794-1868), Chamaraja Wodeyar IX (1862-1894), Krishnaraja Wodeyar IV (1884-1940) and Jaya Chamaraja Wodeyar (1919-1974). The reign of Krishnaraja Wodeyar IV is regarded as particularly important in musical terms.

The instruments normally used to play compositions were the veena, the rudra veena, the violin, the tambura, the ghatam, the flute, the mridangam, the nagaswaram, the *swarabhat*. Instruments such as the harmonium, the sitar and the jaltarang, though uncommon to the southern region, came into use and British influence popularised the saxophone and the piano. The royalty of this dynasty were noted composers and proficient in playing musical instruments both solo and in concert with others. The different styles of compositions included *jati swara, swara jati, varna, kriti, javali* (a light lyric), *tillana* and *pallavi.* It was not unusual for the composers and the kings who patronised them to be experts at instrumental music as well. So proficient were the musicians at their chosen instrument(s) that the name of the instrument became a part of the musician's name, examples being Veena Subbanna and Veena Sheshanna, Veena (or *Veene* as it is known in South India) being their instrument. During these times, Tanjore in modern Tamil Nadu and Mysore in modern Karnataka were the centres of Carnatic music. Mysore developed a distinct school of music which gave importance to the *raga* and the *bhava.* Though many of the musicians in the courts were natives of the Mysore Kingdom, artists from other parts of South India were also patronised. Another important development of this period was the growth of drama. These dramas, original or translated from English and Sanskrit classics, contained many melodious songs and were brought to the stage through the various drama schools established by royalty.

King Krishnaraja Wodeyar III	(1794-1868)
Mysore Musicians	(1638-1947)
Vaikunta Dasaru	(1680)
Krishnaraja Wodeyar III	1799-1868
Mysore Sadashiva Rao	1790
Veena Venkata Subbiah	1750
Shunti Venkataramaniah	1780
Aliya Lingaraja Urs	1823–1874
Chinniah	1902
Chikka Lakshminaranappa	
Pedda Lakshminaranappa	
Devalapurada Nanjunda	
Veena Shamanna	1832-1908
Veena Padmanabiah	1842-1900

Contd...

Veena Sheshanna	1852-1926
Mysore Karigiri Rao	1853-1927
Veena Subbanna	1861-1939
Mysore Vasudevachar	1865-1961
Bidaram Krishnappa	1866-1931
T. Pattabhiramiah	1863
Sosale Ayya Shastry	1854-1934
Jayarayacharya	?-1910
Giribhattara Tammayya	1865-1920
Nanjangud Subba Shastry	1834-1906
Chandrashekara Shastry	
Veena Subramanya Iyer	1864-1919
Muthiah Bhagavatar	1877-1945
Veena Shivaramiah	1886-1946
Veena Venkatagiriappa	1887-1952
Srinivasa Iyengar	1888-1952
Chikka Ramarao	1891-1945
T. Chowdiah	1894-1967
Jayachamaraja Wodeyar	1919-1974
Dr.B. Devendrappa	1899-1986
G. Narayana Iyengar	1903-1959
T. Subramanya Iyer	
Anavatti Rama Rao	1860
Tiger Varadachariar	1876-1950
Chennakeshaviah	1895-1986
T. Krishna Iyengar	1902-1997
S.N. Mariappa	1914-1986
C. Ramchandra Rao	1916-1985
R.N.Doreswamy	1916-2002
Vaidyalinga Bhagavatar	1924-1999

Mridangam

This period heralded the beginning of British control over the administration of Mysore and the start of an important period in the development of vocal and instrumental Carnatic music in south India. King Krishnaraja Wodeyar III was a trained musician, musicologist and composer of merit. Being a devotee of the Hindu goddess Chamundeshwari, he wrote all his compositions under the *mudra* (pen name) "'Chamundi'" or "'Chamundeshwari'". He composed many philosophically themed *javali* (light lyric) and devotional songs in the Kannada language under the title *Anubhava pancharatna. Javali* in Carnatic music have their roots in Mysore and are first mentioned in the king's writings as *javadi.* His scholarship in Kannada is acclaimed and his compositions are seen as parallels to the vachana poems of the Virashaiva poets and to the devotional songs (*pada*) of the Haridasas of Karnataka. Mysore Sadashiva Rao was born in Greemspet in the Chittoor district of modern Andhra Pradesh to a Maharashtrian family. He came to Mysore between 1825 and 1835 and served as a court musician to the incumbent king for nearly fifty years. His compositions are said to have been in the hundreds, though only about one hundred, written in Sanskrit and Telugu under the pen name "Sadashiva", still exist. He is known as the reviver of Carnatic music in the Karnataka region.

Veena Venkatasubbiah came from a Mysorean family of famous veena artists (or "vainika") of the time of King Hyder Ali and belonged to the Badaganadu community. He was appointed music teacher to King Krishnaraja Wodeyar III by his minister (or "Dewan") Purniah, who wanted to make Mysore the cultural centre of south India just as Vijayanagara had been during the rule of the Vijayanagara Empire. His most famous composition is the *Sapta taleshwari gite*. Some historians claim the work was a combined effort by the king and the musician. The king's son-in-law, Aliya Lingraj Urs, was an authority and composer in both the Kannada and Sanskrit languages. A native of Heggadadevanakote (in modern Mysore district), he had several interests in the fine arts. He has over fifty works including compositions, dramas, and Yakshagana to his credit, all of which were written with a pen name beginning with "Linga", such as "Lingendra" or "Lingaraja". His most famous compositions in Kannada are titled "Chandravali jogi hadu", "Pancha vimshati leele" and "Amba kirtana", and in Sanskrit, the "Shringara lahari".

Shunti Venkataramaniah was a musician from Tiruvayyar (modern Tamil Nadu) and an expert at playing the tambura. He was introduced to the king by the court musician Veena Venkatasubbiah under unusual circumstances. When

Venkataramaniah first met Veena Venkatasubbiah, the latter asked him to sing a particular tune. Unable to sing it, Venkataramaniah walked away, only to return a year later having mastered the tune. While singing the tune, Venkataramaniah went into a trance and the court musician hurried to the palace and requested the king to be audience to the singer. The king arrived there and was so pleased with Venkataramaniah's voice he appointed him as a court musician. Venkataramaniah's most famous composition is the *Lakshana gite*.

Chinniah was the eldest son of a family known as the "Tanjore quartet", a quartet of brothers who were singers and composers. Before his arrival in Mysore, Chinniah served at the court of the Tanjore kings Sarabhoji II and Shivaji II. He had learnt music from Muthuswamy Dikshitar. At the court of the king of Mysore, Chinniah created several compositions in praise of his patron king and the local deity Chamundeshwari. Famous among these compositions are *Ninnu koriyunna, Vanajalochana, Nivanti, Chakkani na mohanaguni, Manavigai konarada* and several *javali*.

Veena Chikka Lakshminaranappa, an expert vainika, was a descendant of Krishnappa, a Mysore court musician during the time of Bettada Chamaraja Wodeyar in the 16th century. Chikka Lakshminaranappa became the chief musician in the Prasanna Krishnaswamy temple located within the palace premises. His two sons Krishnappa and Seenappa, who were later patronised by the kings of Mysore, were also proficient players of the veena and violin. Well known visiting musicians to the court during this time included Pallavi Gopalayyar, Veena Kuppayyar, Tiruvattiyur Thyagayyar, Veena Krishnayya and Suryapurada Ananda Dasaru.

King Chamaraja Wodeyar IX (1862-1894)

King Chamaraja Wodeyar IX was also a patron of the fine arts and literature, having been tutored by his own court musicians Veena Sheshanna and Veena Subbanna. The king was well versed in the violin and often participated, along with other musicians, in violin performances at the Krishna temple located in the palace premises. He is known to have helped many budding artists, both by patronage of their talent and in their personal difficulties. He sponsored Mysore Vasudevacharya (who later became a famous musician) to train at Tiruvayyar under the famous Patnam Subramanya Iyer. He also formed the "Amateur Drama Club" to encourage young artists. However, he died at the early age of 32 while travelling in Kolkata. Veena Shamanna was the son of Rama Bhagavatar, an immigrant from Tanjore who came to Mysore during a famine, seeking royal patronage. His birth name was Venkata Subramanya. In 1876, Veena Shamanna was appointed court musician for his talent in both vocal and instrumental classical music. He was known as "Tala Brahma" for his mastery of the veena, violin, ghata and swarabhat. A conservative artist, he played by the norms of theorical classical music and was a tutor to the royal family. In honour of his achievements, a street in Mysore city was named after him. His compositions were published by his son Veena Subramanya Iyer in a book called *Sangeeta samayasara* in 1915.

Veena Padmanabiah, a native of Sriramapura (also known as Budihalu in Chikkanayakanahalli taluk, Karnataka), was trained in classical vocal and veena in his early days by a disciple of Veena Shamanna. Later, under the guidance of Veena Shamanna, Padmanabiah's expertise grew. An incident at the king's palace during his youth made him popular and impressed the king. A well known musician called Veena Sambayya made a mistake in interpreting a *shloka* in the musical treatise *Sangeeta Ratnakara.* Padmanabiah immediately pointed out this error, much to the discomfort of Sambayya, while the rest of the musicians dared not to, out of fear of incurring the senior musician's wrath. Years later, pleased by his talent, the king appointed him to the court and bestowed upon him the title "Mahatapi Khillat". Padmanabiah also served in the same capacity under the next king, Chamaraja Wodeyar IX. He was a music teacher at the "Mysore Maharanis High School", at the "Maharajas Sanskrit School", and he also tutored the royal family. He wrote many compositions in Sanskrit, Telugu and Kannada under the pen name "Padmanaba".

Veena Sheshanna, considered one of the greatest exponents of the veena in India, was born in Mysore in 1852 to Bakshi Chikkaramappa, a court musician of King Krishnaraja Wodeyar III. Once a visiting musician sang a composition (*pallavi*) and challenged the musicians in the king's court to follow. While none of the senior musicians could sing that composition, Sheshanna, who was still a boy, sang it correctly. Impressed, the king gave the boy a chain of pearls he was wearing and a pair of shawls. It was during the rule of King Chamaraja Wodeyar IX in 1882 that

Sheshanna was appointed court musician. His achievements in classical music won Mysore a premier place in the art of playing the veena and he was given the title "Vainika Shikhamani" by King Krishnaraja Wodeyar IV. Veena Sheshanna won laurels and titles from kings and dignitaries including the kings of Travencore, Baroda and Tanjore. He played the veena at the Indian National Congress in Belagavi in 1924 to an audience comprising such leaders as Mahatma Gandhi, Pandit Nehru and others and received the title "Vainika Chakravarthi". A photograph of Veena Sheshanna was taken by King George V to be placed in the art gallery at Buckingham Palace. Sheshanna was proficient at other instruments, including the violin, swarabhat, rudra veena, jalatarang and even the piano, in which he is known to have composed in English. His compositions are largely in Telugu and Kannada, though he also occasionally composed in Hindi.

Mysore Karigiri Rao was the son of Lakshmi Narasimhacharya, who hailed from Tumkur and was a Sanskrit Pandit in the court of King Krishnaraja Wodeyar III. Karigiri Rao learnt music secretly because his family was against that profession. He later travelled, performing in many places before returning to Mysore at the age of fifty when he was appointed court musician by King Chamaraja Wodeyar IX. He was given the title "Sangeeta Vidya Kanteerava" by senior musicians of the day and "Ganakara Durandhara Sangeeta Bhushana" by the king himself. He is credited with writing several Carnatic compositions and more than 200 *devaranama* (devotional songs). Veena Subbanna was born in 1861 in Mysore into a wealthy family of musicians to which he was the only heir. He studied with Prince Chamaraja Wodeyar IX at the Royal school and was well versed in the English language. He was trained in Carnatic vocal music by Mysore Sadashiva Rao and in instrumental music by his father Dodda Sheshanna who was also a famous musician. Veena Subbanna was appointed court musician in 1888 and was a contemporary of the legendary Veena Sheshanna, with whom he was paired in many concerts. A generous man known for his philanthrophic deeds, he has many compositions to his credit and earned such titles as "Vainika Praveena", "Vainika Vara Choodamani" and "Vainika Kesari".

Mysore Vasudevacharya was a musician and composer born on May 28, 1865 in Mysore. He holds the unique distinction of having been patronised by four generations of Mysore kings and of having been court musician to three. He received royal patronage from the age of five owing to his talent. During his time in Sanskrit school, he learned to play the veena from ace musician Veena Padmanabiah. Later, King Krishnaraja Wodeyar IV sponsored him to learn music at Tiruvayyar under Patnam Subramania Iyer. A master of both Carnatic and Hindustani *raga,* he delivered the opening Sanskrit *shloka* (devotional songs) at the Indian National Congress convention at Belagavi in 1924. He represented Mysore in the "Akhila Bharateeya Sangeeta Parishat" concert held in Gwalior. He earned laurels and titles from kings and dignitaries from all over India, including the "Sangeeta Shastra Ratna" and "Sangeeta Shastra Visharada". Numerous compositions in Sanskrit and Telugu are credited to him, as well as one song in Kannada called *Karunisou* under the pen name "Vasudeva".

Bidaram Krishnappa was a Konkani Brahmin and a native of Nandalike in modern Udupi district, Karnataka. When he was a boy he had a chance encounter with a rich businessman who loved music. This happened when hungry Krishnappa, who came from a poor family, was singing a devotional song (*devaranama*) in a local temple. Impressed with his voice, the merchant sponsored Krishnappa to train under the guidance of a musician called Ramaswamy. He later came under the influence of Tammayya and Veena Sheshanna. Bidaram Krishnappa is credited with having popularised the singing of Kannada *devaranama* on stage. He adapted certain concepts of Hindustani music into his Carnatic compositions. For his scholarship in music, he earned the titles "Shudda Swaracharya", "Pallavi Krishnappa" and "Gana Visharada". One of his disciples, T. Chowdiah, went on to become a music legend. Krishnappa was most famous for writing and rendering *devaranama* and *kirtans.*

Among other well known composers of the time, Tiruppunandal Pattabhiramiah from Kumbakonam was well known for his *javali,* with more than fifty to his credit written mostly in Kannada and Telugu under the pen name of "Talavana". Sosale Ayya Shastry was a native of Sosale (in modern Mysore district). His father was a scholar in the court of King Krishnaraja Wodeyar III and his grandfather a minister in Anegondi province (modern Koppal district, Karnataka). He was tutored in music by the well known Periswamy Tirumalacharya. Ayya Shastry became the *Raj Guru* (royal priest) between 1894-1901 and served as a

Kannada and Sanskrit teacher to the royal family. He was noted for his musical and painting abilities and was given the titles *Maha Vidwan* in 1905 and *Kavi Tilaka* in 1912 by King Krishnaraja Wodeyar IV. Among his well known dramas in Kannada are *Karnataka vikramorvasheya natakam, Karnataka ramayana natakam, Karnataka nala charitre* and *Karnataka pratapa simha nataka* with numerous melodious songs in them. In the late 19th-early 20th century, Jayarayacharya (1910) composed *Kalyana Gitavali* containing more than fifty devotional songs to be sung in the king's court and at festivals, and prayers by women; the dramatist Giribhattara Tamayya (1865) wrote the well-known works *Gaya charitre, Droupadi swayamvara, Neeti chudamani, Virata parva* and *Sudhanva charitre* under the pen name "Tammayya". Nanjangud Subba Shastry was a native of Nanjangud (near Mysore). Apart from composing about thirty-five songs, he wrote musical dramas in Kannada and Sanskrit including *Mricchakatika* and *Malavikagnimitra*. Chandrashekara Shastry composed *Javali* in Kannada and Telugu under the pen name "Balachandra". Visiting musicians were Pallavi Sheshayyar, Maha Vaidyanatha Iyer and Patnam Subramanyam Iyer.

King Krishnaraja Wodeyar IV (1884-1940)

This period, as during the time of the predecessor king, was an important era of music in Mysore, especially for Kannada compositions. The King himself was educated in Kannada, English, Sanskrit, the sciences and was knowledgeable in Tamil and Urdu as well. He was well versed in playing musical instruments including the veena, violin, mridangam, nagaswara, sitar, and harmonium as well as Western instruments such as the saxophone and piano. He encouraged his musicians to compose in the Carnatic, Hindustani and Western styles. During this period, Veena Subramanya Iyer wrote an important treatise on music in Kannada, dealing with both its theoretical and practical aspects, called *Sangeeta Samayasara* which was published in 1915. A very influential musician, academic and composer of this period was Harikeshanallur Dr. L. Muthiah Bhagavatar. A native of Tirunalveli (in modern Tamil Nadu), he was a scholar in Sanskrit and was trained in music by Samabasiva Iyer in Tiruvayyar. He was appointed court musician at Mysore in 1927 and was honoured by kings and notables alike. He was given the title "Gayaka

Shikamani" by his patron King Krishnaraja Wodeyar IV. To this famous musician are credited one hundred and eight *Chamundeswari kritis* in Kannada, one hundred and eight *Shivashtottara* compositions in Sanskrit, an important treatise on music in Tamil called the "Sangeeta Kalpadrumam", and a biography in Sanskrit on the life, achievements and contributions of Tyagaraja to Carnatic music called *Srimat Tyagaraja Vijaya*. He wrote a total of over four hundred compositions in all, in Sanskrit, Kannada, Telugu and Tamil under the pen name "Harikesha" and started the "Tyagaraja Sangeeta Vidyalaya" ("Tyagaraja School of Music") in 1920. For his accomplishments, he was given the title of "Sangeeta Kalanidhi" by the Madras Music Academy and received an honorary Doctor of Letters degree from the University of Travencore. Muthiah Bhagavatar died in Mysore in 1945 and is considered one of the most important composers of the post-Tyagaraja period.

Veena Shivaramiah was the son of the Mysore musician Veena Padmanabiah (of Chikkanayakanahalli taluk, Karnataka). Shivaramiah learnt to play the veena from his father and later from Mysore Karigiri Rao and Mysore Vasudevacharya and was appointed court musician in 1900 by King Krishnaraja Wodeyar IV. His one hundred Carnatic compositions are in Telugu, Kannada and Sanskrit, while his Western musical compositions are in English. King Jayachamaraja Wodeyar gave him the title "Vainika Praveena" in 1941. Shivaramiah was also a Kannada writer and co-authored works with such well known Kannada scholars as Devottama Jois, Anavatti Rama Rao and Krishna Shastry. Veena Venkatagiriappa, a native of Heggadadevanakote (in modern Mysore district) and a student of Veena Sheshanna, became a court musician under unusual circumstances. At the end of the very first concert that Venkatagiriappa gave in the king's presence, the king merely gave him a gift of two Indian rupees and left the concert. The musician and his family were disappointed at the king's response. Later the king learnt from one of his attendants that the musician and his family had taken the gift graciously. The king, who had been testing the musician's attitude to music, was pleased and appointed Venkatagiriappa court musician. Over the years, the king gave Venkatagiriappa more responsibility in the functioning of various schools of fine arts in his kingdom. Venkatagiriappa played the veena for fifteen minutes in a well known documentary movie called "Musical Instruments of India" in 1935. He was given the title "Vainika Praveena". His compositions are in Kannada, Telugu and Sanskrit, and he is credited with having created a new kind of Carnatic composition called *nagma,* which resemble the *gats* of Hindustani music.

Belakawadi Srinivasa Iyengar, whose birth name was Kuppaswamy Iyengar, was a native of Srigiripura near Shivaganga (in modern Tumkur district). He came to Mysore in 1912 and was trained in music by Bakshi Subbanna, a musician in the court of King Krishnaraja Wodeyar IV. Srinivasa Iyengar was later appointed a court musician. He was an expert in the gotuvadya and the violin. He was given the title "Mysurina Madhurayi Pushpavanam" by the famous vocalist Subramanya Iyer. Srinivasa Iyengar was a noted dramatist and acted in such well known dramas as *Babruvahana, Rama pattabhisheka, Veera simha charitre, Abhignana shakuntala, Virata charitre,* and *Sudhanva charitre*. Unfortunately, very few of his compositions, which written under the pen name "Srinivasa", are available today. It was Srinivasa Iyengar who popularised Purandara Dasa's Kannada song *Jagadoddharana* by composing its notation. Chikka Rama Rao, a native of Kurudi (in modern Kolar district) was trained under Mysore Karigiri Rao. He was proficient in both the Kannada and Sanskrit languages, and among musical instruments, in the veena, glass tarang and jalatarang. He gained expertise in Western music as well. He is known to have had the gift of playing the veena while singing in a melodious voice. His talent was noticed by the "Raj mata" (queen mother) who brought this to the attention of the king. After listening to him perform, the king appointed him court musician in 1914. Along with Srinivasa Iyengar, Chikka Rama Rao acted in many dramas of the day and was honoured by King Krishnaraja Wodeyar IV with the title "Sangeeta Ratna" (literally, "gem of music") and "pandit" by Hindustani music aces Abdul Karim Khan and Bhaskara Bhuva. To his credit are many compositions in Kannada, Sanskrit and Telugu.

T. Chowdiah, a towering personality in the field of Carnatic music, was born on January 1, 1894 in Tirumakudalu Narasipura (or T. Narasipura, near Mysore). At the age of seven, he received training from Pakkanna and later under T. Subbanna. At the age of sixteen, he was tutored by Bidaram Krishnappa for eighteen years at the end of which Chowdiah emerged as an accomplished violinist. The ambidextrous Chowdiah is known to have played music with all the famous musicians of his day. In 1939, he was appointed court musician by King Krishnaraja Wodeyar IV and received such titles as "Sangeeta Ratna", "Sangeeta Kalanidhi" and "Ganakala Sindhu". He is credited with many compositions in Kannada, Telugu and Sanskrit under the pen name "Trimakuta" (the Sanskrit name for his home town). Dr. B. Devedrappa, a native of Ayanoor in Shivamogga district, was well versed in playing the veena, violin, jalatarang and dilruba. He was a student of the famous Veena Sheshanna and also of Bidaram Krishnappa. He was proficient at the harmonium, flute, ghatam and sitar. He was appointed as a jalatarang player in the court of King Krishnaraja Wodeyar IV and served the palace orchestra as a vocalist and violinist. The titles "Gana Visharada" and "Sangeeta Kalaratna" were bestowed upon him by the king. Later, in 1972, an honorary doctorate was awarded to him. Other famous musicians in the court were Gotuvadyam Narayana Iyengar of Tirunaveli (Tamil Nadu), Tiruvayyar Subramanya Iyer, and Anavatti Rama Rao of Anavatti (in Shivamogga district) who was a scholar, poet and dramatist. The credit of translating many of Tyagaraja's compositions into Kannada goes to him.

King Jayachamaraja Wodeyar

King Jayachamaraja Wodeyar was the last king of the Wodeyar dynasty. An avid fan of music, he was well trained in classical Western music and was an expert pianist. It was only during the later part of his life that he became interested in Carnatic classical music. Several compositions of the Russian composer Medtner were recorded by the king and made available to the public. For his contributions, he was awarded an honorary doctorate and was made a fellow of "Sangeet Natak Academy" (an academy of music and drama). Many important musicians were part of the king's court. Tiger Varadachariar, a native of Kaladipet (modern Tamil Nadu) moved initially to T. Narasipura where he performed music for some years. Later he moved back to Chennai where he served in various music schools. In 1916, he got an opportunity to sing in the presence of King Krishnadavaraja IV. Impressed with this musician's mastery over his art, the king gave him the title "Tiger" In 1944, Varadachariar was appointed court musician at Mysore. He has about eighty compositions to his credit. Chennakeshaviah, a native of Natanhalli (in modern Mandya district) was a Kannada pandit and court musician in 1944. Apart from his compositions, he wrote articles, published three volumes on haridasa compositions, and wrote a book on music. Other well known musicians of the time were Titte Krishna Iyengar, S. N. Mariappa, a native of Sasalu village (in modern Mandya district), Chintalapalli Ramachandra Rao, R. N. Doreswamy, a native of Rudrapatna (in modern Hassan district) and Vaidyalinga Bhagavatar.

Architecture

The architectural style of courtly and royal structures in the kingdom underwent profound changes during British rule – a mingling of European traditions with native elements. The Hindu temples in the kingdom were built in typical South Indian Dravidian style – a modest version of the Vijayanagara building idiom. When in power, Tipu Sultan constructed a palace and a mosque in Srirangapatna, his capital. However, it is the city of Mysore that is best known for its royal palaces, earning it the nickname "City of Palaces". The city's main palace, the Mysore Palace, is also known as the Amba Vilas Palace. The original complex was destroyed by fire and a new palace was commissioned by the Queen-Regent and designed by the English architect Henry Irwin in 1897. The overall design is a combination of Hindu, Islamic, Indo-Saracenic and Moorish styles, which for the first time in India, used cast iron columns and roof frames. The striking feature of the exterior is the granite columns that support cusped arches on the portico, a tall tower whose finial is a gilded dome with an umbrella (*chattri*) on it, and groups of other domes around it. The interior is richly decorated with marbled walls and a teakwood ceiling on which are sculptures of Hindu deities. The Durbar hall leads to an inner private hall through silver doors. This opulent room has floor planels that are inlaid with semi-precious stones, and a stained glass roof supported centrally by columns and arches. The marriage hall (*Kalyana mantapa*) in the palace complex is noted for its stained glass octogonal dome with peacock motifs.

The Lalitha Mahal Palace was built in 1921 by E.W. Fritchley under the commission of Maharaja Krishnaraja IV. The architectural style is called "Renaissance" and exhibits concepts from English manor houses and Italian palazzos. The central dome is believed to be modelled on St. Paul's Cathedral in London. Other important features are the Italian marble staircase, the polished wooden flooring in the banquet and dance halls, and the Belgian cut glass lamps. The Jaganmohan Palace was commissioned in 1861 and was completed in 1910. The three storeyed building with attractive domes, finials and cupolas was the venue of many a royal celebration. It is now called the Chamarajendra Art Gallery and houses a rich collection of artifacts.

The Mysore University campus, also called "Manasa Gangotri", is home to several architecturally interesting buildings. Some of them are in European style and were completed in late 19th century. They include the Jayalakshmi Vilas mansion, the Crawford Hall, the Oriental Research Institute (built between 1887 and 1891) with its Ionic and Corinthian columns, and the district offices (*Athara Kutchery*, 1887). The Athara Kutchery, which initially served as the office of the British commissioner, has an octagonal dome and a finial that adds to its beauty. The maharaja's summer palace, built in 1880, is called the Lokaranjan Mahal, and initially served as a school for royalty. The Rajendra Vilas Palace, built in the Indo-British style atop the Chamundi Hill, was commissioned in 1922 and completed in 1938 by Maharaja Krishnaraja IV. Other royal mansions built by the Mysore rulers were the Chittaranjan Mahal in Mysore and the Bangalore Palace in Bangalore, a structure built on the lines of England's Windsor Castle. The Central Food Technical Research Institute (Cheluvamba Mansion), built in baroque European renaissance style, was once the residence of princess Cheluvambaamani Avaru, a sister of Maharaja Krishnaraja IV. Its extensive pilaster work and mosaic flooring are noteworthy.

Most famous among the many temples built by the Wodeyars is the Chamundeshwari Temple atop the Chamundi Hill. The earliest structure here was consecrated in the 12th century and was later patronised by the Mysore rulers. Maharaja Krishnaraja III added a Dravidian-style gopuram in 1827. The temple has silver-plated doors with images of deities. Other images include those of the Hindu god Ganesha and of Maharaja Krishnaraja III with his three queens. Surrounding the main palace in Mysore and inside the fort are five temples, built in various periods. The Prasanna Krishnaswamy Temple (1829), the Lakshmiramana Swamy Temple whose earliest structures date to 1499, the Trinesvara Swamy Temple (late 16th century), the Shweta Varaha

Swamy Temple built by Purniah with a touch of Hoysala style of architecture, the Prasanna Venkataramana Swami Temple (1836) notable for 12 murals of the Wodeyar rulers. Well-known temples outside Mysore city are the yali ("mythical beast") pillared Venkataramana Temple built in the late 17th century in the Bangalore fort, and the Ranganatha temple in Srirangapatna.

Tipu Sultan built a wooden colonnaded palace called the Dariya Daulat Palace (*lit,* "garden of the wealth of the sea") in Srirangapatna in 1784. Built in the Indo-Saracenic style, the palace is known for its intricate woodwork comprising of ornamental arches, striped columns and floral designs, and paintings. The west wall of the palace is covered with murals depicting Tipu Sultan's victory over Colonel Baillie's army at Pollilur, near Kanchipuram in 1780. One mural shows Tipu enjoying the fragrance of a bouquet of flowers while the battle is in progress. In that painting, the French soldiers' moustaches distinguish them from the cleanshaven British soldiers. Also in Srirangapatna is the Gumbaz mausoleum, built by Tipu Sultan in 1784. It houses the graves of Tipu and Hyder Ali. The granite base is capped with a dome built of brick and pilaster.

Military Technology

The first iron-cased and metal-cylinder rocket artillery were developed by Tipu Sultan, a Muslim ruler of the Kingdom of Mysore, and his father Hyder Ali, in the 1780s. He successfully used these metal-cylinder rockets against the larger forces of the British East India Company during the Anglo-Mysore Wars. The Mysore rockets of this period were much more advanced than what the British had seen, chiefly because of the use of iron tubes for holding the propellant; this enabled higher thrust and longer range for the missile (up to 2 km range). After Tipu's eventual defeat in the Fourth Anglo-Mysore War and the capture of the Mysore iron rockets, they were influential in British rocket development, inspiring the Congreve rocket, which was soon put into use in the Napoleonic Wars.

According to Stephen Oliver Fought and John F. Guilmartin, Jr. in *Encyclopedia Britannica* (2008): "Hyder Ali, prince of Mysore, developed war rockets with an important change: the use of metal cylinders to contain the combustion powder. Although the hammered soft iron he used was crude, the bursting strength of

the container of black powder was much higher than the earlier paper construction. Thus a greater internal pressure was possible, with a resultant greater thrust of the propulsive jet. The rocket body was lashed with leather thongs to a long bamboo stick. Range was perhaps up to three-quarters of a mile (more than a kilometre). Although individually these rockets were not accurate, dispersion error became less important when large numbers were fired rapidly in mass attacks. They were particularly effective against cavalry and were hurled into the air, after lighting, or skimmed along the hard dry ground. Hyder Ali's son, Tippu Sultan, continued to develop and expand the use of rocket weapons, reportedly increasing the number of rocket troops from 1,200 to a corps of 5,000. In battles at Seringapatam in 1792 and 1799 these rockets were used with considerable effect against the British."

Hyder Ali

Hyder Ali was the *de facto* ruler of the Kingdom of Mysore in southern India. He is said to have induced his brother to employ a Parsi to purchase artillery and small arms from the government of Bombay Presidency, and to enrol some thirty sailors of different European nations as gunners, and is thus credited with having been "the first Indian who formed a corps of sepoys armed with firelocks and bayonets, and who had a train of artillery served by Europeans." He induced Shamaiya Iyengar into his ministry as minister of post and police and later Shamaiya served under Tipu Sultan.

Personal Life

Hyder Ali was the great-grandson of an Islamic fakir from Gulbarga, Deccan. His father was a *naik* or chief constable at Budikote, near Kolar in present-day Karnataka. He was born in Budhikote between 1717 and 1722. According to some historians Hyder Ali was born in 1721. As a youth, Hyder assisted his brother, a commander of a brigade in the Mysore Army, and acquired a useful familiarity with the tactics of the French when at the height of their reputation under Joseph François Dupleix.

Rise to Power

At the siege of Devanhalli (1749) Hyder's services attracted the attention of Nanjaraja, the minister of the Raja of Mysore, and he at once received an independent command; within the next twelve years his energy and ability had made him completely master of minister and raja alike, and in everything but in name he was ruler of the kingdom. In 1763 the conquest of Kanara gave him possession of the treasures of Bednor, with which he resolved to make a splendid capital in India, under his own name, thenceforth changed from Hyder Naik into Hyder Ali Khan Bahadur.

Hyder Ali now began to occupy the serious attention of the Madras Presidency, which in 1766 entered into an agreement with the Nizam of Hyderabad to furnish him with troops to be used against the common foe. But hardly had this alliance been formed when a secret arrangement was come to between the two Indian powers, the result of which was that Colonel Smith's small force was met with a united army of 50,000 men and 100 guns. British dash and sepoy fidelity were devastated, first in the Battle of Chengam (September 3, 1767) and again, even more remarkably, in that of Tiruvannamalai (Trinornalai). In February 1768, the British captured Mangalore from Hyder. The Portuguese had offered to help Hyder against the British. But when they betrayed Hyder, he directed his anger towards the Mangalorean Catholics, since they had been converted to Christianity by the Portuguese. Towards the end of 1768, Hyder defeated the British and re-captured Mangalore fort, where the Mangalorean Catholics were taking refuge. Around 15,675 of them were taken as prisoners to Mysore by Hyder.

Peace treaty

On the loss of his recently-made fleet and forts on the western coast, Hyder Ali now offered overtures for peace; on the rejection of these, bringing all his resources and strategy into play, he forced Colonel Smith to raise the siege of Bangalore, and brought his army within 5 miles (8.0 km) of Madras. The result was the treaty of April 1769, providing for the mutual restitution of all conquests, and for mutual aid and alliance in defensive war; it was followed by a commercial treaty in 1770 with the authorities of Bombay. Under these arrangements Hyder Ali, when defeated by the Marathas in 1772 (three wars were fought between 1764 and 1772 by Madhavrao Peshwa against Hyder Ali, in which Hyder Ali lost), claimed British assistance, but in vain; this breach of faith stung him to fury, and thenceforward he and his son did not cease to thirst for vengeance. His time came when in 1778 the British, on the declaration of war with France, resolved to drive the French out of India. The capture of Mahe on the Malabar coast in 1779, followed by the annexation of lands belonging to a dependant of his own, gave him the needed pretext for the Second Anglo-Mysore War.

Losses

With the empire extended to the Krishna River, he descended through the passes of the Western Ghats amid burning villages, reaching Kanchipuram (Conjeevaram), only 45 miles (72 km) from Madras, unopposed. Not till the smoke was seen from St. Thomas Mount, where Sir Hector Munro commanded some 5200 troops, was any movement made.

Then, however, the British general sought to effect a junction with a smaller body under Colonel Baillie recalled from Guntur. The incapacity of these officers, notwithstanding the splendid courage of their men, resulted in the total destruction of Baillie's force of 2800 (September 10, 1780). Warren Hastings sent from Bengal Sir Eyre Coote, who, though repulsed at Chidambaram, defeated Hyder thrice successively in the battles of Porto Novo, Pollilur and Sholingarh, while Tipu Sultan was forced to raise the siege of Vandavasi (Wandiwash), and Vellore was provisioned. On the arrival of Lord Macartney as governor of Madras, the British fleet captured Nagapattinam (Negapatam), and forced Hyder Ali to confess that he could never ruin a power which had command of the sea. He had sent his son Tipu to the west coast, to seek the assistance of the French fleet, when his death took place suddenly at Chittoor in December 1782.

Hyder Ali's Invasion of Tanjore

Hyder Ali invaded Tanjore in 1781, at the height of the Second Mysore War. Col. Braithwaite tried to stem his advance but was defeated and had to surrender. Hyder extracted the allegiance of the Maratha king Thuljaji and plundered the country. Cattle and crops were destroyed. The gross produce of the Tanjore kingdom fell from 10,439,057 in 1780 to 1,578,520 in 1781. It further slid to 1,370,174 in 1782. The ravages of Hyder Ali and his son Tippu Sultan were followed by alleged expeditions of plunder launched by the Kallars. There was scarcity of food and work and the economy was shattered. The kingdom of Tanjore did not recover from the effects of the invasion till the start of the 19th century. The period of suffering referred to in local folklore as *Hyderakalabam* is considered to be one of the darkest periods in the region's history since the invasions of the Kalabhras.

Tipu Sultan

Sultan Fateh Ali Tipu (November 1750, Devanahalli – 4 May 1799, Srirangapattana), also known as the Tiger of Mysore, was the *de facto* ruler of the Kingdom of Mysore. He was the first son of Hyder Ali by his second wife, Fatima or Fakhr-un-nissa. His full name is Sultan Fateh Ali Khan Shahab or Tipu Saheb Tipu Sultan.

In addition to his role as ruler, he was a scholar, soldier, and poet. He was a devout Muslim but the majority of his subjects were Hindus. At the request of the French, he built a church, the first in Mysore.

In alliance with the French in their struggle with the British both Tipu Sultan and Hyder Ali did not hesitate to use their French trained army against the Marathas, Sira, Malabar, Coorg and Bednur. He was proficient in many languages. He helped his father Hyder Ali defeat the British in the Second Mysore War, and negotiated the Treaty of Mangalore with them. However, he was defeated in the Third Anglo-Mysore War and in the Fourth Anglo-Mysore War by the combined forces of the British East India Company, the Nizam of Hyderabad and to a lesser extent, Travancore. Tipu Sultan died defending his capital Srirangapattana, on 4 May 1799.

Sir Walter Scott, commenting on the abdication of Napoleon Bonaparte in 1814, wrote: "Although I never supposed that he [Napoleon] possessed, allowing for some difference of education, the liberality of conduct and political views which were sometimes exhibited by old Haidar Ally, yet I did think he [Napoleon] might have shown the same resolved and dogged spirit of resolution which induced Tipu Sahib to die manfully upon the breach of his capital city with his sabre clenched in his hand."

Early Life

Tipu Sultan was born at Devanahalli, in present-day Bangalore District, some 33 km (21 mi) North of Bangalore city. The exact date of his birth is not known; various sources claim various dates between 1749 and 1753. According to one widely accepted dating, he was born on 10 November, 1750 (Friday, 10th Dhu al-Hijjah, 1163 AH). His father, Hyder Ali, was the de facto ruler of Mysore. His mother Fatima or Fakhr-un-nissa was the daughter of Shahal Tariq, governor of the fort of Cuddapah.

He was also a strongly religious man, there is a conflict between Sunni-Shia practice of religion. He went in daily to say his prayer and paid special attention to mosques in the area. While one of the only Muslim leaders in present-day India, Tipu managed to remain strong in his faith. He built a church, the first in Mysore, at the request of the French. He was a noted linguist, Islamic patriot.

His Rule

During his rule, Tipu Sultan laid the foundation for a dam where the famous Krishna Raja Sagara Dam across the river Cauvery was later built. He also completed the project of Lal Bagh started by his father Hyder Ali, and built roads, public buildings, and ports along the Kerala shoreline. His dominion extended throughout North Bangalore including the Nandi Hills, Kanivenarayanapura, and Chickballapur. His trade extended to countries which included Sri Lanka, Afghanistan, France, Turkey, and Iran. Under his leadership, the Mysore army proved to be a school of military science to Indian princes.

The serious blows that Tipu Sultan inflicted on the British in the First and Second Mysore Wars affected their reputation as an invincible power. Dr. APJ Abdul Kalam, the former President of India, in his Tipu Sultan Shaheed Memorial Lecture in Bangalore (30 November 1991), called Tipu Sultan the innovator of the world's first war rocket. Two of these rockets, captured by the British at Srirangapatna, are displayed in the Royal Artillery Museum in London. Most of Tippu Sultan's campaigns resulted in successes. He managed to subdue all the petty kingdoms in the south. He defeated the Marathas and the Nizams and was also one of the few Indian rulers to have defeated British armies. He is said to have started a coinage system, banking system, a new calendar, and a new system of weights and measures. He was well versed in Urdu, Kannada, Persian, and Arabic. Tipu was supposed to become a Sufi, but his father Hyder Ali insisted he become a capable soldier and a great leader.

Religious Policy

Attitude Towards Hindus

As a Muslim ruler in a largely Hindu domain, Tipu Sultan faced problems in establishing the legitimacy of his rule, and in reconciling his desire to be seen as a devout Islamic ruler with the need to be pragmatic to avoid antagonising the majority of his subjects. His religious legacy has become a source of considerable controversy in the subcontinent. Some groups proclaim him a great warrior for the faith or *Ghazi*, while a large number of groups revile him as a bigot who massacred Hindus.

Some historians claim that he had an egalitarian attitude towards Hindus and was harsh towards them only when politically expedient. In the first part of his reign in particular he appears to have been notably more aggressive and religiously doctrinaire than his father, Hyder Ali. Some historians claim that Tipu Sultan was a religious persecutor of Hindus. In 1780 CE he declared himself to be the *Badshah* or Emperor of Mysore, and struck coinage in his own name without reference to the reigning Mughal Emperor Shah Alam II. H. D. Sharma writes that in his correspondence with other Islamic rulers such as Zaman Shah of Afghanistan, Tipu Sultan used this title and declared that he intended to establish an empire in the entire country, along the lines of the Mughal Empire which was at its nadir during the period in question. His alliance with the French was supposedly aimed at achieving this goal by driving his main rivals, the British, out of the subcontinent.

It is believed that Tipu ordered Shamaiya Iyengar to be blinded. However, Tipu himself forgave Shamaiya when Shamaiya's son bravely defended against the British during the last Anglo-Mysore War, dying due to a gunshot in the chest. Noted historian Hayavadana C. Rao, writing for the Raja of Mysore, wrote about Tipu in his encyclopaedic work *The History of Mysore*. He asserted that Tipu's "religious fanaticism and the excesses committed in the name of religion, both in Mysore and in the provinces, stand condemned for all time. His bigotry, indeed, was so great that it precluded all ideas of toleration". He further asserts that the acts of Tippu that were constructive towards Hindus were largely political and ostentatious rather than an indication of genuine tolerance Brittlebank, Hasan, Chetty, Habib and Saletare, amongst others, argue that stories of Tipu Sultan's religious persecution of

Hindus and Christians are largely derived from the work of early British authors such as Kirkpatrick and Wilks, whom they do not consider to be entirely reliable. A. S. Chetty argues that Wilks' account in particular cannot be trusted, Irfan Habib and Mohibbul Hasan argues that these early British authors had a strong vested interest in presenting Tipu Sultan as a tyrant from whom the British had "liberated" Mysore. This assessment is echoed by Brittlebank in her recent work where she writes that Wilks and Kirkpatrick must be used with particular care as both authors had taken part in the wars against Tipu Sultan and were closely connected to the administrations of Lord Cornwallis and Richard Wellesley, 1st Marquess Wellesley.

Mohibbul Hasan, Prof. Sheikh Ali, and other historians cast great doubt on the scale of the deportations and forced conversions in Coorg in particular, and Hasan says that the British versions of what happened were intended to malign Tipu Sultan, and to be used as propaganda against him. He argues that little reliance can be placed in Muslim accounts such as Kirmani's *Nishan-e Haidari*; in their anxiety to represent the Sultan as a champion of Islam, they had a tendency to exaggerate and distort the facts: Kirmani claims that 70,000 Coorgis were converted, when forty years later the entire population of Coorg was still less than that number. According to Ramchandra Rao "Punganuri" the true number of converts was about 500. The portrayal of Tippu Sultan as a religious bigot is disputed, and some sources suggest that he in fact often embraced religious pluralism.

Tipu Sultan's treasurer was Krishna Rao, Shamaiya Iyengar was his Minister of Post and Police, his brother Ranga Iyengar was also an officer, and Purnaiya held the very important post of "Mir Asaf". Moolchand and Sujan Rai were his chief agents at the Mughal court, and his chief "Peshkar", Suba Rao, was also a Hindu. There is such evidence as grant deeds, and correspondence between his court and temples, and his having donated jewellery and deeded land grants to several temples, which some claim he was compelled to do in order to make alliances with Hindu rulers. Between 1782 and 1799 Tippu Sultan issued 34 *sanad*s (deeds) of endowment to temples in his domain, while also presenting many of them with gifts of silver and gold plate. The Srikanteswara Temple in Nanjangud still possesses a jewelled cup presented by the Sultan.

In 1791 some Maratha horsemen under Raghunath Rao Patwardhan raided the temple and monastery of Sringeri Shankaracharya, killing and wounding many, and plundering the monastery of all its valuable possessions. The incumbent Shankaracharya petitioned Tipu Sultan for help. A bunch of about 30 letters written in Kannada, which were exchanged between Tipu Sultan's court and the Sringeri Shankaracharya were discovered in 1916 by the Director of Archaeology in Mysore. Tipu Sultan expressed his indignation and grief at the news of the raid, and wrote:

People who have sinned against such a holy place are sure to suffer the consequences of their misdeeds at no distant date in this Kali age in accordance with the verse: "Hasadbhih kriyate karma ruladbhir-anubhuyate" (People do [evil] deeds smilingly but suffer the consequences crying)."

He immediately ordered the Asaf of Bednur to supply the Swami with 200 *rahatis* (*fanams*) in cash and other gifts and articles. Tipu Sultan's interest in the Sringeri temple continued for many years, and he was still writing to the Swami in the 1790s CE. In light of this and other events, B.A. Saletare has described Tipu Sultan as a defender of the Hindu dharma, who also patronized other temples including one at Melkote, for which he issued a Kannada decree that the Shrivaishnava invocatory verses there should be recited in the traditional form.

The temple at Melkote still has gold and silver vessels with inscriptions indicating that they were presented by the Sultan. Tippu Sultan also presented four silver cups to the Lakshmikanta Temple at Kalale. Tipu Sultan does seem to have repossessed unauthorised grants of land made to Brahmins and temples, but those which had proper *sanads* were not. It was a normal practice for any ruler, Muslim or Hindu, on his accession or on the conquest of new territory.

The Srikanteswara temple at Nanjungud was presented with a jewelled cup and some precious stones. To another temple, Nanjundeswara, in the same town of Nanjungud, he gave a greenish linga; to Ranganatha temple at Srirangapatana he gifted seven silver cups and a silver camphor burner. This temple was hardly a stone's throw from his palace from where he would listen with equal respect to the ringing of temple bells and the muezzin's call from the mosque.

Tippu sent a letter on January 19, 1790 to Budruz Zuman Khan. It says:

"Don't you know I have achieved a great victory recently in Malabar and over four lakh Hindus were converted to Islam? I am determined to march against that cursed Raman Nair very soon. Since I am overjoyed at the prospect of converting him and his subjects to Islam, I have happily abandoned the idea of going back to Srirangapatanam now".

It is hard to say, however, that Tipu was completely opposed to those with different religious beliefs. Some high officials in his government were Hindu, such as Purnaiya, Krishna Rao, Shamaiya Iyenga. Tipu even offered help and gifted lands to build temples and supported many Brahmins, even some that opposed his regime.

Attitude Towards Christians

Tipu is regarded to be anti-Christian by some historians. The captivity of Mangalorean Catholics at Seringapatam, which began on 24 February 1784 and ended on 4 May 1799, remains the most disconsolate memory in their history.

The Bakur Manuscript reports him as having said: *"All Musalmans should unite together, and considering the annihilation of infidels as a sacred duty, labour to the utmost of their power, to accomplish that subject."* Soon after the Treaty of Mangalore in 1784, Tipu gained control of Canara. He issued orders to seize the Christians in Canara, confiscate their estates, and deport them to Seringapatam, the capital of his empire, through the Jamalabad fort route. However, there were no priests among the captives. Together with Fr Miranda, all the 21 arrested priests were issued orders of expulsion to Goa, fined Rs 2 lakhs, and threatened death by hanging if they ever returned.

Tipu ordered the destruction of 27 Catholic churches, all beautifully carved with statues depicting various saints. Among them included the Church of Nossa Senhora de Rosario Milagres at Mangalore, Fr Miranda's Seminary at Monte Mariano, Church of Jesu Marie Jose at Omzoor, Chapel at Bolar, Church of Merces at Ullal, Imaculata Conceiciao at Mulki, San Jose at Perar, Nossa Senhora dos Remedios at Kirem, Sao Lawrence at Karkal, Rosario at Barkur, Immaculata Conceciao at Baidnur. All were razed to the ground, with the exception of the The Church of Holy Cross at Hospet,owing to the friendly offices of the Chauta Raja of

Moodbidri. According to Thomas Munro, a Scottish soldier and the first collector of Canara, around 60,000 of them, nearly 92 percent of the entire Mangalorean Catholic community, were captured, only 7,000 escaped. Francis Buchanan gives the numbers as 70,000 captured, from a population of 80,000, with 10,000 escaping. They were forced to climb nearly 4,000 feet (1,200 m) through the jungles of the Western Ghat mountain ranges. It was 210 miles (340 km) from Mangalore to Seringapatam, and the journey took six weeks. According to British Government records, 20,000 of them died on the march to Seringapatam. According to James Scurry, a British officer, who was held captive along with Mangalorean Catholics, 30,000 of them were forcibly converted to Islam. The young women and girls were forcibly made wives of the Muslims living there. The young men who offered resistance were disfigured by cutting their noses, upper lips, and ears. According to Mr. Silva of Gangolim, a survivor of the captivity, if a person who had escaped from Seringapatam was found, the punishment under the orders of Tippu was the cutting off of the ears, nose, the feet and one hand.

The Archbishop of Goa wrote in 1800, *"It is notoriously known in all Asia and all other parts of the globe of the oppression and sufferings experienced by the Christians in the Dominion of the King of Kanara, during the usurpation of that country by Tipu Sultan from an implacable hatred he had against them who professed Christianity."*

Tippu Sultan's invasion of the Malabar had an adverse impact on the Syrian Malabar Nasrani community of the Malabar coast. Many churches in the Malabar and Cochin were damaged. The old Syrian Nasrani seminary at Angamaly which had been the centre of Catholic religious education for several centuries was razed to the ground by Tippu's soldiers. A lot of centuries old religious manuscripts were lost forever. The church was later relocated to Kottayam where it still exists to this date. The Mor Sabor church at Akaparambu and the Martha Mariam Church attached to the seminary were destroyed as well. Tipu's army set fire to the church at Palayoor and attacked the Ollur Church in 1790. Furthernmore, the Arthat church and the Ambazhakkad seminary was also destroyed. Over the course of this invasion, many Syrian Malabar Nasrani were killed or forcibly converted to Islam. Most of the coconut, arecanut, pepper and cashew plantations held by the Syrian Malabar farmers were also indiscriminately destroyed by the invading army. As a result, when Tipu's army invaded Guruvayur and adjacent areas, the Syrian Christian community fled Calicut and small towns like Arthat to new centres like Kunnamkulam, Chalakudi, Ennakadu, Cheppadu, Kannankode, Mavelikkara, etc. where there were already Christians. They were given refuge by Sakthan Tamburan, the ruler of Cochin and Karthika Thirunal, the ruler of Travancore, who gave them lands, plantations and encouraged their businesses. Colonel Macqulay, the British resident of Travancore also helped them. Tipu Sultan's invasion of the Malabar had an adverse impact on the Syrian Malabar Nasrani community of the Malabar coast. Many churches in the Malabar and Cochin were damaged. The old Syrian Nasrani seminary at Angamaly which had been the centre of Catholic religious education for several centuries was razed to the ground by Tippu's soldiers. A lot of centuries old religious manuscripts were lost forever.

Tipu's persecution of Christians even extended to captured British soldiers. For instance, there were a significant amount of forced conversions of British captives between 1780 and 1784. Following their disastrous defeat at the battle of Pollilur, 7,000 British men along with an unknown number of women were held captive by Tipu in the fortress of Seringapatnam. Of these, over 300 were circumcised and given Muslim names and clothes and several British regimental drummer boys were made to wear *ghagra cholis* and entertain the court as *nautch* girls or dancing girls. After the 10 year long captivity ended, James Scurry, one of those prisoners, recounted that he had forgotten how to sit in a chair and use a knife and fork. His English was broken and stilted, having lost all his vernacular idiom. His skin had darkened to the swarthy complexion of negroes, and moreover, he had developed an aversion to wearing European clothes.

During the surrender of the Mangalore fort which was delivered in an armistice by the British and their subsequent withdrawal, all the Mestizos and remaining non-British foreigners were killed, together with 5,600 Mangalorean Catholics. Those condemned by Tipu Sultan for treachery were hanged instantly, the gibbets being weighed down by the number of bodies they carried. The Netravati River was so putrid with the stench of dying bodies, that the local residents were forced to leave their riverside homes.

Tipu's Right Hand Man

Sirdar Yaar Muhammad, the right hand man of Sultan Tipu, also known as *Ghazi-e Mysore* (Veteran of Mysore), was born in the 18th century in a Muslim Rajput family to Shah Muhammad, a Sufi saint. It is said that Tippu had become a disciple of Shah Muhammad. Yar joined the Army of Mysore and soon became one of the favourite generals of Tipu Sultan. Seeing his patriotic and dauntless behaviour, Tippu Sultan made him his commander-in-chief. He fought dauntlessly in the Battle of Seringapatam (1799), but after Tippu's death, and later the fall of Mysore, he ran away to the Kullu hills and then to the central Punjab of Maharaja Ranjit Singh. Thus, he managed to evade capture by the English. After the fall of Mysore, he was declared one of the most wanted Mysorean officers. East India Company tried its best to capture him, dead or alive, but couldn't succeed. He carried bounty on his head. Several of Yar's family members and relatives were killed by the conquerors, however, he, along with his wife, his father, and a son Ilahi Bakhsh, escaped. He spent the rest of his life as a fugitive. General Yar Muhammad died in the first half of the 19th century. His descendants still live in Punjab, Pakistan, today.

Description

Alexander Beatson, who published a volume on the Fourth Mysore War entitled *View of the Origin and Conduct of the War with Tipu Sultaun*, described Tippu Sultan as follows: "His stature was about five feet eight inches; he had a short neck, square shoulders, and was rather corpulent: his limbs were small, particularly his feet and hands; he had large full eyes, small arched eyebrows, and an aquiline nose; his complexion was fair, and the general expression of his countenance, not void of dignity"..

He was called the Tiger of Mysore. It is said that Tippu Sultan was hunting in the forest with a French friend. He came face to face with a tiger. His gun did not work, and his dagger fell on the ground as the tiger jumped on him. He reached for the dagger, picked it up, and killed the tiger with it. That earned him the name "the Tiger of Mysore". He had the image of a tiger on his flag. Tippu Sultan was also very fond of innovations. Beatson mentioned that Tippu Sultan was "passionately fond of new inventions. In his palace was found a great variety of curious swords, daggers, fusils, pistols, and blunderbusses; some were of exquisite workmanship, mounted with gold, or silver, and beautifully inlaid and ornamented with tigers' heads and stripes, or with Persian and Arabic verses". Tipu's Tiger, an automaton representing a tiger attacking a European soldier, made for Tippu Sultan, is on display in the Victoria and Albert Museum, London. During Tippu Sultan's reign, a new calendar, new coinage, and seven new government departments, were introduced as well as innovations in the use of rocket artillery.

Early Military Career

Tippu Sultan was instructed in military tactics by French officers in the employment of his father, Hyder Ali (also spelled "Haidar Ali"). At age 15, he accompanied his father Haidar Ali against the British in the First Mysore War in 1766. He commanded a corps of cavalry in the invasion of Carnatic in 1767 at age 16. He also distinguished himself in the First Anglo-Maratha War of 1775–1779.

Second Mysore War

Tipu Sultan led a large body of troops in the Second Mysore War, in February 1782, and defeated Braithwaite on the banks of the Kollidam. Although the British were defeated this time, Tippu Sultan realized that the British were a new kind of threat in India. Upon becoming the Sultan after his father's death later that year, he worked to check the advances of the British by making alliances with the Marathas and the Mughals.

Tipu Sultan defeated Colonel Braithwaite at Annagudi near Tanjore on 18 February 1782. The British army, consisting of 100 Europeans, 300 cavalry, 1400 sepoys and 10 field pieces, was the standard size of the colonial armies. Tipu Sultan seized all the guns and took the entire detachment prisoner. In December 1781 Tipu Sultan successfully seized Chittur from the British. Tipu Sultan had thus gained sufficient military experience by the time Haidar Ali died in December 1782.

The Second Mysore War came to an end with the Treaty of Mangalore. It was the last occasion when an Indian king dictated terms to the mighty British, and the treaty is a prestigious document in the history of India.

The Second Mysore War is also remembered for alleged excesses committed by Hyder Ali and Tipu Sultan in Tanjore.

During the period of occupation which lasted six months, Hyder Ali and Tipu Sultan are believed to have impoverished the country. As late as 1784, the Dutch missionary Christian Friedrich Schwarz describes Tipu's alleged abduction of 12,000 children from the region. It is alleged that the invaders plundered the country and took away the cattle and grain.

The invasion is believed to have had such an impact on the economy of the country that it did not recover until the start of the nineteenth century. The gross domestic product of the kingdom fell by over ninety percent between 1780 and 1781 and took over 15 years to again reach pre-1781 levels. However, this conclusion must be considered in the light of the fact that no real effort to measure the GDP of India was ever made by the British government. The first such attempt was made by Dadabhai Nowroji in 1868 and it suffered from serious limitations. Therefore the veracity of the GDP estimate made in the 18th century is questionable.

Battle of Pollilur

The Battle of Pollilur took place in 1780 at Pollilur near the city of Kanchipuram. It was a part of the second Anglo-Mysore war. Tippu Sultan was dispatched by Haidar Ali with 10,000 men and 18 guns to intercept Colonel Baillie who was on his way to join Sir Hector Munro. Out of 360 Europeans, about 200 were captured alive, and the sepoys, who were about 3800 men, suffered very high casualties. Munro was moving south with a separate British force to join Baillie, but on hearing the news of the defeat he was forced to retreat to Madras, abandoning his artillery in a water tank at Kanchipuram.

Napoleon's attempt at a Junction

One of the motivations of Napoleon's Invasion of Egypt was to establish a junction with India against the British. Bonaparte wished to establish a French presence in the Middle East, with the ultimate dream of linking with Tipu Sahib. Napoleon assured to the Directoire that *"as soon as he had conquered Egypt, he will establish relations with the Indian princes and, together with them, attack the English in their possessions."* According to a 13 February 1798 report by Talleyrand: *"Having occupied and fortified Egypt, we shall send a force of 15,000 men from Suez to India, to join the forces of Tipu-Sahib and drive away the English."*

Napoleon was finally defeated by the Ottoman Empire helped with England at the Siege of Acre in 1799, and at the Battle of Abukir in 1801, so that by 1802, the French were completely vanquished in the Middle-East. Soon however, from 1803, Napoleon went to great lengths to form a Franco-Ottoman alliance against the British and the Russians, sending General Horace Sebastiani as envoy extraordinary. Napoleon also formed a Franco-Persian alliance in 1807, with the continuous aim of linking with India.

Fourth Mysore War

After Horatio Nelson had defeated François-Paul Brueys D'Aigalliers at the Battle of the Nile in Egypt in 1798 CE, three armies, one from Bombay, and two British (one of which included Arthur Wellesley, the future first Duke of Wellington), marched into Mysore in 1799 and besieged the capital Srirangapatnam in the Fourth Mysore War.

There were over 26,000 soldiers of the British East India Company comprising about 4000 Europeans and the rest Indians. A column was supplied by the Nizam of Hyderabad consisting of ten battalions and over 16,000 cavalry, and many soldiers were sent by the Marathas. Thus the soldiers in the British force numbered over 50,000 soldiers whereas Tipu Sultan had only about 30,000 soldiers. The British broke through the city walls, and Tipu Sultan died defending his capital on May 4. When the fallen Tippu was identified, Wellesley felt his pulse and confirmed that he was dead. Next to him, underneath his palankeen, was one of his most confidential servants, Rajah Cawn. Rajah was able to identify Tipu for the soldiers. Tipu Sultan was killed at the Hoally (Diddy) Gateway, which was located 300 yards from the N.E. Angle of the Srirangapattana Fort. The Fort Gateway had been built only 5 Years earlier to Tipu's death.. Tipu was buried the next afternoon, near the remains of his father. In the midst of his burial, a strong storm struck, with massive winds and rains. As Lieutenant Richard Bayly of the British 12th regiment wrote, "I have experienced hurricanes, typhoons, and gales of wind at sea, but never in the whole course of my existence had I seen anything comparable to this desolating visitation".

As Pioneers of Rocket Artillery

Hyder Ali and Tipu Sultan as regarded as pioneers in the use of solid fuel rocket technology or missiles for military use. A military tactic developed by Tippu Sultan and his father, Haidar Ali was the use of mass attacks with rocket brigades on infantry formations. Tippu Sultan wrote a military manual called *Fathul Mujahidin* in which 200 rocket men were assigned to each Mysorean "cushoon" (brigade). Mysore had 16 to 24 cushoons of infantry. The areas of town where rockets and fireworks were manufactured were known as Taramandal Pet ("Galaxy Market"). It was only after Tippu's death that the technology eventually reached Europe. The Royal Woolwich Arsenal's beginning a military rocket R&D program in 1801 that relied on the technology learned from Mysore.

The rocket men were trained to launch their rockets at an angle calculated from the diameter of the cylinder and the distance of the target. In addition, wheeled rocket launchers capable of launching five to ten rockets almost simultaneously were used in war. Rockets could be of various sizes, but usually consisted of a tube of soft hammered iron about 8" long and 1½-3" diameter, closed at one end and strapped to a shaft of bamboo about 4 ft. (1 m) long. The iron tube acted as a combustion chamber and contained well packed black powder propellant. A rocket carrying about one pound of powder could travel almost 1,000 yards. In contrast, rockets in Europe, not being iron cased, could not take large chamber pressures and as a consequence, were not capable of reaching distances anywhere near as great.

Haidar Ali's father, the Naik or chief constable at Budikote, commanded 50 rocketmen for the Nawab of Arcot. There was a regular Rocket Corps in the Mysore Army, beginning with about 1200 men in Haidar Ali's time. At the Battle of Pollilur (1780), during the Second Anglo-Mysore War, Colonel William Braille's ammunition stores are thought to have been detonated by a hit from one of Haidar Ali's Mysore rockets, resulting in a humiliating British defeat.

In the Third Anglo-Mysore War of 1792, there is mention of two rocket units fielded by Tippu Sultan, 120 men and 131 men respectively. Lt. Col. Knox was attacked by rockets near Srirangapatna on the night of 6 February 1792, while advancing towards the Kaveri river from the north. The Rocket Corps ultimately reached a strength of about 5000 in Tipu Sultan's army. Mysore rockets were also used for ceremonial purposes. When the Jacobin Club of Mysore sent a delegation to Tippu Sultan, 500 rockets were launched as part of the gun salute.

During the Fourth Anglo-Mysore War, rockets were again used on several occasions. One of these involved Colonel Arthur Wellesley, later famous as the First Duke of Wellington. Arthur Wellesley was defeated by Tippu's Diwan, Purnaiya, at the Battle of Sultanpet Tope. Quoting Forrest,

"At this point there was a large tope, or grove, which gave shelter to Tipu's rocketmen and had obviously to be cleaned out before the siege could be pressed closer to Srirangapattana island. The commander chosen for this operation was Col. Wellesley, but advancing towards the tope after dark on the 5 April 1799, he was set upon with rockets and musket-fires, lost his way and, as Beatson politely puts it, had to "postpone the attack" until a more favourable opportunity should offer.

The following day, Wellesley launched a fresh attack with a larger force, and took the whole position without losing a single man. On 22 April 1799, twelve days before the main battle, rocketeers worked their way around to the rear of the British encampment, then 'threw a great number of rockets at the same instant' to signal the beginning of an assault by 6,000 Indian infantry and a corps of Frenchmen, all directed by Mir Golam Hussain and Mohomed Hulleen Mir Mirans. The rockets had a range of about 1,000 yards. Some burst in the air like shells. Others, called ground rockets, would rise again on striking the ground and bound along in a serpentine motion until their force was spent. According to one British observer, a young English officer named Bayly:

"So pestered were we with the rocket boys that there was no moving without danger from the destructive missiles...". He continued:

The rockets and musketry from 20,000 of the enemy were incessant. No hail could be thicker. Every illumination of blue lights was accompanied by a shower of rockets, some of which entered the head of the column, passing through to the rear, causing death, wounds, and dreadful lacerations from the long bamboos of twenty or thirty feet, which are invariably attached to them.

During the conclusive British attack on Srirangapattana on May 2, 1799, a British shot struck a magazine of rockets within Tippu Sultan's fort, causing it to explode and send a towering cloud of black smoke with cascades of exploding white light rising up from the battlements. On the afternoon of 4 May when the final attack on the fort was led by Baird, he was again met by "furious musket and rocket fire", but this did not help much; in about an hour's time the fort was taken; perhaps within another hour Tippu had been shot (the precise time of his death is not known), and the war was effectively over.

After the fall of Srirangapattana, 600 launchers, 700 serviceable rockets and 9,000 empty rockets were found. Some of the rockets had pierced cylinders, to allow them to act like incendiaries, while some had iron points or steel blades bound to the bamboo. By attaching these blades to rockets they became very unstable towards the end of their flight causing the blades to spin around like flying scythes, cutting down all in their path.

These experiences eventually led to the Royal Woolwich Arsenal's beginning a military rocket R&D program in 1801, their first demonstration of solid-fuel rockets in 1805 and publication of *A Concise Account of the Origin and Progress of the Rocket System* in 1807 by William Congreve, son of the arsenal's commandant. Congreve rockets were soon systematically used by the British during the Napoleonic Wars and the War of 1812. These descendants of Mysore rockets find mention in the Star Spangled Banner.

Treatment of Prisoners

According to historian Professor Sheikh Ali, the Tippu "took his stand on the bedrock of humanity, regarding all his subjects as equal citizen to live in peace, harmony and concord." However, during the storming of Srirangapattana by the British in 1799, thirteen murdered British prisoners were discovered, killed by either having their necks broken or nails driven into their skulls.

In Fiction

- In Jules Verne's Mysterious Island, Captain Nemo is described as a nephew of Tippu Sultan.
- Tippu Sultan's life and adventures were the central theme of a short-running South Indian television series "The Adventures of Tipu Sultan", and of a more popular national television series "The Sword of Tipu Sultan".
- Naseem Hijazi's novels *Muazam Ali* and *Aur Talvar lum Gaye* (*And The Sword Broke*) describe Tippu Sultan's wars.

- Wilkie Collins's novel *The Moonstone* contains an account of Tippu Sultan and the Fall of Srirangapattana in the prologue.
- In *The Surprising Adventures of Baron Munchausen* by Rudolf Erich Raspe, Munchausen vanquishes Tipu near the end of the novel.
- *Sharpe's Tiger* is a novel in which Napoleonic soldier Richard Sharpe fights at the Battle of Srirangapattana, later killing Tippu Sultan.
- *The Only King Who Died on the Battlefield: An Historical Novel Based on Truth* (published in 2006), was written by a US-Pakistani resident and a young college student Mohammed Faisal Iftikhar. The novel claims that in recent history, Tippu Sultan is the only king who died on the battlefield.
- Tippu Sultan appears as a "Great Person" in the video game, Sid Meier's Civilization: Revolution.

Family and Descendants

Tippu Sultan had four wives, by whom he had 16 sons named below and at least 8 daughters.The fate of his 8 daughters is a mystery.

1. Shahzada Hyder Ali Sultan Sahib (1771-30 July 1815)
2. Shahzada Abdul Khaliq Sultan Sahib (1782-12 September 1806
3. Shahzada Muhi-ud-din Sultan Sahib (1782-30 September 1811)
4. Shahzada Mu'izz-ud-din Sultan Sahib (1783-30 March 1818)
5. Shahzada Mi'raj-ud-din Sultan Sahib (1784?-?)
6. Shahzada Mu'in-ud-din Sultan Sahib (1784?-?)
7. Shahzada Muhammad Yasin Sultan Sahib (1784-15 March 1849)
8. Shahzada Muhammad Subhan Sultan Sahib (1785-27 September 1845)
9. Shahzada Muhammad Shukrullah Sultan Sahib (1785-25 September 1837)
10. Shahzada Sarwar-ud-din Sultan Sahib (1790-20 October 1833), *desc*

11. Shahzada Muhammad Nizam-ud-din Sultan Sahib (1791-20 October 1791)
12. Shahzada Muhammad Jamal-ud-din Sultan Sahib (1795-13 November 1842)
13. Shahzada Munir-ud-din Sultan Sahib (1795-1 December 1837)
14. His Highness Shahzada Sir Ghulam Muhammad Sultan Sahib, KCSI (March 1795-11 August 1872)
15. Shahzada Ghulam Ahmad Sultan Sahib (1796-11 April 1824)
16. Shahzada............. Sultan Sahib (1797–1797).

Tippu Sultan's family was sent to Calcutta by the British. Noor Inayat Khan, who was a major in the British Indian army, is said to be one of Tippu Sultan's descendants who died in France under German occupation.

Sword of Tipu Sultan

Tippu Sultan had lost his sword in a war with the Nairs of Travancore, in which he was defeated. The Nair army under the leadership of Raja Kesavadas defeated the Mysore army near Aluva. The Maharaja, Dharma Raja, gifted the famous sword to the Nawab of Arcot, from where the sword went to London. The sword was on display at the Wallace Collection, No. 1 Manchester Square, London. At an auction in London in 2004, the industrialist-politician Vijay Mallya purchased the sword of Tippu Sultan and some other historical artifacts, and brought them back to India for public display after nearly two centuries.

The Tiger As Tipu's Symbol

Tipu was commonly known as the Tiger of Mysore and adopted this animal as the symbol of his rule. He even had French engineers build a mechanical tiger for his palace. Not only did he place relics of tigers around his palace and domain, he also had the emblem of a tiger on his banners and even on some arms and weapons. Sometimes this tiger was very ornate and had inscriptions within the drawing, alluding to Tipu's faith, including phrases such as "In the name of Allah, the Beneficent, the Merciful" and quotations from the Quran.

7

Trade with Europe

India—The Roaring Trade Partner of Yore

Right from ancient times till the establishment of the British Empire, India was famed for her fabulous wealth. Even during the medieval period, *i.e.* roughly from the 12th to the 16th centuries, the country was prosperous despite the frequent political upheavals. A notable feature of this period was the growth of towns in various parts of the country. This development was the result of the political and economic policies followed by the Muslim rulers. These towns grew into trade and industrial centres which in turn led to the general prosperity. During the Sultanate period, which lasted from the early 13th to the early 16th centuries, the economy of the towns flourished. This was due to the establishment of a sound currency system based on the silver tanka and the copper dirham. Ibn Batuta the 14th century Moorish traveller had visited India during the Sultanate period. He had described the teeming markets of the big cities in the Gangetic plains, Malwa, Gujarat and Southern India. The important centres of trade and industry were Delhi, Lahore, Bombay, Ahmedabad, Sonargaon and Jaunpur. Coastal towns also developed into booming industrial centres with large populations.

During the two hundred years of Mughal rule *i.e.* from the 16th to the 18th centuries the urbanisation of India received a further impetus. The Mughal era witnessed the establishment of a stable centre and a uniform provincial government. During this age of relative peace and security, trade and commerce flourished. The burgeoning foreign trade led to the development of market places not only in the towns but also in the villages. The production of handicrafts increased in order to keep up with the demand for them in foreign countries.

The prime urban centres during the Mughal era were Agra, Delhi, Lahore, Multan, Thatta and Srinagar in the north. The important cities in the west included Ahmedabad, Bombay (then known as Khambat), Surat, Ujjain and Patan (in Gujarat). The flourishing trade centres in the eastern part of the country were Dacca, Hoogli, Patna, Chitgaon and Murshidabad. Most of these cities boasted of sizeable populations.

Products and Manufactures

The accounts of foreign travellers contain descriptions of the wide variety of exquisite goods sold in the markets of those days. India was famous for its textiles, which formed one of the chief items of export. Duarte Barbosa a Portuguese official in Cochin in the early 16th century described Gujarat, in the western region as a leading cotton trade centre. Textiles from Gujarat were exported to the Arab countries and to Southeast Asia. Patola, which is a kind of silk dyed in natural colours, was highly popular in Southeast Asia. It was very much in demand among the wealthy classes in Malaysia, Indonesia, and the Phillipines.

In the east Bengal was another important region for a wide variety of textiles. Ibn Batuta the 14th century Moorish traveller saw many cotton trade centres during his sojourn in Bengal. Silks were also manufactured there. The textile products included quilts of embroidered tussar, or munga on a cotton or jute, silk and brocade edged handkerchiefs. Dhaka muslin was renowned for its fineness. Kasimbazaar in Bengal was an important trade centre for cotton and silk goods. Sirbund, a type of cloth used for tying turbans was manufactured in Bengal. It was highly popular in Europe.

Similarly, Malabar in Kerala was also famous for its coloured and printed cloth material. The other important textiles producing centres in the south were Golconda, Shaliat and Pulicat. The last two were major trading centres for a wide variety of cottons. Golconda was famous for its Kalamkaaris. These were finely painted cotton fabrics with motifs from Hindu mythology. They were exported through the port city of Masulipatnam. Palampores, which were another variety of painted fabrics, were popular in the Mughal and Deccan courts. These were bedspreads made of Calico cloth. The borders of these pieces were block printed while the centre depicted deoicted the 'Tree of Life' motif made by hand. Indian textiles whether from Bengal, Gujarat or the South were highly appreciated abroad for their fine texture, elaborate design and brilliant colours.

Hardwood furniture, embellished with inlay work was a very popular item. The furniture was modelled on the European design but the expensive carvings and inlays were inspired by the ornate Mughal style. The production centres were in Sindh, Gujarat and the Deccan. Mother-of pearl inlay against a black lac background was a traditional design in Gujarat.

Carpets were used both in ancient and medieval India but it was in the 16th century during the Mughal era that the skill of carpet weaving touched new heights. It had become an important profession by then and all the major courts of the country encouraged it. The carpets produced during the Mughal era depicted either animals in combat or flowers. The flowers were woven so meticulously that they could be easily identified. The affinity of the Great Mughals with nature is evident from the designs of the carpets made during their times.

Many varieties of ornamental work in cut stones, ivory, pearl and tortoise shells were produced in South India. Pearl fishing was a major industry here. Diamonds were procured from the Deccan while sapphires and rubies were imported from Pegu and Ceylon. Major centres were established at Pulicat, Calicut and Vijaynagar for cutting and polishing these stones.

Indian arts and crafts were patronised by Indian rulers. They were unmatched for their beauty and skill and were popular in the European countries. During the Mughal era the European traders used to employ local artisans at the manufacturing centres set up by them at various places in India.

Domestic Trade

Foreign travellers gave extensive accounts about domestic trade in medieval India. Ibn Batuta had described Delhi as a major trade centre. The most superior quality rice and sugar from Kannauj, wheat from Punjab and betel leaves from Dhar in Madhya Pradesh found their way to the markets of Delhi.

Well-maintained roads linking various parts of the country facilitated domestic trade. The threat from bandits did not in any way affect the flow of goods as merchants travelled in well-armed groups to ensure their security. According to Barbosa's account, trade between Gujarat and Malwa was possible owing to the routes established in this area. The roads facilitated the exchange of goods between the different parts of the country. Limbodar in Gujarat and Dabhol in Maharashtra were major trade centres, which linked the northern and southern halves of the country. Accounts of foreign travellers give instances of the trade between Vijaynagar and Bhatkal in Goa with 5000-6000 bulls carrying goods between the two places. Vijaynagar traded in diamonds with other southern cities.

River routes also facilitated trade between different parts of the country. Boats carrying goods used to ply on the Indus and the Ganges. Some of the merchants had their own large boats.

Different communities dominated trade in various parts of the country. Multani and Punjabi merchants handled the business in the north, while in Gujarat and Rajasthan it was in the hands of the Bhats. Foreign traders from Central Asia, known as Khorasanis engaged in this profession all over India. Members of the nobility and the royalty took an interest in trading activities. They set up their own manufacturing centres wherein local artisans were employed.

Internal trade flourished due to the organised system set up by the government. The 14th century Sultan Alauddin Khilji for instance, used to strictly supervise the market places. Shopkeepers, who were caught violating the rules, were severely punished. However, the trading community used to face unfair treatment from the government officials. Sometimes they were forced by these officials to sell their products at reduced rates or on credit, thus incurring heavy losses in the process. The price list fixed by the government brought in low returns for the traders.

During the period of the later Mughals in the 18th century, the royalty and the nobility either purchased luxury goods at very low prices or did not pay at all. Such circumstances forced the trader to hoard his wealth and lead a frugal existence.

Foreign Trade

India's exports far exceeded her imports both in the number of items as well as in volume. The chief articles of import were horses, from Kabul and Arabia, dry fruits and precious stones. India also imported glassware from Europe, high grade textiles like satin from West Asia, while China supplied raw silk and porcelain. Foreign luxury goods were highly popular among the royalty and the nobility. These included wines, dry fruits, precious stones, corals, scented oils, perfumes and velvets.

During the Sultanate period articles of everyday use as well as luxury articles were exported to Syria, Arabia and Persia from Bengal and Cambay. These included silks, gold-embroidered cloth caps, exquisitely designed clay pots and pans, guns, knives and scissors. The other prime articles of export were sugar, indigo, oils, ivory sandalwood, spices, diamonds and other precious gems and coconuts.

Arab traders shipped Indian goods to European countries through the Red Sea and the Mediterranean ports. Indian products were also sent to East Africa, Malaya, China and the Far East. In China, Indian textiles were valued more than silk. Trade was also conducted through overland routes with Afghanistan, Central Asia and Persia. The route lay through Kashmir, Quetta and the Khyber Pass. Iraq and Bukhara were the other countries with which India conducted trade via the land route.

Foreign trade was in the hands of both local and foreign merchants. Many European travellers had settled in the coastal regions. Limbodar in Gujarat was a major exporting centre. Horses imported from Arabia were sent from the port of Bhatkal in Goa to the southern kingdoms. Imports like bronze, iron, wax, gold and wool were brought in through Goa, Calicut, Cochin and Quilon. The traders of Malabar, Gujarat and foreign settlers controlled business in the port cities of Calicut, Khambat, and Mangalore. Chinese ships docked at Quilon and Calicut while in Khambat the volume of trade was such that 3000 ships visited this port annually. This fact gives an idea of the magnitude of India's foreign trade during the medieval period.

Trade with China and Southeast Asia was mainly carried on through the port of Sonargaon now known as Dacca. Vijaynagar, which was the richest and most extensive state in the

15th and 16th centuries, enjoyed the most voluminous maritime trade with diverse countries such as Persia, Arabia, Africa, the Malayan Archipelago, Burma, China and the numerous islands in the Indian Ocean. The magnitude of trade can be surmised from the fact that there were 300 ports to facilitate the movement of goods. The shipbuilding industry flourished in the coastal towns.

The city of Vijaynagar was a teeming marketplace for both exports and imports. The fabulous wealth of the Empire left the foreigners dumbfounded. The people, irrespective of which strata of society they belonged to, possessed vast quantities of gold, diamonds and material wealth. Domingo Paes described the citizens as being heavily bejewelled. Abdur Razzak, the Khurasani ambassador to the court of Vijaynagar, refers to the treasury which had chambers filled with molten gold.

The merchant community in the other parts of the country was a prosperous lot. The Gujarati and Marwari businessmen who controlled the trade between the coastal towns and North India were extremely wealthy and spent large sums for the construction of temples. The Multanis who were Hindus and the Khurasanis who were Muslim foreigners controlled the trade with Central and West Asia. Many of these Multanis and Khurasanis settled in Delhi where they lived luxurious lives. Cambay was also home to an affluent mercantile community.

Thus India had always enjoyed a favourable balance in her trade relations with other countries. Her earnings from the export of textiles, sugar, spices and indigo alone went up to crores of rupees. The state coffers were amply stocked with gold and silver.

The Decline in Prosperity

However, the political conditions in India in the 18th century brought about a sea change in the situation. This period was marked by decline of the Mughal government and the rise of the Maratha power. After Aurangzeb, who was the last of the great Mughal Emperors, the state crumbled and it could not protect the mercantile community as before. Though the regional powers did extend patronage to the artisans and manufacturers, they did not have the economic and military means to sustain it. Consequently trade dwindled. The Maratha invasions in northern India also adversely affected trade and commerce.

The rise of the British East India Company in the mid 18th century dealt a fatal blow to the prosperity of the country. The victory of the English over the Nawab of Bengal at the Battle of Plassey in 1757 marked a turning point in the fortunes of the country. In order to disrupt the trade relations between the Indian mercantile community and the foreigners, the Company imposed heavy duties on both imports and exports. After the Company had established its supremacy in Bengal, it prevented merchants from Asian countries from coming to the eastern provinces for trading purposes. The export of Indian textiles to England was totally banned.

The Company increasingly monopolised the foreign trade in India thereby reducing the mercantile community to bankruptcy. Not only did it cripple the indigenous manufactures, but also it started importing various items such as cloth, utensils, horses, etc. from England. This so adversely affected the Indian traders that they turned to other professions for their livelihood. The great trading community, which had flourished during the Mughal rule, had dwindled to non-existence by the end of the eighteenth century. Thus the once glorious arts and crafts of India died a natural death.

The Seventeenth-Century Economy

Interpretations based upon the westernisation and the Marxian approaches tend to start from an assumption of an autonomous and stagnant precolonial society that was, with the imposition of colonialism in the nineteenth century, suddenly subjected to the powerful exogenous forces of Western education and capitalism. Recent historical scholarship, however, has thrown into doubt any static conception of the "traditional" Indian economy. Frank Perlin, a leading figure in this reconsideration, has argued: "India, like Europe, was affected by profound and rapid change in the character of its societies and economies, and state forms, from at least the sixteenth century... a fundamental aspect of that development was a local merchant capitalism which emerged independently of that in Europe, but within a common international theatre of societal and commercial changes." By the early Mughal period, a highly developed commercial system had taken shape in South Asia, one characterised by a number of features once thought to be associated only with modern capitalism: considerable agricultural production for the market, the penetration of merchants and traders into the agrarian economy, the manufacture of large volumes of luxury and nonluxury textiles for domestic and international consumption, a sophisticated monetary system, and extensive trading networks integrating the sub-continent with West Asia, Southeast Asia, China, and Europe.

Located on the western Indian coast in the southern portion of Gujarat-an especially important region of trade and industrial production-Surat was a critical centre in this international economy (see map 1). An indigenous commercial economy, with a history that predated the arrival of the first ships of the English East India Company, thrived in the city. The vibrancy of local commerce was readily apparent to all visitors. Ovington, a late seventeenth-century British traveller, wrote of Surat:

> *Surat is reckoned the most fam'd emporium of the Indian Empire, where all commodities are vendible, though they were never there seen before. The very curiosity of them will engage the expectation of the purchaser to sell them again with some advantage, and will be apt to invite some other by their novelty, as they did him, to venture upon them. And the river is very commodious for the importation of foreign goods, which are brought up to the city in hoys and yachts, and country boats, with great convenience and expedition. And not only from Europe, but from China, Persia, Arabia, and other remote parts of India, ships unload abundance of all kinds of goods, for the ornament of the city, as well as the enriching of the port.*

Under Mughal rule, which began in 1573, Surat replaced Cambay as Gujarat's premier commercial centre. By the seventeenth century the population of the city had expanded to somewhere between 200,000 and 400,000. New neighbourhoods, peopled by artisans and petty traders, sprang up outside the older settlements which had clustered close to the river's edge. As travellers' accounts attest, the city quickly developed its compact, congested, even unsanitary character while becoming India's most important commercial outlet.

By the high point of the Mughal Empire, the city was the hub of a great number of important trade routes: roads and coastal waterways that linked the port with the manufacturing centres of Bharuch, Cambay, and Ahmedabad within Gujarat; the more extended routes along the coastline of the sub-continent to Bengal in the east, Malabar in the south, and Sindh in the west; the overland cart paths to the Mughal heartland in northern India; and overseas routes in the Indian Ocean, particularly to the Persian Gulf and the Red Sea, but also to eastern Africa and Southeast Asia, China, and Japan. Traders based in Surat played critical integrating roles through much of this vast network, coordinating production by artisan family firms, selling commodities through their agents located in all the major cities of India and in numerous commercial centres overseas, and purchasing goods to channel back through the port. Gujarati shippers, mostly Muslims, transported both luxury items and goods for ordinary consumption to international markets in vessels that rivalled the European ships in trade if not in battle. The credit notes (hundi's) of local merchant bankers (sharaf's) which were honoured all over the sub-continent, made possible substantial transactions between towns in India and with ports overseas without large initial cash outlays. Surat's merchants also penetrated into the countryside of South Gujarat as moneylenders and tax-farmers and as traders in the agrarian produce of the region.

With this expansion in business activity came the development of powerful mercantile elites. Merchant princes such as Virji Vohra, a Jain trader and banker during the mid-seventeenth century, and Abdul Ghafar, a Sunni Bohra shipper at the turn of the eighteenth century, were probably among the world's wealthiest persons. They and a few dozen other traders and bankers who had benefited from domestic and international commerce under Mughal rule held a dominant position not only in the economy but also in important areas of the city's social life. As the research of Ashin Das Gupta has demonstrated, the business elite of Surat and Gujarat came from vastly differing social backgrounds. Indian merchants included Brahmans, Hindu and Jain Vaniyas, Muslims (both Shia and Sunni), and Parsis. But foreign traders from Armenia, Arabia, Turkey, Europe, and other distant lands also lived in Surat and participated in its commerce during the seventeenth century.

Despite this sophisticated commercial order, the local economy hardly fit the image of an order built upon the free, amoral exchange that supposedly goes hand in hand with capitalism. A striking feature of economic organisation in the city was the way in which strong social relationships grounded in indigenous moral conceptions intersected with and bolstered trading and production relations. For artisans and traders, both big and small, the joint family served as the basic economic unit. Caste was also essential to the structuring of economic life. It was not uncommon for entire trades to be dominated by particular castes or communities which tried to ward off outside competitors and employed social sanctions to reinforce business agreements. In lines of commerce involving a number of communities these same functions could be performed by guild-like organisations known as mahajan's, which set rules for conducting business, fixed holidays, and established prices and wages for artisans, but which also exercised religious functions, such as building temples and rest houses for Hindu and Jain pilgrims. Such communities of trust often provided much-needed security against the risks of rapidly fluctuating markets, business agreements not backed by legally enforceable contracts, and the provision of finance by individual bankers rather than by impersonal institutions.

Particularly critical to commercial and financial dealings in Surat and in its larger trading networks were perceptions of the reputability of the transacting partners. Merchants frequently conducted their trade as much on the basis of their abru as on their material resources. Even more than its English equivalent, credit, the word abru suggested a family firm's reputation for honouring its agreements and its more general status within urban society. The significance of abru to the commerce of the city is most apparent in the operations of the great sharaf's. The credit of individual merchant bankers was essential to the acceptance of their hundi's in trading centres not only in Surat itself but also elsewhere in the Mughal Empire and in the ports of the Persian Gulf and Red Sea. If these hundi's had lost their viability, then the merchants who carried them would have been unable to make their purchases, and the whole trading network could have collapsed. According to one local saying, the credit of Atmaram Bhukan, an especially prominent eighteenth-century banker of Surat, was so great that even if his hundi's were tied to the branches of a tree, they would still be accepted. Credit also affected the willingness of traders to deposit funds with a banker, as local merchants confirmed in an eighteenth-century petition to the East India Company:

The entire belief that property is perfectly secure in the house of a shroff [sharaf] forms what is called his credit which more than his actual money is the instrument of his dealing and the greater source of his profits. Those who come to trade in this city either bring their bills on the shroffs or lodge the produce of their goods with them during their stay from many parts of India... for all these sums deposited, no receipts are given, the books of the shroffs and the opinion of their faith and substance are the total dependence of the people who deal with them.

As we shall see in the next chapter, opinions of the "faith and substance" of individual merchants were established not in their business dealings alone, but also in patterns of religious giving and the exercise of moral leadership in the community.

Even in the organisation of local industry, business relations were often built around preexisting social ties. Most historians tend to agree that joint-family artisan firms exploiting chiefly family labour and producing in the home were the basic units of industrial activity. Textiles usually were manufactured in distinct steps performed in different workshops by different semiautonomous artisans rather than in larger operations under a single roof supervised by a single industrialist.

Specific caste groupings tended to control the labour in specific stages of the overall process, thus providing group members with some protection against outside competition. Most artisans, however, lacked sufficient knowledge of market conditions and were too vulnerable to the frequent changes in demand to participate in commercial activity directly without seriously endangering the survival of their firms. Usually they relied upon local merchants-with whom they often developed long-standing relationships-for the supply of capital, either in the form of cash advances or of raw materials. These merchants offered low payments to their artisan clients but often provided work during slack periods. Thus, to use Goren Hyden's term, there existed in the domestic manufactures an "economy of affection," in which production relations overlapped strongly with non-economic social bonds. The moral economy of domestic manufacture allowed local artisans and merchants alike to bear better the risks of participation in the unstable market conditions of the precolonial period.

All this suggests special problems with social science models that have viewed joint-family, caste, community, and patron-client relations as "precapitalist" or "feudal" social forms at odds with market-oriented economies. Certainly precolonial is a more satisfactory label. But the perpetuation of these forms after 1800 suggests that, even in using this alternative terminology, we must avoid any teleological reasoning that would suggest the incompatibility of these structures with the altered economic circumstances of colonialism. Under British rule, many precolonial institutions and relations adapted to changes in the larger world rather than disintegrated. Thus, even in the midst of a decaying city, an economy that relied on relationships of affection and trust continued to sustain itself.

Euro-Asian Encounter in the Early Modern Period

The process of decolonisation that the immediate post-World War II period witnessed brought to an end one of the most outstanding-if also the most shameful-characteristic features of the modern age. This was the domination of one people over another generally referred to as colonialism. In its economic dimension, colonialism assumed an extremely important role in determining the nature and the rate of economic growth both in the metropolitan as well as in the colonised world in the nineteenth and the first half of the twentieth century. This served to considerably widen the gap between the income levels and the standard of economic performance generally between the developed countries of the west on the one hand and the underdeveloped countries of the Third World *viz.* Asia, Africa and Latin America on the other.

According to Angus Maddison, one hundred and fifty years ago, the gap in mean per capita share of gross domestic product between the richest and the poorest global regions, namely Western Europe and Africa, was probably three to one. Today this gap between a rich country such as Switzerland and a poor country such as Mozambique is a mind-boggling four hundred to one. To what extent colonialism has or has not been directly or indirectly responsible for this state of affairs has been a subject of intense debate over the last half a century or so. This lecture is not about this debate although some of the issues raised by it will indeed be commented upon. What this lecture will seek to do is to analyse the relationship between Europe and Asia where many countries eventually became the victims of colonialism. The analysis will be confined to the early modern period *viz.* the period from the sixteenth to the eighteenth centuries. In the main, this period formed the backdrop to the phase of the formal colonial relationship between countries in the two continents, although as we shall see there were cases where monopsonistic and monopolistic privileges were sought and obtained by the Europeans in Asia and even formal territorial control established in parts of the continent during this early period. Though economic relationship was by no means the only vehicle of contact between the two continents, the lecture will be confined to this relationship.

Asian Maritime Trade in the Pre-European Period

The history of economic contacts between Europe and Asia goes back into antiquity. Fairly regular commercial contacts are known to have flourished during the days of the Roman Empire. The precise strength and range of these contacts until about the early part of the second millennium A.D., however, remain somewhat obscure. But there can be very little doubt that the rise of long distance Asian maritime trade stretching from Gombroon in the Persian Gulf to Nagasaki in Japan along what I have elsewhere described as the great arc of Asian trade had important implications for the value as well as the composition of the water-cumland trade between west Asia and southern Europe via the Mediterranean. In Asian maritime trade, by far the longest distance was covered by the route that connected Aden to Canton.

There is evidence to suggest that this route was in regular use at least from the seventh century. The principal group which had initiated trade on the route was the Persian merchants who had, however, been supplanted by and large by Arab merchants since about the ninth century. The principal stops on the way were either Cambay or Calicut on the Indian west coast and a port such as Palembang in Sumatra. It would seem that at some time during the twelfth century Chinese junks also began operating on this route in an important way. There is evidence that the Chinese merchants established commercial contacts with places such as Sri Lanka, Kollam on the Malabar coast and Hurmuz in the Persian Gulf. The Chinese participation in trade on this route would appear to have reached important levels by the early years of the fifteenth century. Between 1404 and 1433, a series of seven commercial-cum-naval expeditions was dispatched from China under the command of Admiral Cheng Ho. The first of these expeditions is believed to have consisted of as many as 62 ships and 28,000 men.

The fourth voyage is reported to have reached Hurmuz and Aden, while those that followed claimed to have touched even the East African ports of Mogadishu and Malindi. But in 1433 the Chinese authorities abruptly withdrew from these ventures and, indeed, there is no record of these long-distance voyages having ever been resumed. In the meantime, the Arabs had also gradually pulled out of this long-distance route.

Whatever the reasons behind the Chinese and the Arab withdrawal from long-distance trade, it signalled a basic alteration in the organisational structure of Asian trade. The new structure was based on the segmentation of the great arc of Asian trade into three divisions-the Arabian Sea, the Bay of Bengal and the South China Sea. The ports of Cambay or Calicut and Malacca (founded at the beginning of the fifteenth century), which had until then served essentially as victualling and stopping points on the long route between west Asia and China, now became terminal ports. The role of these ports in providing a reasonably assured market in the goods brought in, as well as in making available those sought after by the visiting ships, besides offering facilities such as anchorage, ware-housing and banking, cannot be overemphasized. In the course of the fifteenth century, Malacca became a truly major centre of international exchange and a meeting point of traders from the East and the West. Increasingly, the participation of the Arab merchants became confined to the trade between west Asia and the west coast of India. This left the trade between the west and the east coasts of India on the one hand, and the eastern Indian Ocean region on the other, almost exclusively in the hands of Indians-the Gujaratis more than anyone else, but also the Chettis, the Chulias and other groups from the Coromandel coast, besides the Oriyas and the Bengalis.

The participation of the Chinese merchants was now restricted by and large to controlling the trade between China and Malacca, while the Indonesian and the Malay merchants hardly seem to have ventured beyond the inter-island and the port-to-port trade in the Malay-Indonesian region. In sum, Indian merchants from different regions of the country constituted an important trading group operating in the Ocean.

It is true that the ships that left Cambay for Malacca each year included many owned and operated by Arab, Persian, Turkish and other merchants from west Asia, but all these groups together were overshadowed by the Gujaratis who controlled the bulk of the trade on the route. The goods that the Malacca-bound ships leaving Cambay carried were, in part, coloured woollen clothes and glassware from the Mediterranean, and items such as rosewater, opium, indigo and silver from west Asia. But a large part of the cargo would seem to have consisted of textiles manufactured in Gujarat-mainly of coarse cotton, though more expensive varieties including those manufactured from fine-quality cotton and silk also seem to have figured in the list. The cargo obtained in exchange at Malacca included Chinese goods such as silk and porcelain, Indonesian spices such as pepper, cloves, nutmeg and mace, besides woods and aromatics, and precious and nonprecious metals such as Malayan tin. In addition to Malacca, the Gujarati ships from Cambay called at ports such as Aceh, Kedah, Tenasserim/Mergui and Pegu. The goods carried to these ports were broadly similar to those carried to Malacca: the goods brought back were largely of local origin, rather than cosmopolitan as in the case of Malacca. A part of the large conglomerate of goods brought to Cambay was obviously destined for consumption in Gujarat, as well as the large north Indian hinterland supplied by it. But a good proportion would seem to have been re-exported mainly to west Asia, the most important ports in the region at this time being Aden and Jeddah. The other important constituent of the cargo to west Asia was textiles manufactured in Gujarat.

These were predominantly those manufactured from coarse cotton and intended for mass consumption, though superior varieties manufactured from fine cotton and silk also figured in the list. The route from Cambay to Aden would seem to have been dominated by the Arab, Persian and other west Asian merchants though the Gujarati merchants also operated on this route in an important way.

The Indonesian spices and other items imported from Cambay into Aden and other west Asian ports found their way in significant quantities, in addition to the markets of west Asia, to Europe via the Mediterranean. The two routes used for the purpose were those via the Red Sea and the Persian Gulf. While the Red Sea route terminated at the Egyptian port of Alexandria on the southern coast of the Mediterranean and involved only a small stretch of overland transportation, the Persian Gulf route made use of the Tigris or the Euphrates rivers and a fair amount of caravan transportation across Iraq and the Syrian desert. Important among the Mediterranean destination ports on this route were Tripoli (of Syria) and Beirut. This traffic was handled exclusively by the west Asian merchants.

At the Mediterranean ports, the goods were procured mainly by the merchants from Venice and Genoa. While both the Red Sea and the Persian Gulf routes had been in use since antiquity, the relative amount of traffic on either at any given point in time depended partly on political circumstances. While during the eighth and the ninth centuries the Persian Gulf route was the dominant one, the decline of the Abbasid caliphate and the rise of the Fatimids of Egypt tilted the balance from the eleventh century onward significantly in favour of the Red Sea route. This was also the period which witnessed a significant expansion in the volume of Euro-Asian trade. Evidence from the end of the fourteenth and the early years of the fifteenth century suggests that volume-wise the Alexandria trade was considerably larger than-nearly double on average-the one via Beirut. However, since the latter handled the expensive spices much more, the difference between the two ports was much smaller in terms of value.

Rise of an Early Modern World Economy

In a well-known passage in his An Enquiry into the Nature and Causes of the Wealth of Nations, Adam Smith, the father of modern economic science, argued that "the discovery of America and that of a passage to the East Indies by the Cape of Good Hope are the two greatest and most important events recorded in the history of mankind." While there clearly is an element of exaggeration in this statement, it nevertheless underscores the critical role of the two events in the emergence of an early modern world economy.

The three principal segments of this economy, namely Europe, the New World, and Asia effectively came together in an interactive fashion for the first time directly as a result of the great discoveries of the last decade of the fifteenth century. The New World was discovered for the first time. As for Asia, what the discovery of the all-water route via the Cape of Good Hope achieved was the overcoming of the transport technology barrier to the growth of the Euro-Asian trade. The volume of this trade was no longer subject to the capacity constraint imposed by the availability of pack animals and river boats in the Middle East. It was indeed a critically important coincidence that the discovery of the Cape route and of the New World took place almost simultaneously. For without the enormous quantities of American silver reaching Europe through the sixteenth century, the enhanced trading opportunities between Europe and Asia opened up by the Cape route would essentially have been frustrated.

Euro-Asian trade had traditionally been one involving the exchange of Asian luxury and other goods basically against European silver and, to a smaller extent, gold. The 'bullion for goods' pattern of trade was an outcome of the inability of Europe to supply goods that could be sold in Asia in reasonably large quantities at competitive terms. Europe at this time had an undoubted overall superiority over Asia in the field of scientific and technological knowledge, but not as yet the distinct cost advantage that came with the Industrial Revolution in the late eighteenth and nineteenth centuries. This put the Asian, and particularly the Indian producers, with their considerably lower labour costs and a much longer history of sophisticated skills in handicrafts of various kinds, in a position of advantage over their European counterparts in the production of a variety of manufactured goods. As a result, Europe really had no option but to pay for the Asian goods overwhelmingly in terms of precious metals.

Ever since the fourteenth century or so, the output of precious metals in Europe had by and large been stagnant raising fears of deflationary tendencies cropping up. This, coupled with the bullionist inhibitions regarding the export of precious metals, would almost certainly have created a situation where the non-availability of significant additional quantities of precious metals for export to the East would by and large have rendered the opportunities opened up by the availability of the Cape route quite redundant. It is in this context that one must appreciate the critical significance of the two great discoveries-that of the New World and of the Cape route to the East Indies-having taken place almost simultaneously. It is from this time onward that one can legitimately speak of the emergence of an early modern world economy embracing in an organic and interactive manner all three of its principal components, namely the New World, Europe, and Asia.

The Portuguese Estado Da India

The Spice Monopoly

Since the Cape route had been discovered by the Portuguese, they immediately monopolised it and even got the Pope to legitimise the arrangement. Was their trade on this route a net addition to the Euro-Asian trade in spices and other goods or did it represent largely a diversion of the trade along the long-established watercum-land route via the Mediterranean? There is very little doubt that in the early years of the sixteenth century the Portuguese policies were indeed instrumental in spelling almost a total disaster for the trade along the old route. The attempt at monopolising the spice trade was unambiguous. It called for a total exclusion of Asian shipping from the Persian Gulf and the Red Sea: the instructions to Pedro Alvares Cabral, in charge of the first major commercial voyage to India that left Lisbon in March 1500, included the initiation of steps designed at blockading the passage to the Red Sea. The rest of the Asian trade would be regulated to exclude trade in spices. The instrument used to implement this policy was the cartaz, a safe-conduct that all Asian ships were obliged to carry on pain of seizure in the event of non-compliance.

The document obliged the Asian ship to call at a Portuguese controlled port and, following the establishment of the Portuguese customs houses there, to pay customs duties before it proceeded on its voyage. Enemies of the Portuguese and banned goods such as spices were not to be carried. There is some evidence that an equivalent of the cartaz existed in the Asian seas before the arrival of the Portuguese, but there can be little doubt that the scale on which this restrictive measure was used by the Portuguese was unprecedented. The measure indeed represented an institutional constraint on the freedom of navigation on the high seas.

The policy of exclusion of the merchants from Calicut, Cambay and other ports on the west coast of India from the Red Sea and the Persian Gulf was highly successful. Hurmuz at the entrance to the Persian Gulf was captured in 1515: the failure to capture Aden was made up for by the dispatch each season from Goa of a fleet to lie off the entrance to the Red Sea, usually cruising between Aden and Bab-el-Mandeb and returning to Hurmuz in

April. Raids on departing fleets at Calicut were common and the result was practically a ruination of the spice trade with the Persian Gulf and the Red Sea. It was reported as early as 1504 that the Venetian galleys calling there found no spices at either Alexandria or Beirut. Two years prior to that, concerned at the loss of the substantial revenues that the spice trade used to bring him, the Mamluk of Egypt had sought the good offices of the Pope to try and dissuade the Portuguese from choking the flow of spices through the Red Sea!

The dislocation in the spice trade, however, proved only temporary. By the second decade of the sixteenth century cracks had already begun to appear in the Portuguese system. A series of circumstances combined to produce this result. A key element in the situation was the financial priorities and compulsions of the Estado da India. Given the rather precarious state of the finances of this body, it was imperative that no opportunity of taxing Asian shipping by making it call and pay duties at Portuguese controlled ports such as Malacca, Goa and Diu be missed. Hurmuz, taken in 1515, was one such strategically located port. Pepper and other spices passing through the port and destined for consumption within west Asia posed no problem: the choice between tax revenue and the cost of the infringement of the European monopoly arose only in respect of that part of the cargo which would eventually reach Venice or Genoa via Aleppo. The choice was made in favour of the tax revenue and, as Niels Steensgaard has suggested, between 1524 and 1543 an average of 90,000 xerafins was earned as customs duties per annum at Hurmuz. Steensgaard's characterisation of the Portuguese enterprise as 'redistributive' in character has in part at its base such parasitical siphoning off of a part of the profits of Asian trade. Another circumstance that prompted the Portuguese to allow pepper shipments to pass Hurmuz was the desire to earn the goodwill of Persia against an increasingly aggressive Ottoman empire. Whatever the motivation, the Portuguese decision involved a diversion of the spice trade from the Aden-Cairo-Alexandria axis to the Basra-Baghdad-Aleppo axis.

But that diversion was strictly temporary, and from the late 1530s onward the Red Sea spice trade began to revive. After an initial vigorous and successful phase, the Portuguese blockade of the Bab-el-Mandeb became increasingly ineffective for a variety of reasons. For one thing, considerations of strategy as well as of economics often obliged the Portuguese authorities to issue a limited number of cartazes for the Red Sea ports. Thus, as early as 1515 Albuquerque found it necessary to grant the Samudri raja a certain number of cartazes for the merchants based at his port, enabling them to resume trade with Aden and Jeddah. On other occasions, a similar concession was extended to other puppet rulers. Important business associates such as Khwaja Shams-uddin Gilani as well as merchants providing credit to the Estado had to be similarly accommodated. In some cases, such as in that of Gilani, trade in pepper was explicitly permitted, while in most others the understanding was that pepper would continue to be treated as a prohibited article. But for all practical purposes, the distinction made little difference and nearly all ships going to the region carried pepper legitimately or clandestinely. And then, of course, there was the trade in pepper carried on by various categories of the Portuguese in contravention of the official policy.

The network of this trade included the Red Sea and there was very little the Portuguese official machinery was able to do about it. It needs to be emphasized that the Estado simply lacked the resources in men and ships to sustain an effective blockade of the Red Sea year after year. The only area in which the Portuguese were reasonably successful was in preventing ships from Malabar from going to the Red Sea. But shipping from Kanara and the Bay of Bengal continued to carry Indian pepper to the Red Sea from the late 1530s and the early 1540s onward, mainly through the agency of the Gujarat merchants. It seems that considering the expense and the poor rate of success, the Portuguese abandoned the Red Sea expeditions around 1569, clearing the way for a full-fledged revival of the Red Sea traffic in pepper. C.R. Boxer, who has traced this revival, is of the opinion that the volume of Aceh pepper reaching Jeddah at the end of the sixteenth century was larger than what the Portuguese were taking to Lisbon by the Cape route.

The Procurement of Pepper

In keeping with the traditional composition of the Asian imports into Europe, the principal item sought by the Portuguese Crown in Asia was spices-overwhelmingly pepper-though some other goods were also procured. Throughout the sixteenth century, an overwhelming proportion of the pepper imported into Lisbon was procured on the southwest coast of India where the first purchases were made at Calicut on the Malabar coast where Vasco da Gama had landed.

But relations with the pardesi merchants of the town as well as the samudri raja deteriorated fast. The conflict with the merchants had its origin mainly in the Portuguese insistence on being provided with pepper before the Red Sea merchants had been served. The Portuguese attack on a sambuk was retaliated by their factory being looted which, in turn, led to an attack on the port and a bombardment of the town in 1501 that lasted for two days.

The era of peaceful trading which, occasional instances of violence notwithstanding, had been the norm in the Asian waters for centuries, had finally been shattered by the Portuguese. At any rate, it was found more expedient to shift the centre of pepper procurement to Cochin where the more cooperative Mappila and the Syrian Christian merchants were used as brokers and intermediaries. With the aid of the dependent raja of Cochin, the Portuguese tried to establish a monopoly in pepper there. But since the raja had no real control over the areas where pepper was grown or over the routes used for its transportation, the monopoly never really worked in any effective sense. At his own level, of course, the raja provided all help by giving protection to the river boats bringing pepper to Cochin, by guaranteeing loans raised by the Portuguese from private sources, as well as by providing loans himself. The friendly relationship between the Estado and the Mappila merchants at Cochin, however, did not last very long. By the end of the third decade of the century, the merchants had declared a holy war-jihad-against the Estado. This hostility continued in one form or another into the seventeenth century.

The procurement of pepper in India was organized by the Estado while the sales in Europe were through contract sales based until the middle of the century at Antwerp and thereafter in Lisbon. The liquidity problems of the Portuguese Crown forced a major reorganization of the trade with Asia in 1564 when the first of a series of contracts giving over trade on the Cape route to private parties was concluded. The remaining part of the century witnessed a variety of experiments being carried out in an attempt to identify the optimal strategy that would ensure to the Crown maximum monopoly revenue without obliging it to be directly involved in the conduct of the trade with Asia. In 1570, the trade in pepper and other spices was opened to free competition, although the Crown also continued to participate in the trade itself and retained its monopoly on the export of precious metals to Asia. The Asian contract system was introduced in 1575.

The first beneficiary of the new arrangement was the Augsburg merchant Konrad Rott and associates who included the Milanese merchant Giovanni Batista Rovalesca. Under this arrangement, Rott received intact the royal monopoly of the Cape route-the procurement of spices in Asia, their shipment to Europe, the provisioning of the carracks in Lisbon and Goa, and the distribution of pepper in Europe. Just before his death in 1580, dom Henrique renewed the Rott-Rovalesca contract for another five years. Each year, the contractors were supposed to purchase in India a total of 30,000 quintals of pepper-15,000 on their own account and 15,000 on the Crown's account. The contractors were free to sell their half of the pepper as they chose; the Crown would also sell all of its 15,000 quintals (which cost it nothing) to the Rott-Rovalesca consortium at 32 cruzados per quintal.

The consortium thus enjoyed exclusive European distribution of Portuguese pepper. A sharp decline in the European price of pepper, however, forced Rott out of business. In February 1586, a new Asian contract was concluded for a period of six years with Rovalesca in association with Giraldo Paris. This group was required to supply to the Crown 30,000 quintals of pepper per annum at a price of 16 cruzados per quintal. The Casa da India sold the pepper to the European contractors at prices negotiated each year in Lisbon. The contract system continued until 1598 when following the English and Dutch intervention in the seaborne spice trade, private enterprise was no longer willing to take up the pepper contracts. In any event, the experiment with the contract system had not been particularly satisfactory for either side. The syndicates were consistently unable to import the quantities specified in the contracts and never managed to make adequate profits. The bankruptcy of Rott has already been noted: his Milanese counterpart Rovalesca was also forced to follow suit.

Redistributive Enterprise

Given the manner in which the Portuguese Crown dealt with the matter of the procurement, the transportation, and particularly the disposal of the Asian pepper in the European market, the

Danish historian, Niels Steensgaard, characterised the Portuguese Euro-Asian pepper trade as a redistributive enterprise. As he so succinctly put it, "the Portuguese pepper monopoly was not a business but a custom house." He had then gone on to contrast this with the productivity enhancing nature of the northern European companies'-particularly the Dutch East India Company's-trading operations between the two continents from the beginning of the seventeenth century onward. The success of the companies was based not upon government monopolies or the use of violence but on their ability to compete in the market. For by adopting specific policies in relation to stocks, pricing and the mode of the disposal of their goods, the companies made impressive gains in the transparency and the predictability of the markets in which they operated. This is essence constituted what Steensgaard described as the Asian Trade Revolution of the early seventeenth century. While certain key elements in Steensgaard's formulation continue to be valid, the overall characterisation of a redistributive enterprise for the entire Portuguese trading operations both between Europe and Asia as well as those within Asia is probably in need of revision. This is partly because the companies were not quite as devoid of the use of monopoly and violence as Steensgaard's model in a pure form would seem to imply. More importantly, we now know that the Portuguese enterprise was indeed very much more than a simple Euro-Asian trade in pepper, the commodity mainly responsible for the characterisation of the trade as redistributive in nature.

It is, therefore, important to keep the matter in perspective and not overstate the redistributive dimensions of the Portuguese Asian enterprise in its entirety. Pepper was indeed the raison d'etre of the Portuguese Euro-Asian trade in the beginning accounting in the first two decades of the sixteenth century for as much as 95 percent of the total Asian cargo imported in physical terms and 85 percent in value terms. However, the situation changed considerably from the 1580s onward with the physical share of pepper coming down to 68 percent during 1587-88, to 65 percent during 1600-03 with an increase to 69 percent during 1608-10. More importantly, a recent study by James Boyajian suggests a dramatic decline in the proportion of pepper to total Portuguese imports over the period 1580-1640 to a mere 10 percent. According to him, by far the most important item of import during this period was cotton and silk textiles accounting for as much as 62 percent of the total value imported, followed by precious stones (14 percent) indigo (6 percent) and spices other than pepper (5 percent). If pepper accounted for no more than 10 percent of the total imports from Asia, the redistributive dimension of the Portuguese Euro-Asian trade as viewed from the European end would assume a very different quantitative profile from that suggested by Niels Steensgaard. At the heart of Boyajian's analysis is his almost revolutionary revision of current orthodoxy in the matter of the relative role of the private Portuguese traders in the Euro-Asian carreira traded over the period. It has traditionally been conceded that the carreira ships did indeed carry on a regular basis a certain amount of private cargo under a variety of arrangements. The novelty of Boyajian's estimates consists in his view of the magnitude of the private cargoes carried abroad these ships overwhelmingly on the account of the New Christian merchants who were descendants of Iberian Jews forcibly converted to Christianity at the end of the fifteenth century. According to Boyajian, private cargoes accounted for an almost unbelievable 93 percent of the total value imported over the period 1580-1640 from Asia. Certain methodological problems with the Boyajian estimates do indeed raise questions about the precise extent of the private Portuguese merchants' trade between Europe and Asia. But there can be little doubt that the significant upward revision of the overall role of these merchants in Euro-Asian trade is in the right direction. This would considerably erode the redistributive dimension of the pepper trade at the European end.

Portuguese Intra-Asian Trade

What about the Asian end of the Portuguese trading operations as an element in the redistributive potential of these operations? We have already seen that the Estado da India's attempt at monopolizing the Indian Ocean spice trade was short-lived. In respect of the bulk of the remainder of the trading activity carried on by the Portuguese either on an official or on a private basis, there was no component of a redistributive enterprise whatever. The Estado itself engaged in a certain amount of trade within Asia, mainly in the Bay of Bengal with Malacca as the principal point of origin and termination of voyages. In the decade of 1511-20, the Fazenda Real (or royal treasury) carried out a number of exploratory commercial voyages and a whole series of crown routes (carreiras) was created. This was done in close cooperation with the Keling merchant community of Malacca, whose doyen at the time was one Nina Chatu. The cooperation often took the form of ventures undertaken jointly by the Crown and Nina Chatu. One such venture was the voyage of the Sao Joao which left Malacca for Martaban in Burma in August 1512, returning in May 1513. The same ship was then sent to Pulicat, again in partnership with Nina Chatu. However, for a variety of reasons, the period over which the involvement of the Portuguese Crown as an entrepreneur in Intra-Asian trade lasted was comparatively brief. The phase of the Crown involvement in Intra-Asian trade was followed from the second half of the sixteenth century onward by a fairly intensive participation in this trade by private Portuguese traders, many of whom were at the same time employees of the Estado. Another major group of private traders participating in Intra-Asian trade was that of the New Christian merchants, also using this channel to obtain a variety of Asian goods for transportation to Lisbon abroad the carreira ships as private cargo. A large number of the private traders operated on the basis of the so-called 'concession' system introduced in the 1550s. This system was essentially in the nature of a benefice conferred by the Crown mainly on the so-called casado merchants. A concession conferred on the grantee the right to make a voyage between two specified ports in the Indian Ocean and/or the China Sea. By the 1580s, the concession system had become a major component of the Portuguese trading network in Asia. Luis Thomaz has listed a total of 34 concession voyages in operation in the 1580s covering the China sea, the Indonesian archipelago, and the Bay of Bengal.

The New Christian merchants of Goa invested in both the carreira da India as well as in Intra-Asian trade. Indeed, the profits from Intra-Asian trade financed a good part of the cargo that the New Christian merchants put on the carreira ships at Goa for Lisbon on their private account. In the 1580, Goa's merchants, according to Boyajian, shipped about 250,000 cruzados in silver and other goods each year to Macao on the China-Japan carracks. In return, they extracted from Japan more than 500,000 cruzados of silver annually, much of which returned to Goa and Cochin as silk, musk and porcelain and gold coin, after yet another exchange in Macao. A large part of this cargo eventually found its way to

Lisbon. This particular trading strategy anticipated in an important manner what the Dutch East India Company did on a much more elaborate scale and with a much greater degree of intensity in the seventeenth century.

A reference to the trading activities of the Dutch East India Company, which we shall analyse in some detail below, also serves to remind one that in so far as the Dutch monopoly of finer spices involved a gross under-payment to the producers in the Spice Islands, the label of redistributive enterprise would apply as much to this segment of the Dutch Company business as it would to the pepper trade of the Portuguese Crown. Indeed, Steensgaard himself recognizes this when he says, "the Dutch East India Company was not a 'pure' type: it contained features in its constitution, in its structure and its policy, more reminiscent of a redistributive enterprise than of a business." Again, the absence of the "use of violence" by the companies is a construct that poses problems. In its trade within Asia, the Dutch East India Company took extensive steps to obtain exclusive right in particular products and markets and minimize competition by indigenous merchants, making a judicious use of violence in the process. The Company also made an optimal use of the pass system to keep Asian competitors out of the trade in monopoly products such as spices and regulate their trade in several others, such as Malayan tin. If some violation of the prescribed policies and procedures, say by the Indian traders, was tolerated, it was only because the cost of unlimited conflict in the form of possible disruptions to its trade in the Indian sub-continent would have been unacceptably high for the Company.

If one goes beyond Steensgaard and defines the notion of "ability to compete" to include both belief and confidence in competitive trade, the sustained opposition of the English and the Dutch companies to the entry of rival European companies into Euro-Asian trade creates problems. The Dutch Company, for example, was clearly hostile to the first Danish expeditions of the 1610s and the early 1620s to India. The VOC's action in seizing two of the Genoese East India Company's vessels in the Sunda Straits in April 1649 was a clear example of the use of force to keep a potential competitor out, though ostensibly the step was taken because the vessels were carrying Dutch crews and merchants. Also, in the 1720s, the Dutch and the English companies successfully formed a coalition both in Europe as well as in Bengal to keep the newly formed Ostend Company out of the lucrative Bengal trade. It was basically the pressure by the two companies that led to the suspension and later the abolition of the Ostend Company. There, of course, was nothing they could do about the same set of merchants regrouping themselves under different nomenclatures. It is, therefore, imperative that the question of the differences between the policies followed by the Portuguese on the one hand, and by the Dutch and the English on the other, which certainly were by no means inconsiderable, be kept in perspective.

The Dutch and the English East India Companies

Even though the Asian Trade Revolution of the early seventeenth century consisted in the English and the Dutch East India companies being different from the Portuguese Estado only in a limited way, there nevertheless was another kind of Asian Trade Revolution under way at precisely the same time. This revolution consisted in an enormous expansion in the volume and value of seaborne Euro-Asian trade as well as a major diversification in the composition of the goods imported into Europe as well as the range of Asian sources where these goods were procured. A related development was the near-wiping out early in the seventeenth century of the water-cum-land route between the two continents that had been in use for centuries.

The Dutch East India was founded in 1602 by a charter granted by the States-General, the national administrative body of the Dutch Republic. The Euro-Asian trade carried on by the Portuguese was running into serious problems in the last quarter of the sixteenth century. This, coupled with the loss, in 1585, of Antwerp's position as the staple market for Asian goods in northwestern Europe as a result of the blockade of the Scheldt, gave the merchants from the northern Netherlands a strong incentive to challenge the Portuguese monopoly of the Cape route and participate directly in the Euro-Asian spice trade. The first stage was the establishment in the 1590s of a number of so-called 'precompanies', the most important of which was the one known as the 'Old Company'. It was on the account of this company that eight vessels were sent out to the East in 1598. The profit on the voyage was estimated at around 400 percent. Since the ships sent to the East on the individual account of different companies competed with each other fiercely, the inevitable result was an increase in the cost price of the pepper and other spices and a decline in their sale prices in the Netherlands. It was with a view to prevent such cutthroat competition that the various companies were merged together in March 1602 to form the United Dutch East India Company. The other major northwest European Company engaged in the Euro-Asian trade was the English East India Company. The great success attendant upon the venture of the Old Company of Amsterdam into the Euro-Asian trade had caused great consternation among the English merchants engaged in the spice trade from the Levant. The fear of the Dutch domination of the spice market in northwestern Europe thus served as the catalyst that led a group of London merchants to apply to the Crown for a monopoly charter for the East India trade. The request was granted and on 31 December 1600 was born the 'Company of Merchants of London trading into the East Indies'.

Initially, both the Dutch and the English concentrated on the procurement of pepper and other spices which, as in the sixteenth century, continued to account for an overwhelming proportion of the total Asian imports into Europe. But unlike, and indeed mainly because of, the Portuguese, the Dutch and the English procured their pepper in Indonesia rather than on the southwest coast of India. The result was a marked shift in the Asian loci of the Euro-Asian seaborne trade from India to the Indonesia archipelago. This was the Asian counterpart of the shift of the European loci of this trade from Lisbon to Amsterdam and London.

It was nearly three quarters of a century before the Asian loci shifted back to India in response to the change in European fashions assigning an increasingly important role to textiles and raw silk in the Asian imports into Europe.

In the case of the Dutch East India Company, for example, spices, including pepper, came down from an imposing 74 percent of the total imports in 1619-21 to 68 percent during 1648-50 and to a mere 23 percent during 1698-1700. On the other hand, textiles and raw silk went up from 16 percent in 1619-21 to an incredible 55 percent at the end of the seventeenth century. There was a decline thereafter, but in 1778-80 textiles and raw silk accounted for half of the total imports. Because of the smaller geographical range of the Asian operations of the English East India Company, goods procured in India accounted for an even greater proportion of the total Asian imports into England. At the end of the seventeenth century, this figure stood at as much as 95 percent and at 84 percent in 1738-40.

The Role of Bullion

The central characteristic feature of Euro-Asian trade, namely the necessity for the Europeans to pay for the Asian goods overwhelmingly in precious metals, however, remained unchanged throughout the entire period between the sixteenth and the eighteenth centuries. This particular phenomenon has sometimes been ascribed to the rigidity of consumer tastes in the East, which rendered the Asian markets for European goods extremely small and static. Alternatively, it has been suggested that the absorption of precious metals by India or China reflected the hoarding habits in these societies. But as pointed out earlier, a more convincing explanation of this phenomenon is the inability of Europe to supply western products with a potential market in Asia at prices that would generate a large enough demand for them to provide the necessary revenue for the purchase of the Asian goods. The only major item Europe was in a position to provide to Asia was precious metals.

The growth of the Euro-Asian trade, therefore, was critically dependent upon an increase in the availability of these metals. In this context, the working of the South American silver mines and the enormous import of American silver into Europe during the sixteenth and the early seventeenth centuries was a development of critical significance.

Although the American silver initially arrived into Spain, a large part of it eventually found its way to Amsterdam, mainly via Hamburg. In fact, from the early years of the seventeenth century the Dutch were the undoubted masters of the European bullion trade and Amsterdam the leading world centre of the trade in precious metals. It is an indication of the international standing of this city as a market for precious metals that the English East India Company also obtained a large part of its requirements of these metals in Amsterdam. An analysis of the Dutch and the English East India companies' exports to the East Indies over the seventeenth and the eighteenth centuries testifies to an unambiguous pattern where precious metals dominated the total exports throughout the period. An important implication of this 'bullion for goods' model of Euro-Asian trade was that as far as the Europeans were concerned, the profit from the trade was derived almost entirely from the sale of Asian goods in Europe rather than also from the sale of European goods in Asia.

Dutch Intra-Asian Trade

If India was at the centre of the European trading companies' Euro-Asian trade, it was equally central to the extensive amount of trade the Europeans, both the corporate enterprises as well as private traders, carried on within Asia using the Indian Ocean-South China Sea trading network. The critical role played by India was as much a function of her capacity to provide cost-competitive manufactured goods-predominantly cotton and other textiles-in the case of the Europeans engaged in Intra-Asian trade, as it had been traditionally in the case of the Indian and other Asian merchants similarly engaged in this trade. The principal European corporate enterprise engaged in Intra-Asian trade in a substantial manner and as an integral part of its overall trading strategy, namely the Dutch East India Company, got involved to this trade in the first place in order to procure Indian coarse cotton textiles at source. These textiles were the principal medium of exchange throughout the Malay Indonesian archipelago and it was nearly impossible for the Company to obtain supplies of pepper and other spices except in exchange for these textiles. While these textiles could have been procured within the region at places such as Aceh, the acute business instinct of the Company took it, within a few years of its arrival in Asia, to their source, the Coromandel coast and Gujarat. The large and assured availability of highly costcompetitive textiles in India with a large demand both in Southeast Asia and West Asia was thus the starting point of the Dutch East India Company's involvement in Intra-Asia trade, which eventually grew to a point where this branch of trade became of as much concern to the Company as its Euro-Asian trade. As early as 1612, Hendrik Brouwer, a future governor-general of the East Indies, had described the Coromandel coast as the "left arm of the Moluccas and the surrounding islands because without textiles that come from there, the trade in the Moluccas will be dead."

The three principal elements in the Dutch strategy of participation in Intra-Asian trade were Indian textiles and raw silk, Indonesian spices, and Japanese silver. The initial supply of investment funds brought in from Holland was invested first in

Indian textiles, a large part of which was then sold against spices. While a part of the spices was sent home, the remainder constituted, together with the remaining Indian textiles, the basis of entry into a number of branches of trade within Asia. Among the most prized of these was the trade with Japan, where nearly half of the value of the goods sent consisted of Indian textiles and raw silk. As of 1639, when the 'closed country' era began in Japan, the Dutch East India Company was the only European entity permitted to operate in the country, giving the Company a significant differential advantage over its rivals. This advantage lay in the large amount of silver, a critical input for the Indian and several other trading areas, that the Japan trade provided. Given the large and persistent differential in the gold-silver bi-metallic ratio between the two countries, it was highly advantageous for the Company to convert a large part of the Japanese silver it procured into gold at Taiwan. The Chinese gold could then be invested profitably in the procurement of textiles on the Coromandel coast, where the basic currency unit in use was the gold pagoda. The point to emphasize is that, by about the middle of the 17th century, the Dutch East India Company had become a major participant in Intra-Asian trade with trading links all along the great arc of Asian trade. Indian textiles, raw silk, and later opium, which turned out to be a highly profitable item, sold in large quantities all over the Indonesian archipelago, were among the key commodities in the Dutch Company's framework of Intra-Asian trade. Given the importance the Company attached to this trade, its employees were not allowed to engage in it on their individual account. That, however, did not prevent them from doing so on a fairly large scale on a clandestine basis. Indeed, in a high-value, low-bulk item such as opium which was ideal for contraband trade, the volume of the clandestine trade was often as large as that on the Company's own account.

Turning next to the English East India Company and the private English traders, one finds that while the involvement of the Company in Intra-Asian trade was negligible and confined essentially to the first half of the 17th century, private English traders based in India constituted by far the largest and the most enduring group of Europeans engaged in the trade of the Indian Ocean and the South China Sea. These traders operated from ports on both the east and the west coasts of India. Over the 17th and the early years of the 18th century, the Coromandel ports witnessed English trading activity on a much larger scale than did ports in Bengal. Masulipatnam was the principal port used on the Coromandel coast, but around the turn of the century more and more private English shipping moved on to Madras. In Bengal, the principal port was Hoogli until it was replaced by Calcutta in the early years of the 18th century. In course of time, Calcutta emerged as the most important port of English private trade in India. On the west coast, English private trade began at Surat in the early years of the 17th century, but moved on to Bombay in the 18th century.

Political and Economic Environment

What was the nature of the political and economic environment in which the European corporate groups and the private traders were obliged to function while carrying on their trading activities in Asia? In other words, if the range of alternative scenarios under which the Europeans functioned in different parts of Asia in the early modern period is conceptualized as a broad spectrum, where precisely would South Asia, for example, figure in that spectrum? One might begin by drawing attention to the fact that in the pre-European phase of the history of commercial exchange in the Indian Ocean-South China Sea complex, there was a well established tradition of foreign merchants being welcome at the Asian ports, since they were perceived as providers of additional business to the local merchants and of additional income by way of customs duties etc. to the ruling authorities. The visiting as well as the resident foreign merchants were, by and large, left to manage their affairs themselves, including the arrangements they might make with their local counterparts, their business dealings in the market, and so on, without the administration unduly interfering in their decision-making processes. The Asian port at which such autonomy was allowed in the most unconstrained fashion was probably that of Malacca, which in the course of the 15th century had become a major centre of international exchange, and a meeting point of traders from the East and the West. Foreign merchants resident in, and operating from, the port could broadly be divided into four groups: (a) the Gujaratis, (b) other Indian merchant groups and merchants from Burma, (c) the merchants from Southeast Asia up to and including the Philippines, and (d) the

merchants from East Asia, including the Chinese, the Japanese and the Okinawans. Each of these four groups was even allowed to have a shahbandar of its own, who managed the affairs of that particular community autonomously of the local authorities.
European naval superiority

To who extent was this scenario modified by the arrival of the Europeans in the Indian Ocean at the beginning of the 16th century? By far the most crucial element in the new situation was the armed superiority of European ships over their Asian counterparts. A glaring example of this disparity was provided in April 1612 when six English ships congregated off the Arabian coast and hijacked, in succession, fifteen passing Mughal ships from India, culminating in the capture of the great 1,000-ten vessel Rahimi, which belonged to the mother of the Mughal emperor. The prizes were taken to a nearby anchorage and plundered at will. It is true that the Rahimi was armed with some fifteen pieces of artillery and that the soldiers aboard her carried muskets, but these were merely anti-personnel weapons. Indian vessels, which often relied on rope and treenails to hold their planks in place, lacked the strength both to withstand heavy artillery bombardment from without, and to absorb the recoil of large ordinance firing from within. The fact that the English could do this with impunity reflected not only the vulnerability of the Indian mercantile vessels but also the absence of a Mughal navy capable of retaliating against such high-handed action. The flotilla at Dhaka and the fleet maintained by the Sidis at Janjira near Bombay were clearly inadequate to support an offensive against European ships. It was indeed not without reason that in 1662, on being approached on behalf of the king of the Maldive islands to use his good offices to persuade Emperor Aurangzeb to impose a ban on English and Dutch shipping to the islands, the faujdar of Balasore pointed out that even if the emperor could be persuaded to oblige the king, he was in no position to do so since he was 'master only of land and not of the sea.'

Dutch Spice Monopoly

In the 17th century, the Dutch and the English also took over the cartaz system from the Portuguese, though in a modified format and under the nomenclature of the 'pass' or the 'passport' system. It was, however, only the Dutch East India Company which, given its high stakes in Intra-Asian trade, took the system with a certain amount of seriousness. The Verenigde Oostindische Compagnie (VOC) also followed the Portuguese precedent in attempting to monopolize both the Euro-Asian and the Intra-Asian trade in spices. By the early 1620s, on the basis of agreements wrested from the authorities in many of the islands in the Moluccas, the Dutch had acquired effective monopsony rights in nutmeg and mace. The case of cloves was somewhat more complex. There was large scale smuggling between the producing areas and Makassar, enabling the English, among others, to obtain large quantities of this spice. Though from 1643 onwards the VOC had managed to reduce such smuggling, it was only after the conquest of Makassar in 1669 that the Dutch fully controlled the trade in cloves. Finally, as far as pepper-which was a substantially more important item of investment in the Indies than all the other spices put together-was concerned, inspite of the conclusion of exclusive agreements with a number of states in the region, the Company never acquired effective monopsony rights in the spice. The totality of the control achieved by the VOC in the case of spices other than pepper in the Euro-Asian trade is exemplified by the almost incredible fact that for the entire period between 1677 and 1744, the Company managed to sell cloves in Amsterdam at the fixed price of 75 stivers per Dutch pound. A similar stranglehold was enjoyed by the Company in the Intra-Asian trade in these spices. The fact that the Moluccas enjoyed world monopoly in the production of these spices, grown in particular islands covering a limited geographical space, which could be effectively policed, was the key to the success of the VOC in controlling the production and the trade in these items. By the same token, pepper, which was grown on the island of Sumatra over extensive tracts, could never be brought under the monopoly net, the formal monopsony agreements with several regional powers notwithstanding. For precisely the same reason, the Portuguese had an essentially similar experience with this spice on the southwest coast of India in the sixteenth century.

What did the Dutch spice monopoly entail for the Company on the one hand, and for the producers and the Asian traders dealing in them on the other? I have argued elsewhere that by increasing the rate of gross profit on these spices to incredibly high levels, often running to a thousand or more percent, the spice monopoly became a major element in the unquestioned domination of Euro-Asian trade by the Dutch through the 17th century. A similar domination was achieved in the Intra-Asian trade by using the spice monopoly as a major entry device into many branches of the network. The unusually high profit was, of course, at the expense of the producers of these spices, as well as the Indonesian and other Asian traders who used to carry on a large-scale Intra-Asian trade in them. This can be seen as institutionalized coercion by one group over another that had not been a feature of Asian trade in the pre-European phase. In terms of the placement in the spectrum discussed earlier, the situation in the Indonesian archipelago would indeed represent one end of the spectrum with a clearcut and substantive differential advantage available to the VOC.

Japan

Together with the spice monopoly, exclusive access to the bullion providing Japan trade was the other principal circumstance behind the VOC's unprecedented success in penetrating the Indian Ocean-South China Sea trading network. But ironically, the conditions under which the Company was obliged to operate in Japan were diametrically opposite to those in the Indonesian archipelago, placing the Company, as it were, at the other end of the spectrum of conditions under which the European corporate enterprises functioned in Asia. In a coercion-based regime, if it was the VOC that resorted to coercion over the producing and the trading groups in the Indonesian archipelago, it was itself the victim of coercion at the hands of the political and the commercial establishment in Japan.

The beginnings of the rise of a non-market governed commercial regime in Japan can be traced to 1604 when, under a new arrangement termed the pancado, the Portuguese were obliged to sell their principal import into Japan, namely Chinese raw silk, at a price determined arbitrarily by a guild monopsony consisting of a group of merchants from the five imperial cities of Edo (Tokyo), Osaka, Kyoto, Sakai and Nagasaki. In 1631, when they protested against the arrangement, the Portuguese were told that they were free to leave the country. In 1633, they actually had to sell at prices lower than even the pancado price. The same year the pancado arrangement was extended to cover a part of the Chinese raw silk brought in by the Dutch East India Company as well. Following the promulgation, in June 1636, of the sakoku or the 'closed country' edict and the expulsion of the Portuguese in 1639 consequent on the suspected involvement of their Catholic missionaries in the Shimbara rebellion in 1637, the Dutch became the only European merchant group to be allowed to operate in Japan. In May 1641, they were ordered to move to the islet of Deshima, off the Nagasaki harbour, to which they were henceforth confined, besides being subjected to a range of commercial restrictions. These included a ban on the export of gold, the prescription of days on which the Company could offer its goods for sale, until which time they had to be kept in sealed warehouses, and the extension of the pancado system to the entire lot of Chinese raw silk the Company imported into Japan. The 1672 introduction of the system of shih shobai which the Dutch translated as taxatiehandel (appraised trade), effectively extended the pancado system to all imports. On the basis of the samples collected from the Dutch factors, the different commodities imported were evaluated unilaterally by selected members of the Nagasaki Chamber of Commerce. This arrangement had an immediate and substantial adverse effect on the profitability of the trade, and in 1675 the Batavia Council wrote to the governor of Nagasaki that although the Company traded with 'all corners of the globe', it had 'never yet found a single other place where the purchaser fixed the price.' The appeal that the 'appraised trade' system be rescinded, however, fell on deaf ears and the Dutch chief at Nagasaki, Martinus Ceaser, could do little but express his frustration as follows, 'But it seems that the Japanese have finally laid aside all sense of honour and decency whilst we perforce must dance to their piping in everything.' The fact that the Japan trade was nevertheless of enormous value for the Company through the 17th century only serves to underscore the critical role that bullion played in the early-modern Asian trade.

India

What was the situation in India like which, as we have seen, was at the centre of the Europeans' trading activities. We have already noted that in the 16th century, the Portuguese managed to obtain monopsonistic privileges in the procurement of pepper on the Malabar coast. On the strength of the assistance provided to the raja of Cochin in throwing the Portuguese out, the Dutch East India Company inherited, in 1663, similar monopsonistic privileges. But given identical problems of policing and enforcement, the situation was indeed comparable to that in Sumatra rather than that in the Molluccas.

Outside of the Malabar coast, however, the situation in India was very much in the mould of the Malacca model, characterized by the absence of coercion on either side. In terms of the spectrum of alternative scenarios, the placement of the Europeans operating in India would be right in the middle of the spectrum. In the sub-continent, the relationship between the ruling authorities and the different European groups was by and large an amicable one, based essentially on perceived mutual advantage. The authorities basically looked upon the European companies' trade in their area as a net addition with the attendant benefits that such growth of trade entailed for the economy. More immediately, the resultant increase in the customs revenue, which in the case of the Mughal empire accrued directly to the central treasury, and probably constituted a head of revenue in importance next only to land revenue, was an important consideration. An equally important consideration would seem to have been the 'bullion for goods' character of the Europeans' trade. The fact that the companies paid for the goods obtained in the sub-continent overwhelmingly in terms of precious metals made them probably the single-most important conduit for the import of these metals into the country. The domestic output of these metals being practically nil, their import, in reasonably large quantities, was critical, among other things, for the successful conduct of the subcontinent's monetary system. As a result, European requests for permission to trade and the establishment of factories were routinely granted by Mughal imperial authorities and by regional authorities in the Coromandel coast. The rate of customs duty that European companies were obliged to pay was ordinarily the same as that payable by the Indian and other Asian merchants operating from the region. Indeed, imperial administration often went a step further and exempted these companies from the payment of transit (rahdari) duties, giving them a differential advantage vis-a-vis their own nationals. It is another matter that local and the provincial authorities, whose income streams would have been adversely affected by such exemption, usually managed to ignore imperial orders and continued charging rahdari duties. Under this dispensation the companies operated in the market basically as yet another group of merchants availing no special privileges in their dealings with the Indian merchants or artisans. By the same token, they were at liberty to function in the system like any other merchant group, without restriction on the use of systematic infrastructures. Their factors and representatives were allowed to travel throughout the empire, buy and sell where they found it most profitable to do so, and deal with their Indian counterparts on terms strictly determined by the market.

Conflict Resolution

The absence of coercion, however, did not preclude occasional conflict between Indian political authorities, on the one hand, and European trading companies, on the other. In such an event, both sides were concerned that the conflict did not escalate beyond a point. At work was, indeed, a rather finely tuned balance between unquestioned European maritime superiority as against their almost total vulnerability on land for a long time. Scholars such as Frederick C. Lane and, more recently, Niels Steensgaard have gone to the extent of arguing that 'the principal export of preindustrial Europe to the rest of the world was violence'. While there is an element of truth in this formulation, it is imperative that it is not torn out of context. Violence on the sea was a weapon of the last resort to be used as sparingly as possible, for the simple reason that it was by no means a costless process. Ordinarily, both sides would first seek to resolve conflict and only in the event of a deadlock would either side resort to actual violence. An example of a potential area of conflict between the authorities and the Dutch East India Company, given its largescale participation in Intra-Asian trade, was the violation of the Company's pass policy by the Indian merchants engaged in the Indian Ocean trade. The trouble the Company faced at Surat in 1648-9 is a case in point. Following the conquest of Malacca in 1641, and the subsequent conclusion of monopsony agreements with the principal tin producing regions in the Malay peninsula, the Company sought to restrict direct access for Indian vessels to the 'tin ports' north of Malacca, and get them to carry out all their trade at Malacca itself. This strategy, however, proved largely ineffective as long as these vessels had continuing free access to the Bay of Bengal port of Aceh on the northern tip of Sumatra. The extensive trade carried on by the Aceh merchants with Sumatran and Malayan ports made Aceh a large market for Indian textiles, as well as a major procurement point for items such as pepper and tin. Indeed, on the basis of the passes issued by the queen of Aceh, it was even possible for the Indian merchants to sail to the east Sumatran and west Malayan ports and carry on trade there. Particularly useful in this regard was the link to Perak, then a vassal state of Aceh and abundantly provided with tin. The implications of this for the VOC were quite severe. In 1646, no tin could be bought in the Malay peninsula and no pepper could be sold at Malacca. A full-scale response was evidently called for and on 3 July 1647, Batavia resolved that 'the Moors of Surat, Coromandel, Bengal Pegu, etc. be prohibited from the trade both in Achin [Aceh] and in the tin quarters [of peninsular Malaya] on pain of seizure [of their vessels] as legitimate prize if they come there in the future'. Patrolling of the approaches to Aceh, as well as to ports such as Kedah, Perak and Johor was intensified. The factors in India were instructed not to issue passes for Aceh or any of the other ports declared out of bounds.

Surat

The reaction to this severely restrictionist policy was sharp, at least at Surat. When passes for Aceh were refused, Mughal authorities banned the loading of Dutch ships at the port. That was not all: in April 1648, the local Dutch factory was stormed by a force of 150 men. One Dutchman was killed, two others wounded and goods worth f.27,000 plundered. The attackers were never identified, but it was a clear message signalling the displeasure of both the Mughal authorities as well as the local merchants. Johan Tack, the Company's man at Agra, sought the Court's intervention in the restitution of the plundered goods. With the help of one of the umara at the Court, Haqiqat Khan, who was generally favourably inclined to the Company, an audience with Shahjahan was obtained. The emperor promised to grant a farman directing the mutasaddi of Surat to compensate the Company for the plundered goods. But before the farman could be issued, a delegation of Surat merchants arrived at the Court. They could not prevent the grant of the farman, but ensured that it was a very different kind of document. All that the farman did was to say that the local authorities at Surat would do their best to trace the plundered goods. The factors saw no point in even bringing the document to the attention of the mutasaddi. The Company then decided to retaliate at sea. A fleet sent from Batavia for the purpose arrived too late in 1648 to attack the Indian ships returning from Mocha. But the following year, two Gujarati ships on their way back from Mocha and carrying a cargo worth more than one and a half million guilders were seized just outside Surat. Following negotiations between the Company, the local authorities, and some of the leading merchants of the city, the Company's two-fold demand for compensation for the plundered goods and a promise to stop the Surat ships' attempted voyages to Aceh, Perak, Kedah and Phuket, etc. was accepted. In return, the Company released the seized ships and the cargo to the lawful owners.

Coromandel

The implications of the Company's pass policy during these years were somewhat less severe on the Coromandel coast. The problems there revolved mainly around the issue of the refusal of passes for the ships of the all-powerful noble, Mir Jumla. Following the seizure in 1647 of tin worth 2,000 rials off Perak, from a ship of the Mir because it did not carry a Dutch pass, the governor of Masulipatnam, a subordinate of Mir Jumla, asked for restitution. Peace was bought temporarily by a promise to do the needful and by agreeing to sell the entire stock of cloves in the Company's warehouses in Coromandel together with a certain amount of copper to the Mir. But the tin had not been returned by 1651 leading to obstruction of the Company's textile trade in the region. It was only after Commissioner Dirck Steur went to see Mir Jumla that an agreement emerged. The Company reiterated its promise to return the tin, besides undertaking to buy its textiles, at specified places only, from the representatives of the Mir. But problems surfaced again following the seizure of one of Mir Jumla's ships, the Nazareth, off Malacca, for flying the Portuguese flag after the Dutch-Portuguese truce had ended. Matters came to a head in 1653 when Mir Jumla threatened to attack Fort Geldria unless the Nazareth and its cargo were released immediately and passes granted for the Portuguese controlled ports in Sri Lanka. It was then decided to meet a part of the Mir's claims in respect of the goods carried by the Nazareth. Besides, passes were to be issued to all subjects of Golconda for ports under the jurisdiction of the king of Kandi and for Aceh. The only stipulation made regarding the latter was that in the event of the blockade of the port by the Dutch, ships sailing for Aceh would agree to proceed to another destination approved by the Company. It was, however, only at the end of 1655 that compensation in respect of the Nazareth was paid. The Company also conceded the Mir's right to trade with Makassar, Bantam and Kedah, as well as to send goods to Malacca aboard the Company's ships. In return, Mir Jumla agreed not to send ships to Jaffanapatnam in view of the ongoing Dutch-Portuguese struggle there.

Economy-wide Implications of European Trade

Trade as an Instrument of Growth

It, however, bears repetition that the occasional areas and phases of conflict notwithstanding, the overall relationship between the European corporate enterprises on the one hand, and the Indian and other Asian authorities they were obliged to deal with on the other, was essentially an amicable one based on a perception of mutual advantage.

What was the situation like at an economy-wide level? In other words, what implications did the Europeans' trade have for the economies of the countries/regions where this trade was carried on? In so far as a country is relatively more efficient in the production of export goods than in that of import goods, an increase in trade between nations is ordinarily to the advantage of both the trading partners, involving an increase in the value of the total output in each of the two economies. The 'gains from trade' tend to become much more substantial in special situations such as in the case of the Euro-Asian trade in the early modern period. This is because the decline in the domestic production of import competing goods, which would usually accompany an increase in the output of export goods in an ordinary trade situation involving the exchange of goods against goods, would be avoided when the imports consisted not of goods but of precious metals (which in any case were not produced domestically in countries such as India). An increase in the output of export goods attendant upon an increase in trade would then involve a net increase in total output and income in the economy. This would be so irrespective of whether the imported precious metals are treated as a commodity import or as a mechanism for settling trade balances.

The increase in the output of export goods in the Indian sub-continent in response to the secularly rising demand for these goods by the Europeans would seem to have been achieved through a reallocation of resources, a fuller utilization of existing productive capacity and an increase over time in the capacity itself. A reallocation of resources in favour of the production of export goods such as raw silk and particular varieties of textiles would have been signalled, among other things, by a continuous rise in the prices of these goods in the markets where they were procured. Evidence regarding such a rise is available in plenty in the European company documentation. The available evidence also suggests both a fuller utilization of existing capacity as well as expansion thereof over time. In the case of textile manufacturing, for example, artisans engaged in the activity on a part-time basis seem to have increasingly found it worth their while to become full-time producers and to relocate themselves in the so-called aurungs-localized centres of manufacturing production, where the Europeans were increasingly concentrating their procurement through the intermediary merchants. Among the other factors of production required, land was clearly in abundant supply practically all over the sub-continent at this time. As far as the necessary capital resources needed for the production of new spindles, wheels and looms etc. was concerned, given the extremely small amounts involved, and the fact that the European companies were ever willing to advance the necessary sums, the availability of funds also is highly unlikely to have been a constraining factor. It need hardly be stressed that across a country of the size of the Indian sub-continent, there are likely to have been regional variations with regard to the degree of dynamism, flexibility and potential for continuing expansion in the scale of production that this scenario envisages. However, evidence available at least in respect of regions such as Bengal, which was by far the most important theatre of company activity on the sub-continent, would generally seem to confirm the presence of such attributes in ample measure.

In this scenario, the Europeans' trade would have become a vehicle for an expansion in income, output and employment in the sub-continent. As far as additional employment generated in the textile manufacturing sector as a result of European procurement is concerned, an exercise carried out in respect of the average annual procurement of textiles and raw silk in Bengal by the Dutch East India Company over the period 1678-1708 suggested that a total of 33,770 to 44,364 additional full-time jobs would have been created by the Company's procurement of these two items. If one extended the exercise to cover the English East India Company, but considered only the early years of the eighteenth century between 1709 and 1718, the number of additional jobs created was estimated at 86,967 to 111,151. The probable total size of the workforce in the textile manufacturing sector in the province of Bengal was estimated at one million. The full-time jobs associated with the Dutch Company's trade thus accounted for between 3.37 per cent and 4.43 per cent of the total workforce in the sector: the proportion went up to between 8.69 and 11.11 per cent when the trade of the Dutch and the English East India Companies was considered together.

The fact that the rate of growth of the Europeans' demand for goods such as textiles and raw silk was almost always greater than the rate at which their output increased turned the market increasingly into a sellers' market. This was reflected in the growing bargaining strength of the merchants vis-a-vis the companies. For example, in 1709 a number of textile suppliers dealing with the Dutch Company in Bengal refused to accept fresh contracts unless the Company gave them an assurance that henceforth in the event of only a limited variation between the quality of the sample given out and that of the pieces actually supplied by them, there would be no deduction made from the price mutually agreed upon at the time of the contract. The suppliers even insisted upon a refund of the price deductions made on this count on textiles supplied during the preceding season. A similar distinct improvement would also seem to have taken place in the bargaining strength of the weavers vis-a-vis the textile suppliers ensuring that the 'gains from trade' indeed percolated all the way down. Writing in 1700, for example, the Dutch factors at Hoogli made the following observation. "The merchants inform us (and on investigation we find that they are speaking the truth) that because of the large number of buyers in the weaving centres and the large sale of textiles, the weavers can no longer be coerced. They weave what is most profitable for them. If one does not accommodate oneself to this situation, then one is not able to procure very much and the supplies go to one's competitors."

The Monetary Domain

Quite apart from the implications of European trade for real variables such as income, output and employment, there was an important range of issues in the monetary domain which were affected by this trade. The import of large quantities of precious metals by the European companies into India on a continuing basis would have had certain consequences for the economy of the sub-continent. There is a considerable body of literature that assigns an important role to the imported American silver in shaping the growth of a number of European economies in the early modern period. According to Immanuel Wallerstein, for example, without the American silver, "Europe would have lacked the collective confidence to develop a capitalist system, wherein profit is based on various deferrals of realized value. This is a fortiori true given the system of a non-imperial world-economy which, for other reasons, was essential. Given this phenomenon of collective psychology, an integral element of the social structure of the time, bullion must be seen as an essential crop for a prospering world-economy."

This is what made South America so valuable. In Wallerstein's words, "The production of gold and silver as a commodity made the Americas a peripheral area of the European world-economy in so far as this commodity was essential to the operation of this world-economy, and it was essential to the extent that it was used as money. In short, they [the Europeans] incorporated the Americas into their world-economy, primarily because they needed a solid currency base for an expanding capitalist system and secondarily to use the surplus in trade with Asia."

But according to the proponents of this position, Asia was different. To quote Wallerstein once again, "At this epoch, the relationship of Europe and Asia might be summed up as the exchange of preciosities. The bullion flowed east to decorate the temples, palaces, and clothing of Asian aristocratic classes and the jewels and spices flowed west. The accidents of cultural history (perhaps nothing more than physical scarcity determined these complementary preferences."

Another western scholar, Rudolph Blitz, makes essentially a similar point: "In the Orient, much of the specie went promptly into hoards or was demonetized and became a commodity satisfying the oriental penchant for ornaments." The otherness of Asia in this view thus derives essentially from the fact tnat while, in the case of Europe, the imported silver involved an accretion to the supply of money in the system, in Asia this valuable asset was frittered away by being used "for hoarding or jewellery?"

There is reason to believe that such a clear-cut dichotomy between Europe and Asia is indeed quite untenable and does not conform to a wide body of evidence available to us. By far the most concrete of the effects associated with the import of American silver into Europe was the so-called 'price revolution' of the sixteenth century. A similar response is ruled out in the case of Asia for the simple reason that the first link in the chain, namely an increase in the supply of money, would not have come about in the Asian economies. But such a position is demonstrably false. In the case of Mughal India, for example, the treasure brought in by the European companies was intended for investment in Indian silk, textiles and other goods. In so far as foreign coins were not allowed to circulate locally, the very first step that would need to be taken by these companies in the matter of raising the necessary purchasing power would be the conversion of imported bullion and coins into Mughal Indian rupees. This could be done either through professional dealers in money known as sarrafs or by recourse to one of the imperial mints in the empire. In either event, there would be an automatic and corresponding increase in the supply of money in the economy. It is, of course, perfectly possible that a part of the increased money supply might eventually have been hoarded or withdrawn from active circulation. But in the present state of our knowledge, it would probably be futile to surmise how significant or marginal this phenomenon might have been. Some observations could nevertheless be made in this behalf. In any society, hoarding of precious metals in the form of bullion or coins would be a function of the structure of asset preferences. Given the virtual absence of deposit banking facilities in India, hoarding on a reasonable scale can very well be interpreted as a perfectly legitimate and rational form of holding liquidity. The point is that the implied irrationality in the 'Oriental penchant for hoarding' kind of story might in fact never have been there except perhaps at the margin.

A growing supply of money in response to a continuing import of precious metals would presumably have had implications for the functioning of an Asian economy along lines not necessarily very different from those in Europe. In relation to late Ming China, this is what William Atwell has to say, "Japanese and Spanish-American silver may well have been the most significant factor in the vigorous economic expansion which occurred in China during the period in question. This is true not only because of its direct impact on the silk and porcelain industries, although this clearly was of great importance; but also because an increase in the country's stock of precious metals upon which economic growth and business confidence seem to have depended would have been determined almost entirely by how much silver entered the country through foreign trade." The situation is unlikely to have been different in Mughal India, where it would seem that the rising supply of money was leading to a significant acceleration in the process of monetization in the economy. The well-known growing monetization of the land-revenue demand during the period was clearly a part of this larger process. Another significant feature of the Mughal Indian economy was the rise of banking firms all over the empire dealing in extremely sophisticated instruments of credit. Many of these firms had enormous resources at their command. Probably the best known of these was the house of the Jagat Seths operating from its headquarters at Murshidabad in Bengal. Along with its other activities, the firm organized the transfer of Delhi's share in the land revenues collected in the province. It need hardly be stressed that there was an important organic link between the rise in the money supply and the growth of the banking firms in the Mughal Indian economy.

What about the relationship between a rise in the money supply and the notional general price level in the economy? In other words, was there a counterpart in India to the European price revolution of the sixteenth century? A considerable body of work done over the past quarter of a century or so on the history of prices in different regions of India during the seventeenth and the first half of the eighteenth century has consistently negated the possibility of a general price rise (as opposed to a rise in the prices of goods procured by the Europeans). This includes my own earlier work on the price history of Bengal based mainly on the evidence available in the records of the Dutch East India Company. The evidence regarding movements in the prices of wage-goods such as rice, wheat, sugar and clarified butter, which I had argued could indeed be treated as proxies for movements in the notional general price level in the economy, suggested considerable fluctuations in the prices of these goods but no statistically significant upward or downward trend.

How does one reconcile the phenomenon of a rise in the supply of money with the absence of a rise in the notional general price level? While no definitive answer is possible, we might consider the following. Together with looking at the supply of money, we ought also to look at the demand for it. We have already noted that the 'bullion for goods' character of the Euro-Asian trade in the early modern period turned the foreign trade sector into an instrument of growth with the savings, investment and production in the economy registering an increase. The rising supply of money in the system would then have been absorbed by rising output, essentially obviating the need for the general price level necessarily to go up. This process would be further reinforced by the increasing monetization in the economy whereby monetized transactions as a proportion of total transactions in the economy would have gone up. Finally, over the fairly long period with which we are concerned, natural increases in population would also have necessitated a secular rise in output and transactions if the per-capita output and availability were not to go down. All these factors would tend to check a general rise in prices consequent upon an increase in the supply of money caused by an increased inflow of precious metals.

Certain deviations from the above scenario across both space and time must be noted. Across space, the above analysis will not be fully applicable to the Malabar coast, for example. The Portuguese had enjoyed special rights in pepper procurement in parts of the region until 1663 when they were thrown out of Cochin by the raja with the active assistance of the VOC. But then the VOC got its pound of flesh consisting, among other privileges, in a monopsony in the procurement of pepper in the area between Purakkad and Cranganur, and a monopoly in the sale of opium. Given the terrain, it was impossible to prevent largescale smuggling by Indian merchants, which substantially limited the scope of the Dutch monopoly privileges. But even so, in respect of that part of the total marketed output of pepper that the Dutch East India Company procured, the price paid to the intermediary merchants, which eventually also determined the return reaching the producers, was lower, possible substantially lower, than what the free market forces of demand and supply would have dictated. The macroeconomic implications of the European procurement would thus have been grossly vitiated.

The Early Colonial Period

Across time, the situation during the second half of the eighteenth century was very different from that in the preceding period. The death of the Mughal emperor Aurangzeb in 1707 was the symbolic beginning of the process of the collapse of the centralized Mughal empire, the rise of the so-called successor states in provinces such as Awadh, Hyderabad and Bengal, and eventually the takeover of large parts of the country by the English East India Company, beginning with Bengal, where it was officially recognized by the Mughal emperor as the diwan of the province in 1765. Aurangzeb was followed in quick succession by Bahadur Shah (1707-12), Jahandar Shah (1712-13), Farrukhsiyar (1713-19) and Muhammad Shah (1719-48). The Emperial fabric was subjected to serious strain during the early part of the century marked by disaffection of the Rajputs, growing militancy among the Sikhs and Jats in the north, and continuing Maratha insurgency in the south. Weakened central authority encouraged governors in several provinces to establish near-autonomous regional states only paying lip-service to the emperor's authority. The financial bankruptcy of the central government-dramatized by episodes such as Jahandar Shah's own troops remaining unpaid from the time of his accession-was further accentuated by the increasing irregularity and default in the receipt of the imperial government's share in the land revenues due from the newly emerging successor states.

The rapid deterioration in the state of law and order seriously affected the flows of long-distance overland trade within the empire. An important route that suffered particular damage was the one that connected the heartland of the empire to Gujarat. Caravans organized by private merchants, even though protected by hired guards, could no longer travel safely from Agra to Surat. In view of the problems faced in the procurement and the transportation of textiles and Bayana indigo from Agra to Surat, the VOC was obliged to close its factory at Agra in 1716. The cost of the bills of exchange between these two cities, which ordinarily used to be no more than 1 to 2 per cent, now shot up to as much as 12 per cent. In Surat, the imperial mint was shut down for several years and numerous dealers in money were reported to have gone bankrupt.

The nature and the extent of the dislocation described above should, however, be kept in perspective and care taken that its negative implications for the overall standard of economic performance are not overstated. Research done over the past two decades or so suggests the strong possibility of various sectors in the Indian economy continuing to perform well during the course of the century. In the words of Burton Stein, scholars maintaining this position "agree that the rural economy over most of the 18th century India enjoyed substantial, if uneven, growth notwithstanding both the destructive wars culminating in those which won the sub-continent for the British, and the supposed political disorder in many areas. It is claimed that new, smaller states with efficient tax-gathering procedures replaced the Mughal military imperial order, that market networks proliferated and became to a degree interlinked, that a more prosperous agriculture came into being with increased commodity production as a result of rural investments by the revenue farmers of the time, that all of this was buoyed up by an ever-increasing level of international trade in which Indian artisans, merchants and especially bankers played key and lucrative roles, and that this phase of political economy obtained until the first quarter of the 19th century."

From the perspective of the European trading companies, the most crucial developments were those taking place in Bengal, by far the most important of the Asian trading regions, supplying at the turn of the eighteenth century as much as 40 per cent of the total Asian cargo that the Dutch and the English East India companies imported into Europe each year. It is vitally important to note that as far as this province was concerned, the situation over the greater part of the eighteenth century was not materially different from that in the heyday of the Mughal empire in the seventeenth. The man mainly responsible for this in the early part of the century was Murshid Quli Khan, who dominated the history of the province between 1701, when he was sent there as the imperial diwan with a specific brief to try and increase the flow of revenues due to the imperial government from the province, and his death in 1727. By scrupulously ensuring that the annual flow of the khalisa revenues to Delhi not only continued uninterrupted but in fact registered an increase over time, Murshid Quli succeeded in creating a mutually beneficial working partnership with the imperial government. In the domain of political stability and the state of law and order, the first four decades of the eighteenth century were certainly no worse than had been the case during the seventeenth. It is true that a certain amount of dislocation was caused in the early 1740s as a result of the Maratha incursions into the province. But that was essentially a temporary phase and things were by and large back to normal by the end of the decade. In brief, the picture of political confusion and unrest usually associated with the declining power of the Mughals in the first half of the eighteenth century is certainly not applicable to Bengal. In fact, the growing weakness of the centre, particularly in the wake of Nadir Shah's invasion during 1739-43, further strengthened regional polities, and successor states such as Bengal, Hyderabad and Awadh stopped paying their customary tribute to Delhi on a regular basis making larger resources available for internal deployment. The Europeans' trade from Bengal also registered a significant increase during the period. Thus of the rising total Dutch exports from Asia to Europe amounting to £19.24 million over the triennium 1738-40 as against £15 million during 1698-1700, the share of goods procured in the province had gone up to 47 per cent as against 41 per cent at the turn of the century. The corresponding figures in the case of the English East India Company were £23 million as against £13.79 million with the share of the Bengal goods being at the all-time peak of 66 per cent during 1738-40 as against 42 per cent during 1698-1700. The second half of the eighteenth century witnessed a fundamental alteration in the nature of the Indo-European encounter.

The takeover of Bengal by the English East India Company following the battle of Plassey in 1757 marked the inauguration of the colonial phase in this encounter. The nawab's army, though ten times the size of Clive's 2,000 sepoys and 900 Europeans, was routed providing the English Company its first foothold in the sub-continent. The formal acquisition of diwani rights in 1765 provided it with access to the province's revenues. These were used in part to strengthen further the Company's military strength. By 1782, the Company was able to maintain 115,000 men in India (90 per cent of them sepoys) enabling it to intervene effectively in other parts of the sub-continent such as the Deccan. A part of the surplus from the Bengal revenues was also used to finance the procurement of goods for export to Europe. To that extent, these exports now became 'unrequited' involving a drain of resources from the country-a theme that has legitimately attracted a great deal of attention in the Indian nationalist historical writings of the nineteenth century. The bulk of the English Company exports during this period, however, were financed by the rupee receipts obtained by the Company locally against bills of exchange issued to English and other European private traders on London and other European capitals enabling these traders to transmit their Indian earnings home. Between the Bengal surplus revenues and the rupees receipts obtained against the bills of exchange, the Company found itself in a position to suspend altogether the import of treasure from home for nearly a quarter of a century. It was only in 1784 that these imports were resumed partly for investment in the procurement of export goods and partly to strengthen further the Company's military presence-a necessary prelude to the conquest of other parts of the sub-continent.

The altered situation held important consequences for the economy of the province. For one thing, the substantial reduction in the silver imports would seem to have been an important element behind the shortage of money that several contemporaries noted and commented upon. More importantly, there was a marked deterioration in the relative share in the total value of the output produced as far as the Bengali artisanal and the mercantile groups engaged in business with the English East India Company were concerned. This was a necessary corollary of the replacement of a market-determined relationship between the Company and these groups until about 1760 by a relationship marked by a clear-cut domination by the Company in the decades that followed. On the basis of its political muscle power, the Company now enforced unilaterally determined below-market terms on the producers of and the dealers in commodities such as textiles and opium. The blatant manner in which this was done, robbing in the process the producers and the merchants of a good part of what was legitimately due to them, would, in turn, have introduced distortions in the incentive structure in the domain of manufacturing and other production in the province. This, combined with the official Company and unofficial private English traders' monopolies in commodities such as salt and opium, is likely to have brought about a certain amount of decline in the value of the total output produced in the province, though in the present state of our knowledge it is not possible to indicate even broadly the extent of this decline.

There is a distinct possibility, however, that this decline was not altogether massive or irreversible and that the structure of both agricultural and non-agricultural production in the province continued to be marked by a reasonable degree of vitality and capacity to deliver. An important, though by no means conclusive, index suggesting this scenario is the continuing growth of both the Euro-Asian and the Intra-Asian trade from the province. It is true that, under the pressure of the increasingly monopsonistic policies adopted by the English Company, the trade of the rival companies operating in the region was on the decline. Thus in the case of the VOC, although the overall value of its Asian exports to Europe between the trienniums of 1738-40 and 1778-80 went up from £19 million of £21 million, the average annual value of the Company's exports from Bengal came down from the all-time peak of £5 million in 1751-2 to a measly £1.32 million in 1784-5. But such a decline was much more than made up for by the English Company's own total exports to Europe going up from £23 million in 1738-40 to £25 million in 1758-60 and to an almost incredible figure of £69 million in 1777-9 giving us an annual average figure of £23 million. Bengal accounted for as much as half of this value. In Intra-Asian trade, the decline in the Dutch Company exports as well as in those by the Indian merchants engaged in this trade was similarly much more than made up for by the spectacular rise in the English private merchants' trade with China.

Conclusion

The Euro-Asian, and more specifically the Indo-European, encounter over the three hundred-year period between 1500 and 1800 was a historical process with extremely significant and wideranging implications for both sides. Within the overall rubric of the desire to procure Indian goods, the precise motivation and mechanism behind the arrival of each of the European trading groups into the sub-continent was different. The Portuguese came basically for pepper, and throughout the sixteenth and the early part of the seventeenth century India provided an overwhelming bulk of the total pepper supplies reaching Lisbon. The Bay of

Bengal figured prominently in the Intra-Asian trading network of the Estado da India, and later also in the trading operations of the private Portuguese merchants both within Asia as well as between Asia and Europe. The Dutch East India Company, on the other hand, procured its pepper and other spices in the Indonesian archipelago and came to India looking mainly for the relatively inexpensive mass-consumption cotton textiles produced on the Coromandel coast, and to a smaller extent in Gujarat, with a view to using them as a medium of exchange to procure the Indonesian spices. This became the first link in a chain that eventually developed into a massive involvement in Intra-Asian trade with other Indian commodities such as Bengal raw silk and opium also playing a critical role in the successful functioning of the complex network. In the last quarter of the seventeenth century, the fashion revolution in Europe put Indian textiles and raw silk at the head of the imports from Asia catapulting India into the position of being by far the most important supplier of goods for Europe.

The key role of India in the Dutch East India Company's overall framework of trade continued well into the early years of the second half of the eighteenth century when the English East India Company, on the strength of its newly acquired special status in Bengal, overwhelmed the Dutch and forced them into reducing the scale of their operations in the sub-continent substantially. The French were late-comers on the scene having set up an East India Company only in 1664. In fact, it was only from the beginning of the second quarter of the eighteenth century onward that the French trade in the sub-continent became quantitatively significant. They were engaged in an almost continuous conflict with the English in south India, but like the Dutch were eventually unable to withstand the English hostility.

The English involvement in the trade of the sub-continent became significant only from the second quarter of the seventeenth century, after they had found it impossible to carry on profitable trade in the Indonesian archipelago due in part to the opposition by the Dutch. From this point on, India figured even more prominently in the total English exports to Europe than was the case with the Dutch. With the English Company's takeover of Bengal in the second half of the eighteenth century, India assumed an altogether new role for Britain. Bengal revenues provided an indirect subsidy to the British exchequer and the enormous opportunities-leg. and clandestine-for private gain now available to the Company servants in their personal capacity created a whole new class of the new-rich 'nabobs' returning to England with fortunes unheard of before. It is, however, highly unlikely that these private fortunes constituted an element of any importance in the financing of the Industrial Revolution in Britain which was then getting under way.

As far as India was concerned, the substantial amount of trade carried on from her ports by the Europeans, both with Europe as well as with other parts of Asia, particularly from the early part of the seventeenth century onward, served to strengthen her status considerably as a premier trading and manufacturing nation in Asia. At the turn of the eighteenth century, India was probably the largest and the most cost-competitive textile-manufacturing country in the world.

An increase in trade being beneficial for a country is an axiom: in India's case the 'bullion for goods' character of the European trade considerably enhanced its positive implications and indeed turned it into an important instrument of growth in the Indian economy. The gold and silver the Europeans imported from Europe and other Asian countries such as Japan led to a substantial increase in the supply of money in the country. The growing level of monetization in the economy, in turn, facilitated reform measures such as the growing conversion of the land revenue demand from kind into cash, which led to a further increase in market exchange and trade. The growing availability of precious metals in the system also helped the rise of banking firms, and generally became an important factor in facilitating the expansion of the Mughal empire.

By not involving a decline in the domestic output of import competing goods, the 'bullion for goods' character of the European trade also implied that the positive implications of the growth in trade for the level of income, output and employment in the economy were considerably more substantial than would have been the case if this trade had been of the ordinary 'goods for goods' variety.

In the agricultural sector, there was an increase in the acreage under cultivation, particularly in the case of highvalue commercial crops such as cotton and opium. The increase in output and employment in the manufacturing sector was clearly on a scale that was not entirely insignificant. Job opportunities in several segments of the services sector such as that providing brokerage services would also have gone up. Besides, the fact that, on average, the rate of growth of the European demand for Indian goods such as textiles and raw silk was greater than the rate of growth of their supply, increasingly turned the market into a sellers' market. The fact that this involved not only an increase in the bargaining strength of the intermediary merchants vis-a-vis the Europeans but also a continuous improvement in the bargaining strength of the weavers vis-a-vis the intermediary merchants, implied that the benefits of the continuing rise in the level of output, income and employment were not confined to the intermediary groups but percolated all the way down to the weavers and the other constituents of the producing groups.

During the early colonial phase in the post-1760 period, this situation continued unaltered in many respects but underwent major modification in others. The composition of the trade with Europe remained unchanged, and except for the 'unrequited' part of the exports financed through the investment of the Bengal surplus revenues, the 'bullion for goods' character of the trade continued to be valid, though in a more restrictive and limited way. From the point of view of the English Company, the suspension of silver imports for a while and the financing of the exports mainly through the bills of exchange only meant that the payment in silver was now made in Europe rather than in India.

But of course, this silver never reached India. Also, in so far as the relationship between the English East India Company on the one hand and the Indian intermediary merchants and producers on the other was no longer governed by the market but was dictated by the Company, a good part of the legitimate share of the producers and the merchants in the total output was now appropriated by the Company.

As the Industrial Revolution began to mature in Britain, more fundamental changes followed. From the second quarter of the nineteenth century onward, India began to lose the European market for its textiles. Later in the century, the so-called colonial pattern of trade came into operation in a full-fledged manner and India was converted into an important market for textiles manufactured in Manchester and Lancashire.

From Trade to Colonization-Historic Dynamics of the East India Companies

> *"In the middle of the seventeenth century, Asia still had a far more important place in the world than Europe." So wrote J. Pirenne in his 'History of the Universe', published in Paris in 1950. He added, "The riches of Asia were incomparably greater than those of the European states. Her industrial techniques showed a subtlety and a tradition that the European handicrafts did not possess. And there was nothing in the more modern methods used by the traders of the Western countries that Asian trade had to envy. In matters of credit, transfer of funds, insurance, and cartels, neither India, Persia, nor China had anything to learn from Europe." (Quoted in Auguste Toussaint's 'History of the Indian Ocean')*

Such was the situation when the East India Company began its trading activities in the early 17th century. Initially, the British traders had come to India with hopes of selling Britain's most popular export item to Continental Europe-British Broadcloth, but were disappointed to find little demand for it. Instead, like their Portuguese counterparts, they found several Indian-made items they could sell quite profitably in their homeland. Competing with other European traders, and competing with several other trade routes to Europe (the Red Sea route through Egypt, the Persian Gulf Route through Iraq, and the Northern Caravan Route through Afghanistan, Persia and Turkey), the early British Traders were in no position to dictate terms. They had to seek concessions with a measure of humility and offer trade terms that offered at least some benefits to the local rulers and merchants. While Aurangzeb (who had, perhaps, seen the connection between growing European Trade concessions and falling revenues from the overland trade) attempted to limit and control the activities of the East India Company, not all Indian rulers had as many compunctions about making trade concessions. Besides, the East India Company was willing to persevere; fighting and cajoling for concessions, it built trading bases wherever it could along either side of the lengthy Indian coastline.

In this period, relations between Indians and Britishers were not lacking in cordiality and the East India Company included employees from both worlds. Friendships between the two nationalities developed not only within the context of business relations, but even beyond, to the point of intermarriage. Unaffected by the pompous stuffiness of the British gentry, the British employees of the East India Company made the most of life in India-dressing in cool and comfortable Indian garments, enjoying Indian pastimes and absorbing local words in their dialect. With as yet unprejudiced eyes, these British traders delighted in the delicate craftsmanship and attractiveness of Indian manufactures and took good advantage of their growing popularity in Britain and France. So lucrative was the trade that even though India would accept nothing but silver (or gold) in return, the East India Company prospered.

Considering the long route (around the African Cape) that the British had to take in reaching England, it was surprising that they made as much money as they did. But other factors outweighed this disadvantage. First, owing to their legally sanctioned monopoly status in England, they had substantial control on the British market. Second, by buying directly at the source, they were able to eliminate the considerable mark-up that Indian goods enjoyed en-route to Europe. Thirdly, the East India Company probably enjoyed better economies of scale since their ships were amongst the largest in the Indian Ocean. In addition, they were able to develop new markets for Indian goods in Africa, and in the Americas.

And finally, (and perhaps, most significantly), as Veronica Murphy reports in 'Europeans and the Textile Trade' (Arts of India 1550-1900), "although the East India Company was not itself engaged in the transatlantic slave trade, the link was very close and highly profitable." In fact, in the 18th century, the British dominated the Atlantic slave trade transporting more slaves than all the other European powers combined. In 1853, Henry Carey-author of 'The Slave Trade, Domestic and Foreign' wrote: "It (the British System) is the most gigantic system of slavery the world has yet seen, and therefore it is that freedom gradually disappears from every country over which England is enabled to gain control." The Atlantic slave trade was hence, a vital contributor to the financial strength of the East Indian Trading Companies.

So much so that by the middle of the 17th century, the East India Company was re-exporting Indian goods to Europe and

North Africa and even Turkey! Unsurprisingly, this was to have a severely deleterious effect on the Ottomans, the Persians, the Afghans, since much of the revenues of these states came from the India trade. It also seriously impacted the revenues of the Mughals, and while the activities of the Arab and Gujarati traders were not entirely eliminated, their trade was much curtailed, and largely reduced to the inter-Asian trade which continued unabated. In any case, the Mughal state was unable to resist centrifugal forces and rapidly disintegrated. This left the East India Company with considerably more leverage and emboldened it to expand its activities, and demand even greater concessions from Indian rulers.

But even as the Indian rulers were granting more concessions, there was a rising chorus of voices bemoaning the loss of "European" silver to Asia. At the end of the 17th century, the silk and wool merchants of France and England were unwilling to put up with the competition from Indian textiles which had become the rage in the new bourgeoisie societies of Europe. Not only did they seek bans on such trading activities of the East India Company, they also sought and won restrictions on the purchase of these items in their respective nations.

These prohibitions, while not entirely eliminating the smuggling of such items, nevertheless squeezed out most of the trade, impacting the revenues of the regional Indian states that had only recently broken off from the centralized Mughal state and Bengal was the first to face the consequences.

Having lost the opportunity to profit from the Indian textile trade, the East India Company was not hesitant in changing character. In 1616, Sir Thomas Roe, an envoy of the East India Company had declared to the Mughals that war and trade were incompatible. But already in 1669 (even before the bans on the textile trade), Gerald Ungier, chief of the factory at Bombay had written to his directors: " The time now requires you to manage your general commerce with the sword in your hands" In 1687 came the reply from the directors, advocating a Goa like British dominion in India. The French Dupleix was more or less of similiar view. Still earlier, in 1614, the Dutch Jan. Pieterzoon Coen, had written to his directors: "Trade in India must be conducted and maintained under the protection and favour of your weapons, and the weapons must be supplied from the profits enjoyed by the trade, so that trade cannot be maintained without war or war without trade." (from Auguste Toussaint's: History of the Indian Ocean)

The Opium Trade of the 18th century (which eventually led to the Opium Wars), when the Royal British Navy worked more or less hand in hand with the commercial interests of the East India Company, exemplified precisely such a link between war and trade. From the intertwining of war and trade, colonization was only a small step away. Plassey was a portentious indicator of a new dynamic in Indo-British relations.

Contrary to the views of several apologists for colonial rule, who still argue that the defeat of India had solely to do with "congenital flaws" or the centuries old "ennui" or " weak character of the Asian", or the "inability of the Indians (and other Asians) to govern themselves", R. Mukerji (in Rise and Fall of the East India Company) advanced a different thesis. He argued that there were compelling economic imperatives that drew the European India Companies into the path of imperialism. He pointed out that although monopoly rights assured the India Companies of the exclusive privileges of buying and selling, it did not guarantee that they could buy cheap. For that, political control was essential.

A second problem for the East India Company was that their profits were in direct conflict with those of their British-based competitors. Under these circumstances, as long as the profit motive was paramount (which it was), the Battle at Plassey, and the Opium Wars could be seen as logical outcomes of circumstances where continued profits by legal and honourable means were simply not possible. But, had the East Company comprised of "Gentlemen Traders" as some historians have claimed, they could not have switched so easily from trading in Indian Textiles, to trading in Opium for Tea which, in modern language-would surely be described as a form of "drug-running"! Had the traders of the East India Company been "men of honour", denied the right to profitable trade, they would have simply gone bankrupt, as so many do in the world of business!

Yet, what is even more significant is that even after The East India Company had regained sizeable profits from the Opium trade, it served as no deterrence to future acts of aggression. It had become like the proverbial man-eating tiger, that having tasted blood once, would be driven to tasting it again and again. After

Plassey, the East India Company had been able to force the cultivation of opium in sufficient quantities in India, and hence, procure sufficient volumes of tea for the British market, reaping significant profits. Yet, now military attacks were also to be directed against Indian (and other Asian) ships engaged in the inter-Asian trade. These attacks were to lay the groundwork for the battles against the Coromandel rulers and the Marathas whose revenues from this trade dwindled. While Plassey may have been a matter of "survival" for the East India Company, the subsequent battles were not in that category. Some historians tried to argue that competition with the French precipitated the battles in South India, but such a view is contradicted by a Frenchman, no less!

Abbe de Pradt, author of "Les Trois Ages des colonies, Paris, 1902" wrote that with the victory at Plassey and the establishment of sovereign rights, England had demonstrated to all of Europe that it was no longer necessary for it to send precious metals obtained from the "New World" to India. She could trade on the basis of revenue acquired from taxing subjects and commodities, whereas other European countries had to trade at a "loss", with "metal currency". The extension of English sovereignty in India, would exempt Europe from sending capital into India. Specifically, Abbe de Pradt wrote: " the people who have enough control over India to reduce substantially the exportation of European metallic currency into Asia rule there as much for Europe's benefit as for their own; their empire is more common than particular, more European than British; as it expands, Europe benefits, and each of their conquests is also a real conquest for the latter." Chastizing European opponents of the British conquest, he wrote: "all the sound and fury now echoing across Europe about England's hegemony in India are the shrieks of a blind delirium, as an anti-European uproar; it might be thought that England was taking away from every European state what it was conquering from those of Asia, whereas, on the contrary, every part of Asia that she takes for herself, she, by that very fact, takes for Europe."

In fact, this view tallies quite closely with the observations of several later analysts who found it paradoxical that inter-European rivalries and conflicts reduced in the 18th century when compared to the 17th century, and decreased still further after Plassey. In essence, the race for the colonization of India had been won by the British, and what Abbe de Pradt was saying was that it was in French interest to enjoy the "general" benefits of this victory and not bemoan the loss of "specific" benefits from the British victory.

N.K Sinha, author of an "Economic History of Bengal" summarizes the situation in these words: "For more than two centuries the Europeans had found that the trade with Bengal whether carried on by companies or by the individual free traders or by illicit means had always been so much in favour of Bengal that the balance had to be supplied in cash. Now after Plassey supplies were at last found in Bengal " by means independence of commerce"-referring to the forced taxes that were extracted by the East India Company from the people of Bengal.

He continues: "The trade of the country merchant began to stagnate. Armenian, Mughal, Gujarati and Bengali merchants found their free trade daily fettered and loaded." The export, import, and manufacture of goods moved from the hands of independant Indian merchants to intermediaries hired by the British East India Company. Often this required force. Sepoys of the East India Company were sent to destroy the factories owned by Indian rivals to the East India Company. Independent weavers who refused to work for the pitiful wages that the East India Company offered had their thumbs cut off. After Plassey, the East India Company also moved to impose it's monopoly on the internal overland trade. In a matter of three decades after Plassey, the East India Company achieved a virtual stranglehold on the economic and political life of Eastern India.

Just as Abbe de Pradt had predicted, the benefits of colonization did not go exclusively to the British. French, Dutch and Danish rivals were also able to take advantage of the trade monopoly established by the British East India Company. With the decline of the Indian merchants, they were able to buy Indian goods at lower prices. Secondly, corrupt employees of the British East India Company engaged in considerable price gouging, cheating and local thuggery. They preferred to repatriate this illegally acquired wealth from India through French and Dutch rivals to escape detection of their cheating and to avoid taxes and customs duties in Britain. Even as Indian rivals to the British East India were wiped out, European rivals continued to survive and flourish for another 30-40 years.

The American Furber who published his research on the East India Company in 1948 (in Cambridge, Mass.) pointed out that its French and Dutch rivals continued operating until 1769 and 1798. He also indicates that it was a very cosmopolitan association. At least one-fifth of its nominal capital of pound 3,200,00 was in Dutch hands, and a large proportion of that capital came from financiers in Amsterdam, Paris, Copenhagen, and Lisbon, who were also directly concerned in the company's affairs. Furber noted that the commercial activity of the French, the Dutch, and the Danes in the Indian Ocean during the eighteenth century clearly showed that "the time had arrived when Europeans at home or overseas who had a stake in the maintenance of European power anywhere on the Indian continent were one and all forced to take part in the work of building a British empire in India". What Furber was pointing out was not only the substantial and cosmopolitan nature of the backing the East India Company enjoyed, but also the motivations and direct self-interest of its backers.

Thus, Plassey was to be only the first of several assaults that no regional Indian power was able to fend off successfully. While united India had largely held off the Europeans, and divided India had temporarily held off divided Europe, divided India was no match for united Europe. The conquest of India continued with conclusive defeats of the Marathas in 1818, the Sikhs in 1848 and the annexation of Awadh in 1856. 1857 was a brave attempt to rollback the victories of the East India Company, but instead it now brought on the might of the entire British imperial government. The Indian colonies of the British East India Company became British Colonial India-and so began a new phase of colonial plunder from the sub-continent. A phase that saw constant challenges to British hegemony in the region, but it was not till 1947 that a new era could be ushered.

Hence, for almost 200 years, there was a systematic transfer of wealth from India to Europe. Although Britain may have been the primary beneficiary, it's allies in Europe and the new world benefited no less. British Banks used their Indian capital to fund industry in the US, Germany and elsewhere in Europe. The industrial revolution and the development of modern capitalism was based on the colonization of India and the rest of the world. It was the forced pauperization of the colonized world that allowed nations such as Britain, or the US to industrialize and "modernize". Any serious analysis of modern capitalism must take this into account.

European Domination of the Indian Ocean Trade

Prior to the arrival of the Portuguese in the Indian Ocean in 1498, no single power had attempted to monopolize the sea lanes that connected the ports of the Indian sub-continent with the Middle East and East Africa on the West, and the ports of South East Asia and China to the East. Unlike in the Mediterranean where during Roman (and earlier) times, rival powers attempted to control the oceanic trade through military means, peaceful trade had remained the norm in the Indian Ocean. Although there were periods when coastal rulers of the Malabar coast and Southern India were powerful enough to demand toll taxes from passing ships, (and Arab rulers had attempted to control the shipping lanes through the Red Sea) there had not been any systematic attempt by any single political power to eliminate all others from the oceanic trade that touched the Indian sub-continent.

Indian ports that demanded high taxes from docking ships invariably lost out to "free ports", *i.e.* ports that demanded very low tariffs from docking ships. In fact, several of the Indian ocean ports were politically neutral entities-giving free and equitable access to shippers of varied nationalities and religious affiliations.

Whereas pre-15th century Arab and Chinese geographical texts spoke of various natural hazards involved in long-distance shipping, they did not cite any significant political or military impediments to undertaking long-distance voyages other than the risk from pirates. Thus, evidence left behind by chroniclers such as Marco Polo, Ibn Batuta, Persian ambassador Abdur Razzaq, the Venetian Nicolo Conti, and Genoan Santo Stefano-all indicate that the Indian Ocean was the scene of thriving trade in the 14th and 15th centuries. But once the Portuguese had discovered their new route to India, they displayed considerable zeal in seizing the most profitable ports of East Africa, the Persian Gulf, and the Saurashtran, Konkan and Malabar regions in India. A chain of fortified coastal settlements backed by regular naval patrols allowed the Portuguese to gradually eliminate many rivals, and enforce a semi-monopoly in the spice trade by the middle of the 16th C. Local traders were coerced into buying safe passes and paying customs duties to the

Portuguese. However, this attempt at a monopoly was challenged by the maritime powers of North Sumatra based in Aceh, as well as by the Omanis, and by Gujarati traders. And as the Portuguese expanded with settlements in South East Asia, China and Japan-the Western monopoly became harder to maintain.

Initial success came to the Portuguese because they had been shrewd enough to develop a strategy of divide and conquer-first concentrating on isolating Muslim traders from the Hindu monarch of Calicut and demonstrating their fire power by launching a two-day bombardment of the vital port city (which was then the largest spice market of the Indian Ocean). These intimidating tactics worked in the favour of the Portuguese who repeated this strategy at other key trading destinations. In 1510, Bijapur's Adil Shahi ruler ceded the control of Goa to the Portuguese. Having realized that the bulk of trade moving out of India landed at one of three ports in the Indian Ocean-*i.e.* Hormuz in the Persian Gulf, Aden on the Red Sea, and Malacca in the Malay Peninsula-Goa's Indian Governor, Alfonso Albuquerque then shifted his attention to capturing each of these crucial ports. Malacca fell in 1511 and Hormuz in 1515. Only Aden proved elusive.

In 1505, the spice trade from Asia to Europe was declared a 'royal monopoly' by the Portuguese, who saw in this the possibility of extorting tribute through military means. Once Hormuz and Malacca came under the military and political control of the Portuguese, the Portuguese then attempted to expand their monopoly to the inter-Asian trade. For this they needed to seal off independent access to the Gujarati traders who although cut off from Malacca could continue to trade through the Red Sea. For twenty years, the Portuguese kept attacking the ports of Gujarat, even gaining a military victory in 1509 (after an earlier defeat against the combined defences of Diu and an Egyptian naval fleet that had been sent to aid the defences of Diu's Amir Hussain). But nevertheless, Diu did not fall; and attempts to defeat Malik Ayaz, (the next governor of Diu) also failed in 1520-21. In 1530, the Portuguese colonists looted and burned the ports of Cambay, Surat and Rander, but it was only in 1534, when in a moment of weakness, Sultan Bahadur of Gujarat relinquished control of the small port of Bassein. Diu-which had held out for two decades, suddenly became vulnerable when Mughal emperor Humayun cut a deal with the Portuguese to defeat Sultan Bahadur. The

Portuguese were given permission to build a fort on the island, which allowed the Portuguese to garner complete political control over the territory by 1555. Portuguese naval control over the Gulf of Cambay became complete when they also captured the port of Daman in 1559. Thus the merchants of Gujarat were brought under control by the Portuguese, and Gujarat-(which on account of its thriving industry and trade may have been one of the richest of India's provinces) saw its fortunes steadily decline.

Following their conquests in Gujarat, the Portuguese then proceeded to augment their control in Sri Lanka by taking over Colombo, and founding a settlement in Meliapur (Sao Tome) on the Coromandel coast. Realizing that the trade from Goa to Bengal was even more lucrative than the Coromandel trade, they then turned their aggressive energies on Bengal. After initial resistance, they were allowed to settle in Chittagaon and Satgaon (near Kolkata), and later moved up to river Hooghly. This enabled them to establish a virtual monopoly on the trade out of West Bengal by the end of the 16th C, until they were expelled by the Mughal armies in 1632. The Livra das cidades, e fortalezas documented in detail Portuguese control over numerous Indian ocean ports (in addition to those previously mentioned), such as Sofala in Mozambique-a major supplier of African gold, Mangalore, Cannanore, Cranganore, Cochin and Quilon-all important sources for spices and other tropical produce.

This success had come about mainly because unlike the trading ships of their Asian predecessors, the Portuguese ships were extremely well-armed for their times. Moreover, they were fortunate to arrive in the Indian sub-continent at a time when many of the ports were outside the political control of any powerful local ruler who could mount any effective resistance against their superior fire-power and their willingness to use it without hesitation. This was also due to the fact that the great Asian economies of the time were essentially land-based self-reliant economies. External trade did not comprise a significant portion of the economy, and the rulers had little stake in defending the interests of the sea-faring merchant classes. Where the merchant class was of some local significance-such as in Gujarat, the Portuguese did meet with considerable resistance (as also in Sumatra). But when squeezed between two enemies (the Mughals to the North and the Portuguese to the South), Gujarat had little choice but to give in. Smaller and less-established traders from the Southern and Eastern Indian coast were completely eliminated from the inter-Asian trade, and were never able to recover. Others survived by accepting Portuguese conditions and lemands of tribute for safe passage. However, some Gujarati and other Indian traders (along with their counterparts from East Africa, the Middle East and Indonesia) tried hard to bypass the Portuguese monopoly by using smaller ports that were relatively free from Portuguese domination. In addition, Gujarati traders began to emulate the Portuguese practice of arming their fleets, so as to resist the attacks from their Portuguese rivals.

However, the bulk of the profits went to the Portuguese who shipped highly-prized Indian textiles to Indonesia-picking up valuable spices in return for shipment to Europe. But the very profitability of this trade brought competitors. First the Dutch, and soon after the English and the French. In 1656, Colombo fell to the Dutch, and in 1663, the Portuguese lost Cochin to the Dutch. Competition with the British East India Company had led to the loss of Hormuz earlier.

Very quickly, the Dutch and then the English attempted to replace the monopoly of the Portuguese with a monopoly of their own. This led each of them to form their own fortified settlements along the chief trading routes as alternatives to the former Portuguese trading bastions. At first, the Dutch appeared to be more successful than their British and French rivals, and succeeded in establishing their pre-eminence in Indonesia, and once they had outmanoeuvred the Portuguese, also came to dominated the shipping out of Gujarat and Sindh. It was now the Dutch that imposed their will on most Indian shippers, exacting the taxes that were earlier levied by the Portuguese. At the same time, each of Portugal's European rivals began setting up local factories and trade outlets that matched or exceeded Goa.

Surat (1612), Madras (1639), Bombay (1668), Pondicherry (1674) and Calcutta (1698) thus gradually overshadowed Goa, and took over as the main centres of Indo-European trade. Nevertheless, the Indian (and other Asian) ship-building industry continued to thrive, as ships built in the ports of the Indian Ocean often matched (or even exceeded) the European-built ships in finish and craftsmanship. Impressed by the range of Indian manufactures (especially textiles), and to supplement their trade, Dutch and

British merchants established factories not only in their new port settlements, but also inland. Factories in the centres of textile weaving-such as Bahruch and Ahmedabad in Gujarat, and further inland in Burhanpur, Agra and Lahore were set up. Masulipatam, Pipli, Balasore and Dhaka also drew their attention as did Patna later. In this way, the Dutch and British merchants could keep a much more significant share of the profits that would have otherwise gone to local Indian middlemen. Manufacturing and trading emporiums were also set up in Indonesia by the Dutch.

But even as European-initiated manufacturing grew quite dramatically in the period leading up to direct colonial rule, a successively smaller proportion of the revenues that were generated in Europe reached the highly skilled and industrious Indian or Indonesian workers.

However, with only limited political control in India, British and Dutch traders could not entirely control the price of skilled labour, and had to deal somewhat respectfully with local factory owners, traders and tax officials. India continued to maintain a positive trade balance with respect to its European trade, and European traders were compelled to cover this trade deficit with a steady supply of precious metals. And as long as the European traders furnished the Indian sub-continent with gold and silver, Indian monarchs had some incentive to tolerate the European traders even as they continued to expand their presence, and artfully resisted political control over their Indian activities.

For a while, an equilibrium was maintained; but the European trading companies were always trying to increase their bargaining power by exhibitions of their steadily improving military might. They were constantly testing their powers-probing any weakness on the part of the Indian rulers. In 1691, the East India Company even attempted to challenge Mughal authority, but lost to Aurangzeb's armies, who was determined not to allow the European traders any more concessions than what they had already won.

But once the Mughal empire began to disintegrate, it was only a matter of time before one or the other of the European powers that dominated the Indian Ocean trade would find a way to extend its domination on the Indian heartland as well. In the end, it was the British who won the battle to rule over India, edging out their

European rivals who found other territories to colonize in Asia and Africa. The colonization of India was followed up by the colonization of Burma, Indo-China, the Middle East and virtually all of Africa. China's coastal areas also come under European domination. By the dawn of the 20th century, the US had also emerged as a colonial power, as it took over Spanish colonies in the Caribbean and in the Philippines.

Thus what began as a war against the unarmed free-trading merchants of the high seas, ultimately led to the almost complete subjugation of much of the planet by the Western European (and American) powers, and an enormous and unprecedented flow of wealth from the colonies to Europe and North America. For a century, the Portuguese managed to exact tribute from most of the regional traders who were active in the Indian Ocean. This was followed by a period of Dutch domination, although there were also pockets (and periods) of competitive trade as other European rivals attempted to outflank the Portuguese (and later the Dutch). But in the end, it was the British who won the largest prize-direct colonial rule over two-thirds of mainland India (and indirect rule of the rest)-allowing for the extraction of tributes far greater in magnitude than what had accrued to the Portuguese and the Dutch before them.

But even as much of Asia and Africa were forced into a state of unprecedented poverty and misery, Europe and North America witnessed astonishing developments in science, technology and culture. What was for the West, a triumph of awesome proportions, became an unmitigated tragedy for those that had to suffer the tortuous ordeal of colonization. It is important not to ignore this tragic dialectic of history-that the wealth (that in large part) funded the foundation and sustenance of "Western Civilization" came from the South and the East.

Western champions of "free trade" might also note that it was the armed and willing European monopoly traders who destroyed the free trade of the Indian Ocean. Not the other way around. Protected trade, at the barrel of the gun, not "free" or "fair" trade was at the very heart of the West's early contacts with the South and the East, and to this date, it is the West that appears most unwilling to bring down its own trade barriers even as it attempts to preach "free trade" to the rest of the world.

8

Development of Rail Transport

A rail system in India was first put forward in 1832 in Madras but it never materialised. In the 1840s, other proposals were forwarded to the British East India Company who governed India. The Governor-General of India at that time, Lord Hardinge deliberated on the proposal from the commercial, military and political viewpoints. He came to the conclusion that the East India Company should assist private capitalists who sought to setup a rail system in India, regardless of the commercial viability of their project.

On September 22nd, 1842, British civil engineer C. B. Vignoles, FRS, submitted a *Report on a Proposed Railway in India* to the East India Company. By 1845, two companies, the East Indian Railway Company operating from Calcutta, and the Great Indian Peninsula Railway (GIPR) operating from Bombay, were formed. The first train in India was operational on 1851-12-22, used for the hauling of construction material in Roorkee. A few years later, on 1853-04-16, the first passenger train between Bori Bunder, Bombay and Thana covering a distance of 34 km (21 miles) was inaugurated, formally heralding the birth of railways in India. Prior to this there was in 1832 a proposal to build a railroad between Madras and Bangalore and in 1836 a survey was conducted for this line.

The British government encouraged the setting up of railways by private investors under a scheme that would guarantee an annual return of 5% during the initial years of operation. Once completed, the company would be passed under government ownership, but would be operated by the company that built them. Robert Maitland Brereton, a British engineer was responsible for the expansion of the railway from 1857 onwards. In March

1870, he was responsible for the linking of both the rail systems, which by then had a network of 6,400 km (4,000 miles). By 1880 the network had a route mileage of about 14,500 km (9,000 miles), mostly radiating inward from the three major port cities of Bombay, Madras and Calcutta. By 1895, India had started building its own locomotives, and in 1896 sent engineers and locomotives to help build the Ugandan Railways.

In 1900, the GIPR became a government owned company. The network spread to modern day states of Assam, Rajasthan and Andhra Pradesh and soon various independent kingdoms began to have their own rail systems. In 1901, an early Railway Board was constituted, but the powers were formally invested under Lord Curzon. It served under the Department of Commerce and Industry and had a government railway official serving as chairman, and a railway manager from England and an agent of one of the company railways as the other two members. For the first time in its history, the Railways began to make a profit.

In 1907 almost all the rail companies were taken over by the government. The following year, the first electric locomotive makes its appearance. With the arrival of World War I, the railways were used to meet the needs of the British outside India. With the end of the war, the state of the railways was in disrepair and collapse. In 1920, with the network having expanded to 61,220 km, a need for central management was mooted by Sir William Acworth. Based on the East India Railway Committee chaired by Acworth, the government takes over the management of the Railways and detaches the finances of the Railways from other governmental revenues.

The period between 1920 to 1929 was a period of economic boom. Following the great depression, the company suffered economically for the next eight years. The Second World War severely crippled the railways. Trains were diverted to the Middle East and the railways workshops were converted to munitions workshops. By 1946 all rail systems were taken over by the government.

Start of Indian Railways

Following independence in 1947, India inherited a decrepit rail network. A large chunk of the railways now passed through the newly formed Pakistan. A large number of lines had to be rerouted through Indian territory had to be undertaken. A total of forty-two separate railway systems, including thirty-two lines owned by the former Indian princely states existed at the time of independence spanning a total of 55,000 km. These were amalgamated into the Indian Railways.

In 1951, the rail networks were abandoned in favour of zones. A total of six zones came into being in 1952. As India developed it economy, almost all railway production units started to be built indigenously. Broad Gauge became the standard, and the Railways began to electrify most lines to AC.

In 1985, steam locomotives were phased out. Under Rajiv Gandhi, reforms in the railways were carried out. In 1987, computerisation of reservation first was carried out in Bombay and in 1989 the train numbers were standardised to four digits. In 1995 the entire railway reservation was computerised through the railways intranet. In 1998, the Konkan Railway was opened, spanning difficult terrain through the Western Ghats. A Calcutta Metro has been built.

Chronology of Railways in India

1832

- First proposal for a railway in India, in Madras. This remained a dream on paper.

1840s

- Various proposals for railways in India, especially around Calcutta (EIR) and Bombay (GIPR).

1844

- R MacDonald Stephenson's "Report upon the Practicability and Advantages of the Introduction of Railways into British India" is published.

1845

- Survey work carried out for Bombay-Kalyan line and an extension up the Malay Ghat for proposed connections to Khandwa and Pune.
- Madras Railway Company is mooted.
- East India Railway Company is formed.

1848

- Governor-General Lord Dalhousie while advocating railway construction in India also says, *"No one can safely say whether railways in this country will earn or not"*.

1849

- August 1: Great Indian Peninsular Railway incorporated by an Act of Parliament.
- "Old Guarantee System" providing free land and guaranteed rates of return (5%) to the private English companies willing to work on building railways. Agreed upon in March, finalised on August 17.

1851

- Locomotive Thomason is used for construction work in Roorkee, beginning on December 22.
- Construction begins of an "experimental" section of track (Howrah-Rajmahal) for the proposed Calcutta-Delhi link via Mirzapur (EIR).

1852

- Construction of a line out of Bombay begins, and a locomotive, *Falkland*, begins shunting operations on February 23. The line is ready by November, and on the 18th of November, a trial run of the Bombay-Thane trip (35 km) is held. (Some accounts suggest another locomotive, *Vulcan* might have also been used for shunting operations here.)
- The Madras Guaranteed Railway Company is formed.

1853

- On April 16th, at 3:35pm, the first train in India leaves Bombay for Thane (see above for details). Initial scheduled services consist of two trains each way between Bombay and Thane and later Bombay and Mahim via Dadar.
- Madras Railway incorporated; work begins on Madras-Arcot line.
- Lord Dalhousie's famous Railway Minute of April 20 lays down the policy that private enterprise would be allowed to build railways in India, but that their operation would be closely supervised by the government.

1854

- On August 15th, the first passenger train in the eastern section is operated, from Howrah to Hooghly (24 miles). The section is soon extended to Pundooah.
- By May, GIPR Bombay-Thane line is extended to Kalyan and is a double tracked line; inaugurated by Lord Elphinstone. Dapoorie viaduct is completed.
- GIPR opens its first workshops at Byculla.
- Stations are classified into 4 groups on some railways, according to traffic and the proportion of European and Indian passengers.

1855

- BB&CI Railway incorporated, and begins work on a Surat-Baroda line.
- Thane-Kalyan line extended to Vasind on the northeast.
- February 3: EIR's "experimental" track for a Calcutta-Delhi route now consists of a Howrah to Raneegunj (Raniganj, collieries near Asansol) section of 121 miles.
- August: EIR 21 and 22 ("Express" and "Fairy Queen") begin work. The Fairy Queen is still working!

1855-1856

- HMS Goodwin carrying railway carriages for East Indian Railway Co. sinks. Another ship carrying a locomotive is mis-routed to Australia.

1856

- On July 1st, the first train in the south was operated, from Royapuram/Veyasarapady (Madras) to Wallajah Road (Arcot) (approx. 100km) by the Madras Railway Company.
- A combined Loco, Carriage and Wagon Workshop is set up by the Madras Guaranteed Rly. (later part of the MSMR) at Perambur, near Madras, later to become the Carriage and Wagon Workshops of SR (and the Loco Workshops at Perambur).
- Sindh (later Sindh, Punjab and Delhi) Railway is formed, a guaranteed railway.
- GIPR line extended to Khopoli via Palasdhari on the

southeast. Regular services are now run from Mumbai to Vasind and from Mumbai to Khopoli. Stations opened at Dadar, Kurla, Titwala, Badlapur, and Neral.

1858

- Eastern Bengal Railway and the Great Southern of India formed (guaranteed railways).
- June 14: Khandala-Pune section of GIPR open to traffic. The 21km gap over the Bhore ghat (Karjat-Khandala) is crossed by palanquin, horses, or on foot. In some cases the passenger cars were also carried over each way.

1859

- On March 3rd, the first train in the north was operated, from Allahabad to Kanpur (180km).
- BBCI Railway obtains permission to extend its lines southwards from Surat, and opens its Grant Road terminus for its proposed line from Surat.
- Eastern Bengal Railway begins construction on Calcutta-Kushtia line (175km).
- Calcutta and South-Eastern Railway formed, with 5% guarantee from the government.

1855-1870

- Several (about a dozen) railway companies are incorporated.
- Early 1860s
- Various early experiments with providing passenger amenities such as toilets, lights, etc. These naturally tended to be introduced first in the First Class carriages and only later in the lower classes of accommodation.
- Sindh and Punjab Railway is engaged in construction of a northward line from Karachi, a Lahore-Multan line, and a Lahore-Delhi line.
- Kanpur-Etawah section opened.

1860

- Bhusawal station set up by GIPR.
- Vasind-Asangaon line opened.

1861

- Madras Railway's trunk route from Madras extended to

Beypur/Kadalundi (near Calicut). Work begins on a northwestern branch out of Arakkonam.

- Great Southern Railway of India completes 125km BG line between Nagapatnam and Trichinopoly. (Some sources suggest the line was till Tanjore, and extended to Trichinopoly by March 1862.)
- Churchgate station opened by BBCI Railway as its new terminus for Bombay.
- January 1: GIPR's Kasara line opens (extended from Asangaon).
- May 13: Karachi-Kotri section of the Scinde Rly. opens to public traffic, the first section in the region that would later become Pakistan.

1862

- Feb. 8: Jamalpur Loco Works established.
- Khanderao, the Gaekward of Baroda, opens 8 miles of an NG railway line from Dabhoi towards Miyagam. Oxen were used as the motive power!
- EIR's Delhi-Calcutta route progresses as far as the west bank of the Yamuna, via Mughalsarai. Sahibganj Loop.
- Sealdah station commissioned.
- Bhore ghat incline constructed, connecting Palasdhari to Khandala.
- November: EBR's Calcutta-Kushtia line open for traffic.
- Calcutta and South-Eastern Railway's 45km line from Calcutta to Port Canning is constructed.
- Amritsar-Attari section completed on the route to Lahore.
- The Indian Branch Railway Co. formed to construct short branches and feeder lines in northern India, with a 20-year subsidy but no guarantee.
- The Indian Tramway Co. is formed for building short lines around Madras, also with a 20-year subsidy. This suffered losses later, was reorganised to become the Carnatic Railway and finally was taken over by the South Indian Railway.

- Two-tier seating is introduced in Third Class (on EIR, GIPR, etc.) as a measure to alleviate overcrowding. A typical coach carries 50 passengers on the lower seats, and 70 on the upper level, nearly doubling the capacity of the already overcrowded third-class coaches. These were the first double-decker coaches to be used in India, and perhaps in the world.
- Madras Railway extends its lines to Renigunta.
- GSIR's Nagapatnam-Trichinopoly line opened to traffic.

1863

- May 14: GIPR line from Bombay across the Bhore Ghat to Pune constructed.
- BB&CI Railway completes Surat-Baroda-Ahmedabad line.
- EIR completes Arrah bridge over the Sone.
- Port Canning-Mutlah line opened by the Calcutta & South-Eastern R Railway.
- Nalhati-Azimganj 4' gauge line built by the Indian Branch Railway Co.
- First luxury carriage in India is built for the Governor of Bombay.

1864

- August 1: First train into Delhi. Though trains run between Delhi and Calcutta; coaches are ferried on boats across the river at Allahabad.
- Bombay-Surat line completed by BB&CI Railway.
- Jolarpettai-Bangalore Cantt. branch added by Madras Railway; Bangalore Mail begins running.
- First proposals for (horse-drawn) trams in Bombay.

1865

- Sindh and Punjab Railway's Multan-Lahore-Amritsar line is completed. Works begins on line from Delhi to Amritsar.
- BB&CI completes Bombay-Ahmedabad rail link.
- Yamuna bridge at Allahabad opened, allowing EIR trains to cross over without using ferries.
- Arakkonam-Conjeevaram 3'6" line built by the Indian Tramways Co.

- Kasara line extended to Igatpuri over the Thull (Thall) ghat.
- GIPR timetables show 'local trains' separately for the first time. These are in the sections to Mahim and Kalyan.
- Alambagh Workshops set up by the Oudh and Rohilkhand Rly. (formerly the Indian Branch Rly. Co.).

1866

- Railway Branch formed in Central Public Works Department.
- Delhi and Calcutta are linked directly by rail as the completion of the Yamuna bridge (road and rail) in Delhi allows the trains to reach what later became Delhi Junction. The 1 Dn/2 Up Mail begins running—this is the predecessor of the Howrah-Kalka Mail.
- Bhusawal-Khandwa section opened.
- W. Newman & Co. begins publishing the "Newman's Indian Bradshaw" for train timetables in India.
- Indian Branch Rly. Co. begins construction of Lucknow-Kanpur light MG line.

1867

- Virar-Bombay Backbay suburban service commences (BB&CI); one train in each direction each day.
- Some Indian locos are sent overseas for the Abyssinian expedition.
- GIPR branch line extended to Nagpur; Bhusawal-Badnera section opened.
- EIR branch line extends from Allahabad to Jubbulpore (Jabalpur).
- Lucknow-Kanpur line opened by the Indian Branch Railway Co.

1868

- Madras Railway extends its network (with a new terminus at Royapuram) to Salem, and also finishes the Jolarpettai-Bangalore Cantonment branch.
- November: Sindh, Punjab, and Delhi Railway's line towards Amritsar from Delhi (Ghaziabad) is open for traffic up to Ambala.

- Calcutta and South-Eastern Railway, having suffered extensive losses on their Sealdah-Canning line because of floods and other problems, decide to transfer the line to the government in return for capital costs, becoming the first railway to be taken over by the state.
- GSIR's line reaches Erode, connecting to the Madras State Rly.
- Charbagh workshops set up by the Oudh and Rohilkhand Rly.

1869

- Governor-General Lord Lawrence suggests that the Government of India itself undertake all future construction of railway lines. But GIPR's guarantees and leases are extended, and also those of the Bombay, Baroda, and Madras Railway Companies. Still, this year marks a turning point in government policy away from the guarantee system.
- GIPR locals extended from Mahim to Bandra.
- Jan. 25: Runaway train on the Bhore Ghat derails and crashes after failing to be stopped by a catch siding, and is made (in)famous by pictures in the Illustrated London News.
- Total trackage in India is about 4000 miles.

1870

- March 7: GIPR connection over the Thull Ghat reaches Jubbulpore (Jabalpur) from Itarsi, linking up with EIR track there from Allahabad, and establishing connectivity between Bombay and Calcutta.
- BBCI Railway runs direct trains between Ahmedabad and Bombay.
- October: Sindh, Punjab, and Delhi Railway completes Amritsar-Saharanpur-Ghaziabad line, linking Punjab Railway with the EIR and providing connectivity between Multan and Delhi.
- Mughalsarai-Lahore main line is also completed.
- Lord Mayo introduces meter gauge as a compromise

between proposals for narrow gauges less than 3' and broad gauge, for use in areas with limited traffic.

- Mobile post-office services in trains on EIR.
- The Nizam of Hyderabad pays for the construction of a railway linking Hyderabad to the GIPR.
- Jamalpur workshop gets a rolling mill of its own.

1871

- Southeast of Kalyan, the GIPR line extended over the Bhore Ghat to reach Raichur, connecting with the Madras Railway, whose branch line out of Arakkonam reaches Raichur by now.
- BB&CI line to Viramgam.
- The 'Shorter Main Line' on the Delhi-Calcutta route (via Jhajha, Patna) is in place with the completion of the section from Raniganj to Kiul.
- EBR line from Calcutta to Goalundo opens.
- EIR trackage totals 1350 miles; other railways: GIPR—875, Madras Railway—680, Sindh and Punjab—400, BBCI—300, East Bengal—115, and Great Southern—170.

1872

- Bombay suburban services extended to Arthur Bunder in Colaba.
- First, MG line from Delhi to Farukh Nagar is built.
- The Saunders system of air-cooling first-class coaches is introduced on the GIPR.
- BB&CI line to Wadhwan (Surendranagar)
- GSIR merged with the MG Carnatic Rly.
- Oudh & Rohilkund Rly. opens line from Benares (Varanasi) to Lucknow.

1873

- Colaba Terminus commissioned, envisioned as a temporary station pending completion of a permanent line between Marine Lines and Churchgate, making Marine Lines the new terminus.
- The world's first commercial MG service runs from Delhi to Rewari.
- Dabhoi-Miyagam line (the first 2'6" line) is re-laid with

stronger rails to allow locomotives to be used (earlier oxen were the motive power) although locomotives were not used regularly on this until 1880. This later becomes part of the Gaekwad's Baroda State Railway.

- Early attempts to set up a horse-drawn tram system in Calcutta, between Sealdah and Armenian Ghat Street (3.8km). This service opened on Feb. 24 and closed by Nov. 20 for lack of patronage.
- Stearnes and Kittredge get contract for horse-drawn tram system in Bombay.

1874-1880

- Famines in several areas of India result in more railway lines being bulit for relief.

1874

- Wadi-Secunderabad railway line built with financing from the Nizam of Hyderabad, and later becomes part of the Nizam's Guaranteed State Railway. Secunderabad railway station built by this railway.
- Delhi-Bandikui, Bandikui-Agra lines of Rajputana State Railway opened, and Alwar line is under construction (all MG).
- Fourth Class accommodation is introduced on several railways, consisting of coaches with no seats in them, or just a few benches, as a way of alleviating overcrowding.
- Lord Salisbury, Secretary of State for India, stipulates the use of BG to settle the gauge debate, and work begins on relaying many MG lines to BG.
- "F" class 0-6-0 MG locomotives are introduced, soon to be among the most widely-used in India for just about all kinds of duties. Dubs & Co. of Glasgow built the first few.
- GSIR and Carnatic Rly. merger is now renamed the South Indian Railway.
- ORR extends line from Lucknow to Moradabad.
- Tirhoot State Rly. opens MG lines to Samastipur and Darbhanga.
- SIR on July 1 takes over GSIR (BG) and Carnatic Rly. (MG).

- May 9: Horse-drawn tram system begins operation in Bombay, between Parel and Colaba. Operated by Stearnes and Kittredge with a stable of 900 horses.

1875

- Hathras Road-Mathura Cantt. section opened to traffic. The first train runs here on Oct. 19.
- Rajputana State Railway MG line reaches Ajmer.
- Special train built for the Prince of Wales on his visit to India; this train is later used as the vice-regal train for the next 3 decades.
- Former GSIR Nagapatnam-Trichinopoly BG line converted to MG.

1877

- Construction work begins on the Ajmer workshops of the Rajputana-Malwa State Rly.
- Masjid, Parel, Ghatkopar, Diva, and Chinchpokli stations opened for Mumbai local services.
- (Possibly 1876?) Emile Moreau, a French author, and TK Bannerjee, an Indian businessman, start the bookstore chain 'AH Wheeler & Co.', which later spread to have its book stalls in a great many small and big railway stations in India, especially in the north. The company was also the one that published Rudyard Kipling in 1988 when he was all but unknown. The company's name was borrowed from a then-successful London bookstore, Arthur Henry Wheeler's.

1878

- Punjab Northern State Railway builds the Lahore-Jhelum line (parts that opened as MG in 1876 are converted to BG).
- Railway line laid across the Bolan Pass to help move men and materiel during hostilities in Afghanistan.
- Indus Valley State Rly. opens Multan-Kotri line.
- Khandwa-Indore MG line of Holkar State Railway under construction, passing the Mhow ghat section by 1878.

- Construction of Victoria Terminus begins in Bombay.
- Construction of the Siliguri-Darjeeling line, the first hill railway in India (not counting the ghat sections near Bombay).

1879

- In a reversal of the broad-gauge policy instituted under Lord Salisbury, the Rajputana-Malwa Railway is authorised to build its lines to meter-gauge.
- Continuous vacuum brakes are brought into use for passenger rakes.
- BB&CI extends BG network to Wadhwan (Surendranagar) in Kathiawar.
- Ahmedabad-Palanpur MG section opened.
- All of the former GSIR lines (now in SIR) are converted to MG from BG.
- The state takes over the Nizam's Railway.
- North Bengal State Rly. opens Parbatipur-Kaunia MG line.
- (1877) Following an agreement between the British and the French, an MG line is laid between Pondicherry and Villupuram.

1880

- About 9,000 miles of railways in India, of which 2,175 miles are state-owned. Famine Commission suggests creating another 5,000 miles of railways, and private construction of railways is resumed.
- EIR taken over by the state (1879), but the construction and operation of the railway are handed back to the company.
- The Kandahar State Railway from Ruk to Sibi is formed; 133.5 miles of track are laid in 101 days!
- The Darjeeling Steam Tramway (later the Darjeeling Himalayan Railway) starts services on its first section, the Siliguri-Darjeeling line.
- The durable 'L' class 4-6-0 tender locos make their appearance.
- GIPR runs about 14 local services in each direction in

Mumbai, including five terminating at Kurla. It is believed that at this time Currey Road station is used for loading and unloading horses for the races at Mahalaxmi.

- Bhavnagar-Wadhwan (Surendranagar) line opened by Kathiawar State Rly. (later part of Bhavnagar State Rly.). (MG)
- Kanpur-Farukhabad section is operational.
- Dec. 22: Calcutta Tramways Co. incorporated.

Early 1880's

- Bengal and North Western, Bengal Central, Rohilkhand-Kumaon, and Indian Midland Railways formed without guarantees; Southern Mahratta Railways formed with guarantees.

1881

- Ajmer-Ahmedabad line (MG) opens, and becomes part of the Rajputana State Railway.
- September: Darjeeling Steam Tramway becomes the Darjeeling Himalayan Railway.
- The Maharaja Sindia of Gwalior opens the Agra-Gwalior line of what became the Sindia State Rly.
- Jan.: Horse-drawn trams begin regular operation in Calcutta.

1882

- BB&CI trunk route reaches Godhra.
- Khandwa-Indore line extended to Ajmer.
- Rajputana State Rly. merged into Rajputana Malwa Rly.
- Bangalore-Mysore MG line opened by the Mysore State Rly. (this line later went to the Southern Mahratta Railway Co. which was chartered in 1882 to operate some famine-relief lines opened by the state).
- Marwar-Pali section opened on June 24 as part of the new Jodhpur Railway.
- Bangalore City linked to Bangalore Cantonment by Madras Railway.
- Assam Rly. and Trading Co. opens Dibrugarh/Amlapatty-

Dinjan Stream MG section as part of the Dibru-Sadia Railway (section operational on Aug. 15).

- Railway Watch and Ward, the predecessor of the RPF, constituted.
- Post of Director General of Railways is created in the Central Public Works Department.
- Jan. 1: Victoria Terminus, still under construction, is opened to the public.
- First 'A' class tank locomotives built for the DHR.
- Nagpur-Rajnandgaon MG line opened.
- Steam tramway system begins operating in Calcutta.

1883

- Punjab Northern State Railway line extended from Jhelum to Peshawar.
- Attock bridge across the Indus is constructed.

1884

- Bengal-Nagpur Railway (a private company) sanctioned, with guarantees.
- A Select Committee in the House of Commons recommends continuing the policy of using MG for local and secondary lines only, and suggests that feeder lines to BG should also be BG.
- Amlapatty-Dinjan route extended to Tinsukia and Margherita.
- Pali-Luni section of Jodhpur Railway opens on June 17.
- Delhi-Mathura line opened
- Calcutta-Khulna line opened by Bengal Central Rly.
- Bhopal-Itarsi line opened by the Begum of Bhopal.
- Southern Mahratta Rly. Co. opens Hospet-Bellary and Gadag-Hotgi lines.
- April: Bengal & North-Western Rly. opens Nawabganz-Gonda-Bahraich line (MG).
- MG lines: Assam Behar State Rly. builds to Parbatipur; Bangalore-Tumkur-Gubbi (Mysore State Rly.); Rohilkund-Kumaon Rly. builds line to Kathgodam.

- Budni-Burkhera ghat section opened.
- NG lines: Two lines from Kaunia to Dharlla river (part of the East Bengal State Rly.)
- Meridian Conference in Washington, DC, sets the foundation for worldwide standard time zones from which, eventually, Indian Standard Time emerged in the 20th century.

1885

- Jodhpur is connected (via Luni) to the Rajputana Malwa Railway network (first train on March 9) (MG). This line later becomes part of the Jodhpur Bikaner Rly.
- Seats are provided in Fourth Class accommodation. Simultaneously, accommodation classes are reorganised so that the Fourth Class becomes Third Class, Third Class is renamed Second Class, and Second Class is transformed to "Inter" Class.
- First coaches (wooden-bodied) with steel underframes introduced.
- Assam Rlys. & Trading Co. builds Dibru-Sadiya Rly. (MG)
- Narayanganj-Mymensingh MG line opened by Dacca State Rly.
- DHR line extended to Darjeeling Bazaar.
- April 20: A steam tramway opens in Karachi.
- Victoria Terminus-Byculla track is doubled.

1886

- ORR line extended to Saharanpur.
- NG lines: Cherra-Companyganj Rly. (Cherrapunjee Mountain Rly.) builds line from Companyganj to Therria Ghat and across it to Cherrapunji with 7 gradients worked by rope mechanisms.
- Miraj-Pune MG line opened.
- Karachi's steam tramway is replaced by a horse-drawn system.

1887

- Dufferin Bridge constructed over the Ganga at Varanasi, allowing EIR trains to go from Mughalsarai to Varanasi.

- Victoria Terminus named after Queen Victoria on Jubilee Day.

1888

- Madras Railway trunk route from Madras extended along the west coast to Calicut.
- Construction of Bombay's Victoria Terminus building is completed. The cost was estimated at Rs 1,640,000
- Landsdowne bridge over the Indus (at Sukkur).
- Kushtia-Siliguri line (MG) of North Bengal State Railway.
- A.H. Wheeler and Co. introduce their Indian Railway Library series of publications.
- Southern Mahratta Rly.'s main eastward route connects with other lines going until Bezwada (Vijayawada), which were later taken over by the SMR. The section in Goa worked by SMR for West of India Portuguese Rly. terminating at Marmagoa opens.

1889

- Nizam's State Railway's main line is extended to Bezwada (Vijayawada).
- Delhi-Ambala-Kalka line laid.
- A Select Committee in the House of Commons recommends against laying any new MG lines outside areas where MG was dominant.
- Jamshedpur workshops work on putting together some locos (but the first complete loco is not built in India until 1895 at Ajmer).
- EIR appoints the first Signal Engineer in India (Mr S T Dutton).
- Jodhpur Bikaner Railway formed.
- First 'B' class locomotives of the DHR built.
- Indian Midland Rly. opens lines from Jhansi to Gwalior, Kanpur, Manikpur, and Bhopal.
- Assam Behar State Rly.'s Parbatipur MG line is extended to Katihar.
- Jamalpur-Jagannathganj Rly. open to traffic.

- Gubbi-Birur-Harihar MG line opened by Mysore State Rly.
- Six platforms constructed at Bombay Victoria Terminus.

1890

- Goa-Guntakal MG line completed by the Southern Mahratta Rly Co., with branches from Londa to Poona (connecting to Mysore via Bangalore, and also with Gadag-Hotgi), and Bezwada (Vijayawada) to Marmagoa.
- East Coast State Railway (government-owned) sanctioned.
- SIR taken over by the state, but working of lines is by a reconstituted SIR company (1891).
- NG lines: Wadhwan-Morvi-Rajkot line opened (later converted to BG); Shahjahanpur-Powayan (Powayan Steam Tramways).
- (Approximate date) Some time in the 1890s third class passengers are allowed on the prestigious Mail trains.
- Railways Act passed by the government defining the framework for railway construction and operation.

1891

- Jodhpur connected to Bikaner by MG (Jodhpur-Merta Road opened April 8, Merta Road-Nagaur on Oct. 16, and Nagaur-Bikaner on Dec. 9).
- Following political and passenger demands, toilet facilities are introduced on a large scale in first class carriages.
- Khojak tunnel opens, the westernmost point of the Kandahar State Rly. (Chaman Extension Rly.) which was to reach Afghanistan but which in fact never crossed the frontier from British India beyond Chaman. At the time, this was the longest railway tunnel in the sub-continent.
- Construction begins for the Nilgiri railway.
- Delhi-Ambala-Kalka line opened.
- Rope-worked section over Therria Ghat of Cherra-Companyganj Rly. dismantled.

1892

- Assam Bengal Railway incorporated (MG).

- Early use of simple mechnanical interlocking devices (List and List & Morse systems) at six single line crossings of NWR.
- BB&CI line to Godhra
- Yeshwantpur-Dodballapur MG line by Mysore State Rly.

1893

- The government-built Godhra-Nagda link is handed over to the BB&CI Railway for operation.
- Cabin interlocking introduced in some places by the GIPR on the Bombay-Delhi route. (Equipment supplied by Saxby and Farmer.)
- First railway foundry set up at Jamalpur Workshops
- Merta-Kuchaman section opened to carry salt traffic from the Rajputana areas.
- Bengal Dooars Rly. opens (MG).
- Cuttack-Khurda Road-Puri line opened by the East Coast Rly.
- MG line from Yeshwantpur extended to Mysore frontier by Mysore State Rly.

1894

- List & Morse interlocking system introduced for 29 single line crossings between Lahore and Ghaziabad.
- NG lines: Powayan Steam Tramways extended to Mailani on the Rohilkund-Kumaon Rly.

1895

- First locomotive built in India at the Ajmer works, an 'F' class 0-6-0 MG loco for the Rajputana Malwa Railway (F-734). This is now preserved at the National Rail Museum.
- Udaipur-Chittorgarh MG line built by the Mewar Darbar.
- NG lines: Tezpore-Balipara; Tarakeshwar-Howrah (Bengal Provincial Rly. Co.)
- Madras trams begin operating, with a conduit system. (This is replaced in 1905 with electric traction.)

1896

- Indian railway staff and some MG locos are sent overseas to help build the Uganda Railway.
- BB&CI line to Nagda and Ujjain.

1897

- The first section of the NG Barsi Light Railway is built from Barsi Road Junction to Barsi Town.
- (Late 1890's) Lighting in passenger coaches introduced by many railway companies. Lower classes tended to get gas lamps, whereas upper classes sometimes got electric lights, but often gas or oil lamps.
- First Godavari bridge built near Rajahmundry, helping Chennai-Howrah traffic.
- Hoogly (Hooghly) bridge built.
- Strategic considerations from the War Department force all new narrow-gauge lines to be laid to 2'6" gauge instead of 2' gauge from 1897 onwards. 2'6" was the narrow-gauge standard for all the imperial colonies.
- Rajkot-Jamnagar MG section opened by Jamnagar Rly.
- Mettupalayam-Coonoor rail line constructed.
- Delhi-Bhatinda-Samasatta line opened by Southern Punjab Railway Co.

1898

- August: Mettupalayam-Coonoor rail line opens, but is soon closed after heavy rains cause severe damage to the track.
- NG lines: Howrah-Amta, Howrah-Sheakhala (2' gauge, Martin & Co.).

1899

- Maharaj Scindia of Gwalior opens NG (2') railway lines from Gwalior to Bhind and Shivpuri. These later become part of the Gwalior Light Railways.
- Jamalpur Workshops officially begin producing steam locomotives (earlier they were putting together locomotives with parts from other locomotives, etc.). The first engine is CA 764, *Lady Curzon*.

- Nov. 1: Through BG connection between Bezwada (Vijayawada) and Madras (Chennai) opens.
- Mettupalaiyam-Coonoor section of the Nilgiri Mountain Rly. reopens after repair and restoration.
- Bina-Baran line opened.
- South Indian Railway begins Madras-Tuticorin service connecting with the boat to Ceylon, using vestibuled coaches for both First and Second class. The trip takes nearly 22 hours for the 443 mile route.
- Electric traction for trams introduced in Calcutta.

1900

- GIPR network becomes state property on July 1, but the company is allowed to continue operating the services.
- Upper Sone bridge built, the longest in India at 10,052 feet.
- Balotra-Hyderabad section of Jodhpur Bikaner Rly. opens.
- Doon Railway opens (Haridwar-Dehradun).
- Tapti Valley Railway opened.
- Connection to Gaya added on the Calcutta Delhi route
- Assam Bengal Rly. opens branch line to Guwahati.
- Bengal Dooars Rly. open link to EBR at Lalmonirhat.
- Rajputana Malway Rly. becomes part of the BB&CI Rly.
- Brahmaputra-Sultanpur Branch Rly. opens MG line from Santahar east (with a ferry section) to Mymensingh.
- Manmad-Secunderabad MG line opened by the Hyderabad Godavary Valley Rly.
- Calcutta tramways' electrification and conversion to standard gauge from meter gauge begins. Total system size is at 30km.
- NG lines opened: Parlakimedi Light Rly. from Navpada (BNR); Rajpur-Dhamtari (BNR). Planning begun for Matheran Light Railway.

1901

- Sir Thomas Robertson Committee submits recommendations on administration and working of the railways. An early version of the railway board is constituted, with three members serving on it at first.

- Railway mileage now at about 24,750 miles in India, of which 14,000 miles are BG, and most of the rest MG (with only a few hundred miles of 2' and 2'6" gauge lines).
- The railways also start returning some modest profits; for the last 40 years they had been making large losses.
- Indian Midland Railway merged into BBCI Railway.
- EIR's "Grand Chord" section finished connecting Sitarampur-Gaya-Mughalsarai.
- BB&CI line to Cambay.
- East Coast Rly. line to Waltair becomes part of the Madras Railway.
- MG lines: Kaunia-Dharlla Rly. lines converted to MG; Jodhpur-Hyderabad (by Jodhpur Bikaner Rly., after a section near Hyderabad is converted from BG to MG).
- NG lines: Gitaldaha-Jainti (Cooch Behar State Rly.); Nawshera-Dargai State Rly. (later NWR).
- Burn & Co. sets up a workshop at Howrah.

1902

- Shoranur-Cochin line is built, owned by the state but operated by the SIR.
- A monorail of the Ewing system (double-flanged wheels and an outrigger wheel for balance) powered by ponies is installed for transporting tea and other light goods at the High Range near Keranganie.
- The Luni-Shadipalli line is completed in the Thar desert. The Shadipalli-Hyderabad (now Pakistan) line is regauged to MG.
- BNR takes over part of the East Coast Rly. lines (Cuttack-Vizianagaram, branch line to Puri).
- NG lines: Khushalgarh-Kohat (later NWR).
- Mar. 27: Electric trams begin operating in Calcutta.
- The Jodhpur Railway becomes the first to introduce electric lights as standard fixtures. (Electric lighting had been tried by other railways starting in the 1890s.)

1903

- BESA standards for new loco types are formulated.
- The Robertson Report recommends re-laying all BG and

MG lines to standard gauge, but this report seems to have been completely ignored.

- Nov. 9: Kalka-Shimla Railway line opened, built at 2'0" gauge (but relaid later, see below).
- The first bogie-mounted coaches appear, including bogie dining cars on some railways.
- Assam-Bengal Rly. joins Dibru-Sadiya Rly. at Tinsukia from Chittagong via Lumding (MG).
- GIPR appoints its first Signal Engineer (following belatedly in EIR's footsteps), Mr I W Stokes.
- Interlocking introduced for 9 stations (3 on Bombay-Thane section, 6 on Thane-Kalyan section)—including Bombay VT.
- NG lines: Gondia-Nainpur (BNR); Kohat-Thal (later NWR).

1904

- The Moghulpura workshops near Lahore build six 0-6-2T "ST" class locos by using parts from other locos, making them the only works other than Ajmer to build locomotives in (British) India.
- The Kharagpur Locomotive and Carriage and Wagon Workshop is set up.
- Railway Board expanded, given more powers.
- Agra-Delhi chord line opened.
- NG lines: Nainpur-Chhindwara (BNR); Howrah-Tribeni (Bengal Provincial Rly. Co., connecting to Katwa line); Gwalior light railway sections: Gwalior-Jora Alapur (Jan. 1), Jora Alapur-Sabalgarh (Dec. 1). Construction begun on Matheran Light Railway.

1905

- Powers of the Railway Board are formalised under Lord Curzon. The Board is under the Department of Commerce and Industry, and has government railway official serving as chairman, and a railway manager from England and an agent of one of the company railways as the other two members.
- The visit of the Prince and Princess of Wales gives EIR a chance to build a special train with coaches rivalling the luxury saloons used by nobility in Europe.

- A petrol-driven 0-4-0 loco from Kerr Stuart is in use by the Morvi Railway and Tramways company.
- Kalka-Shimla Railway regauged to 2'6" gauge under guidelines from the War Department seeking to ensure uniformity in all imperial narrow gauge systems.
- "F" class 0-6-0 MG locomotives are introduced, soon to be among the most widely-used in India for just about all kinds of duties. Dubs & co. of Glasgow built the first few.
- Railway Board decides that lavatories will be provided in all lower class carriages for trains running more than 50 miles.
- BNR's Satpura Railway complete's Gondia-Nainpur-Jabalpur link.
- Surendranagar-Rajkot MG section opened.
- A short MG spur is built into Afghanistan along the Kabul river.
- NG lines: Wadhwan-Rajkot line of Morvi Rly. converted to BG; Rupsa-Barapada line of Mourbhang (Mayurbhanj) Rly. opens (BNR); Tirupattur-Krishnagiri; Gondia-Nainpur line extended to Jabalpur (BNR); Tuna-Anjar by the Maharaja of Cutch, later part of the Cutch State Rly.
- GIPR line quadrupled up to Currey Road.
- The first electric trams run in Madras with overhead electrification.
- Entire Calcutta tram network is now electrified and converted to standard gauge. The Howrah Station to Bandhaghat line opens in June.

1906

- The 'General Rules' are framed, governing operation of railways.
- Howrah Terminus rebuilt and inaugurated, the largest railway station in India.
- Madras Rly. builds Morappur-Dharmapuri MG line for famine relief.
- Barsi Road Jn.-Pandharpur section of Barsi Light Railway opens.

- Kalka-Shimla Rly. taken over by the state.
- Rajputana-Malwa Rly. taken over by state and made part of BB&CI Rly.
- BB&CI Rly. starts a Weekend Special from Bombay to Surat, the forerunner of the Flying Ranee.
- Kasganj-Kathgodam section opens to passenger rail traffic.
- Kurla-Chembur single line built for garbage trains.
- Dec. 6: The Grand Chord via Gaya, which significantly shortens the distance between Delhi and Calcutta, opens on the EIR's Calcutta-Delhi trunk route (inaugurated by the Earl of Minto, the Viceroy and Governor-General of India.
- Indian Standard Time (IST) comes into force for timekeeping in British India (except for Calcutta and some other regions).

1907

- The government purchases all major lines and releases them to private operators, with the exception of Rohilkhund & Kumaon Rly. and Bengal & North-Western Rly.
- Sirhind-Morinda section of the Patiala State Monorail is opened, powered by oxen and army mules from 1907 until 1927.
- By now, toilets are standard in most lower class carriages, except for short suburban lines.
- Railway Mail Service (RMS) is established.
- 22 March: Matheran Light Railway opens, with 4 articulated 0-6-0T locomotives.
- Madras Railway trunk route extended from Calicut to Mangalore.
- Jaipur-Sawai Madhopur MG line opened by the Jaipur State Rly.
- NG lines: Purulia-Ranchi (BNR); Tuna-Anjar extended to Bhuj (Cutch State Rly.); Shahdara-Saharanpur Light Rly. (Martin & Co.).
- The Sir James Mackay Committee suggests further enhancements to financial and administrative procedures.

- May 7: Electric trams begin operating in Bombay.
- June: Kanpur's electric tram system begins operation.

1908

- Kaunia-Dharlla MG line of East Bengal Railway extended to Amingaon, where a ferry across the Brahmaputra connected to the rail system of the Assam Bengal Railway through Guwahati.
- BB&CI Railway constructs a line from Baroda to Mathura.
- India's first internal combustion locomotive, a petrol-driven MG loco, is delivered to the Assam Oil Co. by McEwan Pratt & Co. of Wickford, Essex.
- Patiala State Monorail obtains the four famed Orenstein and Koppel monorail locomotives for some of its lines.
- Inward-opening doors are introduced on passenger coaches.
- The spur from the northwest territories into Afghanistan, the only railway line in Afghanistan at this time, is dismantled.
- NG lines: Gwalior-Sheopur Kalan (2' gauge, Gwalior Light Rly.), Sabalgarh-Birpur (Nov. 1).
- Karachi's horse-drawn trams are replaced by petrol trams.
- Calcutta tram network extended to Sibpur via G.T. Road.

1909

- India's first electric locos (two of them) are delivered to the Mysore Gold Fields by Bagnalls (Stafford) with overhead electrical equipment by Siemens. Also among the earliest electric vehicles, electrically operated rail trolleys (" White's patented rail motor trolleys") are brought into use (by EIR's Carriage & Wagon workshops, by the Oudh and Rohilkhund Rly., by the Eastern Bengal State Rly., etc.).
- A petrol-driven 0-4-9 loco is supplied to Morvi Railway and Tramways by Nasmyth Wilson. A couple of Thornycroft petrol-driven parcel delivery vehicles are also in use by the EIR.

- Saharanpur marshalling yard under construction by the North Western State Rly. and the Oudh and Rohilkhund Rly.
- 23-ton BG bogie hopper wagons brought into use by Bengal Nagpur Rly. for transporting iron to the Tata Iron and Steel Works.
- South India Rly.'s contract is renewed despite widespread support for appropriation by the state among local interests.
- South India Rly. is engaged in ultimately abandoned attempt to build a direct railway between India and Ceylon with a viaduct over the Panban viaduct.
- The Harbour Line opens from Kurla to Reay Road as the terminus (double track).
- Syke's Lock and Block system of interlocking introduced on the BB&CI Rly. and other railways.
- NG lines: Gwalior Light Rly.: Birpur-Sheopur (Jun. 15)

1911

- Kanpur-Chachran line opened by princely state of Bahawalpur (now in Pakistan, closed in the 1980s).
- NG lines: Barsi Light Railway extended until Latur; Champaner-Shivrajpuri Light Rly. (later part of BB&CI); Dehri-on-Sone-Rohtas (Dehri-Rohtas Light Rly.); Bukhtiarpur-Bihar Rly. (Martin & Co.).

1912

- June 1: Punjab Mail (GIPR) makes its inaugural run.
- Cabin interlocking completed for the entire length of the Bombay-Delhi route (GIPR).
- Work begins on Mysore-Arsikere link.

1913

- Bowringpet-Kolar 2'6" line (part of the Kolar District Rly.) opened by the Mysore State Railways.
- Madras Rly. extends MG line from Dharmapuri to Hosur.
- NG lines: BB&CI lines to Godhra, Nadiad; Jessore-Jhenidah (McLeod's).

- NG lines: Kalabagh-Bannu (Trans-Indus Rly.; later NWR).
- In the Mumbai area, suburban terminals are opened at Kurla, Kalyan, Thane, and one at the BB&CI station at Bandra for GIPR trains.

1914-1919

- World War I places heavy strain on the railways. Railway production is diverted to meet the needs of British forces outside India. At the end of the war Indian railways are in a total state of dilapidation and disrepair. All services are downgraded or restricted.

1914

- Ceylon Government Railway extends the line from Polgahawela to Talaimannar at the northern tip of Ceylon (now Sri Lanka), to enable connecting services with SIR trains with a ferry crossing across the Palk Strait. Steamer services from Dhanushkodi (India) to Talaimannar (Ceylon) start on March 1.
- RBS standards for rails adopted (90lb/yd for BG, 60lb/yd for MG).
- Double line between Ravli Cabin and Mahim on Harbour Branch.
- NG lines: Dholpur-Bari line extended to Tantpur; Dhond-Baramati (Central Provinces Rly.; later GIPR); Murtazapur-Achalpur/Yavatmal; Arrah-Sasaram, Baraset-Basirhat (Martin & Co.); Larkana-Jacobabad and Jacobabad-Kashmore (NWR, now in Pakistan after conversion to BG).

1915

- Two new branches of the Darjeeling Himalayan Railway opened to traffic. The Kalimpong Road (now Gelkhola) branch followed the Teesta valley (hence known as the Teesta Valley Line) and the Kishanganj branch (built in the preceding year, 1914) ran west-southwest of Siliguri.
- Lower Ganges Bridge (Hardinge Bridge) opened on the trunk route to Siliguri on the EIR.
- Burdwan-Katwa line opened.

- Mandra-Bhaun and Sialkot-Narowal lines opened (both now in Pakistan; the former was closed in the 1990s).
- First ever diesel locomotive in India, a 2'6" gauge unit from Avonside (Bristol) is supplied to the India Office for use on a tea plantation (in Assam??).
- Currey Road-Thane line is quadrupled.
- Calcutta-Santahar MG line of East Bengal State Rly. opens.
- NG lines: Yeshwantpur-Devanahalli-Chikaballapur section of what would become the Bangalore Chikaballapur Light Rly. opens (2'6"); Ellichpur-Yeotmal (Central Provinces Rly.; later GIPR); Burdwan-Katwa (McLeod's).

1916

- Bowringpet-Kolar 2'6" line extended to Chintamani/ Chikkaballapur (forming the Kolar District Rly.) by the Mysore State Railway.
- Kacheguda station built by the Nizam of Hyderabad.
- Parsik tunnel (1.3km) opened to traffic.
- NG lines: BB&CI lines to *Pani* mines.

1917

- Ahmadpur-Katwa line opened.
- Thane-Kalyan line is quadrupled.
- Yeshwantpur-Yelahanka MG line is made mixed gauge to allow NG 2'6" traffic.
- NG lines: Pulgaon-Arvi (Central Provinces Rly., later GIPR); Khanai-Hindubagh (Zhob Valley Rly.; later NWR); Bankura-Damodar, Kalighat-Falta, and Ahmadpur-Katwa (McLeod's).
- Nushki Extension Rly. towards Iran opened till Dalbandin, from Spezand on the Sibi-Quetta line.

1918

- Bangalore-Chikkaballapur Light Railway (2'6") opens the Bangalore-Yeshwantpur section.
- Mysore-Arsikere MG line opened by the Mysore Darbar.
- Nushki Extension Rly. is completed until Zahidan (Duzdap) in Iran.

1919

- Wagon pooling comes into wide use among the various regional railways.

- Oct. 1: Mysore Darbar takes over Nanjangud-Mysore-Bangalore and Birur-Shimoga lines.
- NG lines: Pachora-Jamner (Central Provinces Rly.; later GIPR).
- Batasia Loop constructed on the DHR.
- Bhusawal loco shed set up by GIPR; at the time the largest loco shed in Asia and the third largest in the world.

Early 1920's

- Vacuum braking comes into wide use.
- Track-circuiting introduced on WR suburban lines.
- Telephones are brought into use for train control purposes in some suburban sections.

1920

- Total trackage at 37,000 miles (about 15% privately-held). The East India Railway Committee (chaired by Sir William Acworth, hence also known as the Acworth Committee) points out the need for unified management of the entire railway system. On the recommendations of this committee, the government takes over the actual management of all railways, and also separates railway finances from the general governmental finances (the latter step led to the practice, followed to this day, of presenting the Railway Budget separately from the General Budget every year).
- Superheating makes its appearance in India.
- Electric lighting of signals is introduced between Dadar and Currey Road.
- A 2' gauge diesel loco is delivered to Bengal by Baugleys of Burton-on-Trent. (1921)
- Sep.: Double-decker electric trams are introduced in Bombay.

1921

- The Peninsular Locomotive Company is founded at Jamshedpur for the purpose of building locomotives; this would have been the third loco manufacturing plant in India after Ajmer and Jamalpur, but unfortunately it failed even before it manufactured a single loco.

- July 1: Chikjajur-Chitradurg line opened by MSMR.
- Total trackage stands at 61,220 route km.
- The Railway Board is reorganised with a Chief Commissioner of Railways having overriding powers on technical matters. (1921)

1922

- Retrenchment Committee under Lord Inchcape recommends drastic cuts in working expenses and other measures designed to produce a fixed annual profit for the state.
- An electric loco with overhead power collection is delivered to the Naysmyth Patent Press Co. at Calcutta, by British Electric Vehicles.
- Jamnagar-Khambaliya-Gorinja-Okha MG section opened.
- Locomotive Standards Committee publishes a paper with details of proposed standardisation of locomotive classes.
- Jamnagar-Kuranga MG line opened by the Jamnagar & Dwarka Rly., and the Kuranga-Okha MG line by the Okhamandal Rly.
- NG lines: Larkana-Jacobabad (NWR); Futwah-Islampur (Martin & Co.).

1923

- Two diesel locos delivered to Barsi Light Railway by Ruton Proctor of Lincoln.
- Total trackage at 60,540 route-km.

1924

- Railway finances separated from general finances in the general government budget after the first Railway 'Convention'. Railway board expanded to have a Financial Commissioner, a member in charge of ways, works, stores and projects, and a member in charge of administration, staff, and traffic.
- Uniform system of loco classification codes based on an initial letter for the gauge comes into use.
- Jodhpur Bikaner Rly. split into Jodhpur State Rly. and Bikaner State Rly.
- Kurla-Chembur line open for passenger traffic.

- Rajkot-Morvi 2′6″ line of Morvi Rly. converted to BG.
- Rupsa-Barapada NG line extended to Talband.

1925

- February 3: First electric railway operates on Harbour branch of the GIPR from Victoria Terminus to Kurla (16 km), using 1500V DC overhead traction. The section is designated as a suburban section. EMUs from Cammell Laird and Uerdingenwagonfabrik are used. In the same year electrification of VT-Bandra is also completed and EMU services begin there as well, with an elevated platform at Sandhurst Road. The GIPR suburban line is later electrified up to Kalyan.
- Feb. 3: The EF/1 (later WCG-1) "crocodile" loco is introduced.
- VT-Kurla section is also completely track-circuited.
- Oudh and Rohilkhund Rly. amalgamated with EIR.
- Locomotive Standards Committee adopts several IRS loco classes as standards.
- First Railway Budget.
- East Indian Railway Company taken over by the state on January 1; Great Indian Peninsular Railway taken over on June 30.
- Khyber Railway opened from Peshawar Cantt. to Landi Kotal.

1926

- Ex-GIPR suburban line is electrified up to Kalyan. Main line electrified up to Poona and Igatpuri over the Bhore and Thal Ghats (1500 V DC).
- Order placed with Vulcan Foundry for the new classes of locos (XA, XB, XC, etc.).
- Lucknow's Charbagh Station built.
- East Bengal State Rly.'s line to Siliguri is converted to BG.
- Khyber Railway's last section from Landi Kotal to Landi Khana, 2km short of the frontier with Afghanistan, is opened.
- NG lines: Bhavnagar-Talaja section of Bhavnagar Tramways.

1927

- The BB&CI suburban lines extended to Borivili and Virar. In the Bombay area tracks in some places are doubled and even tripled or quadrupled (*e.g.*, between Bandra and Borivili).
- Patiala State Monorail stops operations.
- NG lines: line from Barsi Road Jn. to Pandharpur is extended to Miraj; Dehri-Rohtas extended to Rohtas Fort. In Nepal, the Raxaul-Amlekhganj line is opened (Martin & Co.).
- 8-coach EMU rakes are introduced on the main line in Mumbai and 4-coach rakes on the Harbour line.

1928

- Work begun on Madras suburban line.
- Jan. 5: Colaba-Borivili section electrification completed by BB&CI Rly.
- Two suburban tracks of the Bombay-Borivli section are electrified, but the two mainline tracks are left for steam traction. The first batch of electric EMUs for Bombay arrive (made by British Thompson Houston/Cammell Laird).
- Sep. 1: The Frontier Mail is flagged off from Colaba Terminus, with Peshawar as its destination.
- First automatic colour-light signals in India, on GIPR's lines between Bombay VT and Byculla.
- Kanpur Central and Lucknow stations inaugurated.
- Golden Rock workshops near Trichy set up by the South Indian Railway.
- Bahawalnagar-Fort Abbas line opened by princely state of Bahawalpur (now in Pakistan, closed in the 1990s).

1924-1929

- Railways build more than 1,000 miles of tracks each year. General period of prosperity for the railways—generous provisions are made for passenger amenities (waiting rooms, etc.).

1929-1937

- Railways (like everything else!) hit by the 1929 Wall Street Crash and the ensuing global depression; severe economy measures undertaken.

1929

- Kazipet-Balharshah link completed, connecting Delhi and Madras directly.
- The Grand Trunk Express begins running between Peshawar and Mangalore.
- Kalyan-Igatpuri-Pune section is now completely electrified, and the quadruple line between Bombay and Kalyan is also electrified.
- A 2' gauge diesel loco from Maffei is supplied to C K Andrew and Co. (Probably used on a plantation?)
- Burma Railways taken over by the state.
- Chola Power House near Thakurli built by the GIPR for supplying power for the newly electrified Kalyan-Igatpuri-Pune section.
- Punjab Limited Express begins to run between Mumbai and Lahore, leaving Mumbai on Thursdays.
- Bombay's Victoria Terminus undergoes some reconstruction work so that it gets 14 platforms.
- Automatic colour-light signalling extended to the Byculla-Kurla section.
- The Kurla car shed is opened.
- NG lines: BB&CI line to Piplod; Kangra Valley Rly. (NWR).
- Railway Board reorganised with separate members in charge of traffic and labour matters.

1930's

- Experiments with railcars on the Jamnagar & Dwarka Rly.
- Power signalling introduced; upper-quadrant semaphore signals introduced.

1930

- The Times (London) nominates the Frontier Mail "the most famous express train in the British empire".
- Through electric services begin on the Kalyan-Pune section.
- June 1: The Deccan Queen begins running, hauled by a WCP-1 (No. 20024, old number EA/1 4006) and with 7 coaches, on the GIPR's newly electrified route to Poona (Pune).

- Two BG diesel shunters from William Beardmore in use on the North Western Railway.
- NWR procures two 420hp diesel-electric shunters from William Beardmore.
- Hyderabad Godavary Valley Rly. merged into Nizam's State Rly.
- Axle boxes with roller bearings come into use.
- The route of the Grand Trunk Exp. is changed to Delhi-Madras.

1931

- Madras MG suburban railway line completed. ((April 2) May 11: Tambaram-Beach has electric traction). The first MG EMU service.
- The YCG-1 DC MG locos are introduced in the Madras area.
- Samdari-Raniwara section opens as the first phase of a rail connection between Jodhpur-Bikaner and Gujarat. Phalodi-Jodhpur section opens.
- Total trackage in India at about 43,000 miles. Hardly any new construction until after World War II.
- NG lines: Darwha-Pusad (Central Provinces Rly; later GIPR).
- More than 700 stations have interlocking by now.

1932

- MSMR's workshops at Perambur split into the Carriage and Wagon Workshops and the Locomotive Workshops.
- NG lines: Agar-Ujjain (Gwalior Light Rlys.)
- Nok Kundi-Zahidan section of Nushki Extension Rly. is closed.

1933

- Kaunia-Dharlla MG lines north of the Brahmaputra are extended to Rangapara.
- May 16: Kanpur trams stop operating.

1934

- Shoranur-Cochin line converted to BG.

1935

- NWR procures two 1200hp diesel-electric locos from Armstrong-Whitworth with the intention of using them for a new Bombay-Karachi route. They were deployed on the Karachi-Lahore mail route, but then were withdrawn soon afterwards, having manifested many problems as they were not designed for Indian conditions.

1936

- Borivli-Virar electrification complete. The two mainline tracks on the Bombay-Borivli section are also electrified.
- BBCI obtains one diesel shunter from Armstrong Whitworth.
- Air-conditioning introduced in some (first-class) passenger coaches. Matunga workshops manufacture 5 air-conditioned coaches, the first such to be made locally.
- Indian Railway Committee under Sir Ralph Wedgwood constituted to look into the position of the state-owned railways and how to improve their finances.
- Mavli-Marwar MG line opened.
- Jodhpur Rly. acquires two Drewry railcars, one for the Maharaja and the other an inspection car.

1937

- Wedgwood Committee makes recommendations for public relations, advertising, etc. which until then had been neglected. Also recommends faster and more reliable passenger services and expansion of freight activities, for the railways to compete with road transport.
- The post of Minister for Transport and Communications is created; the Minister was a civil servant, and could decide on matters dealt with by the Railway Board.
- The infamous Bihta accident, in which the excessive oscillations of an XB class loco caused the derailment of the Punjab-Howrah mail, killing 154 persons.
- NG lines: In Nepal, the Nepal Jaynagar-Janakpur Rly. opens.

- May 1: The Flying Queen (predecessor of Flying Ranee) is introduced between Bombay and Surat, hauled by an H class 4-6-0 and making her run in 4 hours.

1938

- All lines of the MSMR in Mysore are taken over by the Mysore Darbar.
- NG lines: Bhavnagar Tramways line extended to Mahura.

1939

- World War II. Railways under strain again. Locomotives, wagons, and track material are taken from India to the middle East; 28 branch lines were completely cannibalised for this. Railway workshops are used to manufacture shells and other military equipment. The entire railway system is in poor shape by the end of the war.
- Diesel railcars from Ganz are tried out on the Nizam's State Railways.
- A light railcar built at Bikaner is used on the minor lines around there.
- The power systems of the Chola Power House and the Tata Hydroelectric plant are combined for supplying traction power to Bombay-area suburban trains as well as for long-distance trains across the ghats.

1940

- The Jamnagar and Dwarka Railway procures a single MG diesel loco for its Saurashtra Passenger service, from Brookville.
- Jodhpur-Phalodi section extended to Pokharan.
- All-steel BG coaches manufactured for the first time in India.

1940's

- Large numbers of American and Canadian locos are imported (AWD, CWD, along with AWC, AWE, and MAWD classes).
- Neale's Ball Token Instruments come into use.

1941

- Hosur-Dharmapuri NG line de-commissioned.
- The 'Following Trains' system of train working is introduced as an emergency measure in some areas out of necessity because of wartime requirements.

1942

- Most of the remaining large railway companies are taken over by the state.
- July 11: A flash flood washes out portions of the tracks on the Chappar Rift of the Sindh Peshin State Railway (now in Pakistan), and though running never resumes on this line.
- Nok Kundi-Zahidan section of the Nushki Extension Rly. is reopened.

1943

- Bengal and North-Western Railway is taken over by the state, after being merged with the Rohilkund and Kumaon Rly., the Mashrak-Thane Extension Rly., the Lucknow-Bareilly Rly., and the Tirhut Rly. The new railway is known as the Oudh and Tirhut Rly.
- The opening of the Howrah bridge in February allows the Calcutta routes of trams to be connected to the Howrah routes; total system is at 67km.

1944-45

- Fifteen diesel locos from GE supplied by USATC and deployed on WR, among the first diesel locos to be successfully used in many locations in India. Most of these were classified as WDS-1.

1944

- April: MSMR merged with the lines worked by the SIR company, and taken over by the state.
- Oct. 1: BNR taken over by the state.

1945

- Indian Railway Standards renamed Indian Government Railway Standards. Locomotive classification codes updated to include diesels and electrics.

- Tata Engineering and Locomotive Co. (TELCO) formed as a company.
- Bandra station has the country's first all-electric interlocking.
- Apr. 1: Jacobabad-Kashmore line taken over by state (now in Pakistan).

1946

- A Skelton system monorail (locomotive with rubber tires guided by a rail, and wagons carried on the rail with outrigger wheels for stability) is installed for the 18km section from Bhanvad to Khambalia in Gujarat, powered by a modified diesel loco.
- 16 prototypes of the new WP class Pacifics ordered.

Bibliography

Adikaram, E. W.: *Early History of Buddhism in Ceylon,* D. S. Puswella, Migoda, 1946.

Agrawala, V. S.: *Shiva Mahadeva: The Great God,* Veda Academy, Varanasi, 1966.

Ahmad, Imtiaz: *State and Foreign Policy: India's Role in South Asia,* Vikas, New Delhi, 1993.

Ahmad, Jamil-ud-din: *Some Recent Speeches and Writings of Mr. Jinnah,* Lahore, Ashraf, 1952.

Aiyar, R. Krishnaswami: *Outlines of Vedaanta,* Chetana, Bombay, 1978.

Archer, W. G.: *The Kama Sutra,* Unwin Hyman, London, 1990.

Ashton, S.R. : *British Policy Towards the Indian States, 1905-1939,* London, Curzon, 1982.

Aurobindo, Sri: *Vyasa and Valmiki,* Acharya Press, Pondicherry, 1956.

Avalon, Arthur and Ellen: *Hymns to the Goddess,* Ganesh and Co., Madras, 1964.

Aziz, Ashraf: *Light of the Universe: Essays on Hindustani Film Music,* Three Essays Collective, New Delhi, 2003.

Bagchi, P. C.: *Studies in Dharmashastra,* University of Calcutta Press, Calcutta, 1939.

Bahadur, K.P.: *The Wisdom of Vedaanta,* Sterling Publishers Private Limited, New Delhi, 1996.

Banerjea, J. N.: *Pauranic and Vedanta Religion,* University of Calcutta, Calcutta, 1996.

Bankimchandra, C.: *Essentials of Dharma,* Sanskrit Book Depot, Calcutta 1979.

Basu, Manoranjan: *Dharmashastra: A General Study,* Shrimati Mira Basu, Calcutta, 1976.

Beaumont, Roger : *Sword of the Raj: The British Army in India, 1747-1947*, Indianapolis, Bobbs-Merrill, 1977.

Benjamin, Joseph : *Scheduled Castes in Indian Politics and Society*, New Delhi, Ess Ess Publications, 1989.

Bhattacharyya, B.: *Nispannayogavali of Mahapandita Abhyakara Gupta*, Oriental Institute, Baroda, 1949.

Borchert, Bruno: *Mysticism: Its History and Challenge*, Samuel Wiser, York Beach, 1994.

Bose, D. N.: *Dharmashastra: Their Philosophy and Occult Secrets*, Kali Press, Calcutta, 1965.

Bowle, John: *The Imperial Achievement: The Rise and Transformation of the British Empire*, Little, Brown, 1974.

Brockington, J. L.: *Righteous Rama: The Evolution of an Epic*, Oxford, London, 1984.

Bromley, D.: *Krishna Consciousness in the West*, Bucknell University Press, Lewisburg, 1989.

Brooks, E.: *The Original Analects: Sayings of Confucius and His Successors*. Columbia University Press, New York, 1988.

Bruhn, Klaus: *The Jina-Images of Deogarh*, MacMillan, Leiden, 1969.

Burke, Mary Louise: *Swami Vivekananda in America: New Discoveries*, Advaita Ashrama, Calcutta, 1966.

Chaudhary, M.: *Partition and the Curse of Rehabilitation*, Calcutta, Bengal Rehabilitation Organization, 1964.

Chaudhuri, Nirad: *Thy Hand, Great Anarch! India: 1921-1952*, London, Chatto & Windus, 1987.

Coomeraswamy, Ananda K.: *Buddha and the Gospel of Buddhism*, MacMillan, London, 1928.

Crawford, Cromwell S.: *Ram Mohan Roy: His Era and Ethics*, Acharya Press, New Delhi, 1984.

Dalton, Dennis : *Gandhi's Power : Nonviolence in Action*, New Delhi, OUP, 2001.

Danielou, Alain: *The Complete Kama Sutra*, Park Street Press, Rochester, 2000.

Dasgupta, Shahana: *Rani Lakshmibai: The Indian Heroine*, Rupa & Company, Calcutta, 2002.

Datta, V.N.: *Sati: Widow Burning in India*, Manohar, New Delhi, 1990.

David, M. D.: *John Wilson and his Institutions*, Mumbai, 1957.

De Bary: *Self and Society in Ming Thought*, Columbia University Press, New York, 1970.

De, Sushil Kumar: *Ancient Indian Erotics and Erotic Literature*, Firma K. L. Mukhopadhyay, Calcutta, 1959.

Deak, Istvan: *The Lawful Revolution: Louis Kossuth and the Hungarians 1848-1849*, Columbia University Press, 1979.

Dhar, Niranjan: *Vedanta and Bengal Renaissance*, Minerva Associates, Calcutta, 1977.

Dikshit, D.P. *Political History of the Chalukyas of Badami*. New Delhi: Abhinav, 1980.

Donat, K.: *Meditate the Tantric Yoga Way*, George Allen and Unwin, London, 1973.

Doniger, W.: *The Rig Veda: An Anthology*, Penguin, New York, 1981.

Duboi, Abbe: *Hindu Manners, Customs and Ceremonies*, Fifth Indian Impression, CUP, 1985.

Dwivedi, M.: *The Principal Upanishads*, Adyar Library, Madras, 1931.

Eaton, Richard M.: *Sufis of Bijapur, 1300-1700: Social Roles of Sufis in Medieval India*, Princeton University Press, Princeton, 1978.

Edwardes, Michael: *Battles of the Indian Mutiny*, London; B. T. Batsford Ltd., 1963.

Erickson, Erik H.: *Gandhi's Truth: On the Origins of Militant Nonviolence*, Norton, New York, 1970.

Farquhar, J.N.: *Modern Religious Movements in India*, Munshiram, New Delhi, 1967.

Fay, Peter Ward: *The Opium War, 1840-42*, University of North Carolina Press, 1975.

Fisher, Michael H.: *The Politics of British Annexation of India - 1757-1857*, Oxford, 1996.

Frauwallner, E..: *History of Indian Philosophy*, Motilal, Delhi, 1973.

Gambhirananda, S.: *Brahma Sutra Shamkar Bhasya*, Adavita Ashrama, Calcutta, 1977.

Gambhirananda, Swami: *Brahma Sutra Shamkar Bhasya*, Adavita Ashrama, Calcutta, 1977.

Gandhi, M. K.: *The Story of My Experiment With Trust*, Washington, Public Affairs Press, 1948.

Garbe, R.: *The Philosophy of Ancient India*, Chicago University Press, Chicago, 1899.

Goradia, Nayana: *Lord Curzon: The Last of the British Moghuls*, New Delhi, Oxford University Press, 1993.

Goudriaan, T.: *Ritual and Speculation in Early Tantrism*, State University of New York Press, New York, 1992.

Gough, A.E.: *The Philosophy of the Upanisads and Ancient Indian Metaphysics*, MacMillan, London, 1882.

Grant, G. P.: *Philosophy in the Mass Age*, Copp Clark, Toronto, 1959.

Grisenold, H.D.: *Insights into Modern Hinduism*, Oxford, New York, 1934.

Growse, F. S.: *The Ramayana of Tulasidasa*, Motilal Banarsidass, Delhi, 1995.

Gurumurthy, S. : *Hindu Heritage, Assimilative, Not Divisive*, Vigil, Madras 1993.

Haich, E.: *Sexual Energy and Yoga*, Aurora Press, New York, 1982.

Hasan, Murhirul: *Legacy of a Divided Nation: India's Muslims Since Independence*, New Delhi, Oxford, 1997.

Hasan, Mushirul: *India's Partition: Process, Strategy and Mobilization*, New Delhi, Oxford UP, 1993.

Heifetz, Hank: *The Origin of the Young God: Kalidasa's Kumarasambhava*, University of California Press, Berkeley, 1985.

Heimann, Betty: *Facets of Indian Thought*, Geroge Allen & Unwin, London, 1964.

Heinsath, Charles: *Indian Nationalism and Hindu Social Reform*, Princeton University Press, Princeton, 1964.

Heschel, J.: *God in Search of Man: A Philosophy of Judaism*, Noonday Press, New York, 1997.

Hirschman, Edwin: *White Mutiny: The Ilbert Bill Crisis in India and the Genesis of the Indian National Congress*, New Delhi, Heritage, 1980.

Hixon, L.: *Mother of the Universe: Visions of the Goddess, Tantric Hymns of Enlightenment*, Quest Books, Wheaton, 1994.

Hopkins, J.: *Kalachakra Tantra Rite of Initiation*, Wisdom Publications, Boston, 1982.

Hopkirk, Peter: *The Great Game: The Struggle for Empire in Central Asia*, Kodansha, 1992.

Hume, R.E.: *The Thirteen Principle Upanishads*, Oxford University Press, London, 1971.

Hutchins, Francis: *Spontaneous Revolution: The Quit India Movement*, New Delhi, Manohar, 1971.

Irene, S.: *Vedic Heritage Teaching Program*. Arsha Vidya Gurukulam, Coimbatore, 1994.

Iyar, K.: *Vedanta: The Science of Reality*, Ganesh and Co., Mardas, 1930.

Iyengar, B.K.S.: *Light on the Yoga Sutras of Patanjali*, Aquarian Press, London 1993.

Jacob, K.: *Religion and Ethics in Advaita*, C.M.S. Press, Kottayam, 1982.

Jafar, Malik Muhammad: *Jinnah as a Parliamentarian*, Lahore, Afzar Publications, 1977.

Jain, Kailash Chand, *Lord Mahavira and His Times*, Saraswati Press, Delhi, 1974.

James, Lawrence: *The Rise and Fall of the British Empire*, St. Martin's, 1997.

James, Robert Rhodes: *The British Revolution, 1880-1939*, New York, Knopf, 1976.

Jean, M.: *Tantrik Yoga*, The Aquarian Press, Wellingborough, 1970.

John, B.: *Mantras: Sacred Words of Power*, George Allen and Unwin, London, 1977.

John, Elsner: *Pilgrimage: Past and Present in the World Religions*, Harvard University Press, Cambridge, 1995.

John, K.: *The Origin and Development of the State Cult of Confucius*, Paragon Book, New York, 1966.

Karmarkar, D.: *Sankara's Advaita*, Karnatak University, Dharwar, 1976.

Kaushik, Asha : *Globalization, Democracy and Culture : Situating Gandhian Alternatives*, Jaipur, Pointer, 2002.

Kaviraj, G.: *Aspects of Indian Thought*, University of Burdwan, Calcutta, 1966.

Kavlekar, K.K. : *Non-Brahmin Movement in Southern India, 1873-1949*, Kolhapur, Shivaji University, 19790

Keith, A.B. : *Rigveda Brahmanas*, Harvard University Press, Cambridge, 1920.

Keith, Arthur Berriedale: *The Religion and Philosophy of the Veda and Upanishads*, MacMillan, Delhi, 1925.

Kishwar, Madhu : *Religion at the Service of Nationalism, and Other Essays*, OUP, Delhi, 1998.

Klaus, K.: *A Survey of Hinduism*, State University of New York Press, Albany, 1989.

Knipe, M.: *Hinduism: Experiments in the Sacred*, Harper, San Francisco, 1991.

Knott, K.: *Hinduism, A Very Short Introduction*, Oxford University Press, New York, 1998.

Kosambi, D. D. : *The Culture and Civilisation of Ancient India in Historical Outline*, London, Routledge and Kegan Paul, 1956.

Kottackal, Jacob: *Religion and Ethics in Advaita*, C.M.S. Press, Kottayam, 1982.

Kuiper, F.B.J. : *Aryans in the Rigveda*, Rodopi, Amsterdam, 1991.

Kuppuswamy, Sastri S.: *Compromises in the History of Advaitic Thought*, Kalyani Press, Madras, 1940.

Louis, Fischer: *Essential Gandhi: An Anthology of His Writings*, Vintage, New York, 1983.

Low, D. A. and Brasted, Howard: *Freedom, Trauma, Continuities: Northern India and Independence*, New Delhi, Sage Publications, 1998.

Maheshwari, Shriram: *Rural Development in India: A Public Policy Approach*, New Delhi, Sage, 1995.

Makhan, L.: *The Ramayana of Valmiki*, Munshiram Manoharlal, New Delhi, 1978.

Mathew, Arnold: *Culture and Anarchy*, The University Press, Cambridge, 1935.

Mayer, A. : *Caste in an Indian Village: Change and Continuity 1954-1992*, Delhi, OUP, 1996.

Mazumder, Sukhendu : *Politico-Economic Ideas of Mahatma Gandhi: Their Relevance in the Present Day*, New Delhi, Concept Pub., 2004.

Mearns, David J.: *Shiva's Other Children: Religion and Social Identity amongst Overseas Indians*, Sage, Walnut Creek, 1995.

Mearns, J.: *Shiva's Other Children: Religion and Social Identity amongst Overseas Indians*, Sage, Walnut Creek, 1995.

Mehra, Parshotam: *A Dictionary of Modern Indian History, 1707-1947*, New Delhi, Oxford University Press, 1985.

Metcalf, Thomas R.: *The Aftermath of the Revolt: India, 1857-1870*, Princeton, Princeton University, 1964.

Mohan, K.: *The Mahabharata*, Munshiram Manoharlal, Delhi 1997.

Mookerjee, Ajit: *Kali The Feminine Force*, Thames and Hudson, London, 1988.

Mookerji, Satkari: *Modern Polity and Vedanta*, Sanskrit College, Calcutta, 1972.

Moon, Penderel: *The British Conquest and Dominion of India*, London, Duckworth, 1989.

Morris-Jones, W.H.: *The Government and Politics of India*, London, Hutchinson, 1971.

Nanda, B. R. : *Gandhi and His Critics*, Oxford University Press, Delhi, 1993.

Neale, Walter C.: *Economic Change in Rural India: Land Tenure and Reform in the United Provinces, 1800-1955*, New Haven, 1962.

Nevile, P.: *Lahore: A Sentimental Journey*, New Delhi, Penguin, 1993.

Oddie, G.A. : *Hindu and Christian in South-East India*, London, Curzon Press, 1991.

Pathak, Dr S.P.: *Jhansi during the British Rule*, Ramanand Vidya Bhawan, Delhi, 1987.

Preston, Diana: *The Boxer Rebellion*, Berkley Books, 2000.

Raimundo Panikkar: *The Vedic Experience: Mantramanjari*, Longman Todd, London, 1977.

Raja, C. Kunhan : *The Taittiriya Sarvanukramani of Yaska*, Madras, 1931.

Ramamurti, A.: *Advaitic Mysticism of Sankara*, Visvabharati, Santiniketan, 1974.

Ranajit Guha: *A Construction of Humanism in Colonial India*, CASA, Amsterdam, 1993.

Renou, Louis: *The Nature of Dharmashastra*, Walker and Co., New York, 1997.

Robson, Brian: *Sir Hugh Rose and the Central India Campaign*, Sutton Publishing Ltd for the Army Records Society, UK, 2000.

Satyapal Verma: *Role of Reason in Sankara Vedanta*, Parimal Publication, Delhi, 1992.

Savarkar, Vinayak Damodar : *The Indian War of Independence* 1857 Rajdhani Granthagar, Delhi, 1988.

Scheftelowitz, Isidor : *Die Kasmirische Rezension von Katyayanas Sarvanukramani,* Zeitschrift fur Indologie und Iranistik, 1922.

Shukla, D. N.: *Vastu-Shastra,* Motilal Banarsidass, Delhi, 1966.

Singh, Birendra Kumar: *Early Chalukyas of Vatapi, circa A.D. 500 to 757,* Delhi, Eastern Book Linkers, 1991.

Smith, Col. J. T. : *Silver and the India Exchanges,* Effingham Wilson, London, 1876.

Strauss, L.: *Political Philosophy,* The Bobbs Merrill Co., New York, 1975.

Swami Vishnu Tirtha: *Devatma Shakti,* Swami Shivom Tirth, Rishikesh, 1962.

Talageri, Shrikant : *Aryan Invasion Theory and Indian Nationalism,* Voice of India, Delhi, 1993.

Tejomayananda, Swami: *Hindu Culture: An Introduction,* Chinmaya Publications, Piercy, 1993.

Thapar, Romila : *Ashoka and the Decline of the Mauryas,* London, Oxford University Press, 1961.

Thompson, Edward: *The Making of the Indian Princes,* Oxford University Press, London, 1943.

Trautmann, Thomas R.: *Kautilya and the Arthasastra: A Statistical Study,* Leiden, Brill, 1971.

Trimingham, J.: *Sufi Orders in Islam,* Oxford University Press, New York, 1998.

Utpat, V.N.: *Riddles of Buddha and Ambedkar,* Itihas Patrika Prakashan, Thane 1988.

Vable, D.: *The Arya Samaj. Hindu without Hinduism.* Vikas Publ., Delhi, 1983.

Vedalankar, Pandit Nardev : *Basic Teachings of Hinduism,* Veda Niketan, Durban, 1978.

Visvantha, K.: *Essentials of Hinduism,* Narosa Pub. House, New Delhi, 1989.

Wendy Doniger: *Siva: The Erotic Ascetic,* Oxford University Press, Delhi, 1998.

Zaidi, A. Moin: *Evolution of Muslim political Thought in India,* New Delhi: S. Chand, 1975.

Index

S

T

U

V

W

Y

Z

□□□